PAINTING THE SIDEWALK WITH WATER

WITH WATER

Talks & Dialogues About Non-Duality

JOAN TOLLIFSON

NON-DUALITY PRESS
An Imprint of New Harbinger Publications

PAINTING THE SIDEWALK WITH WATER

First edition published October 2010 by Non-Duality Press

© Joan Tollifson 2010
© Non-Duality Press 2010

Non-Duality Press | An imprint of New Harbinger Publications

ISBN: 978-0-9566432-1-6

www.newharbinger.com

Neither the dharma world nor empty space is anything other than the painting of a picture.

-Dogen

Consciousness itself is the greatest painter. The entire world is a picture.

-Nisargadatta Maharaj

If you cannot find the Truth right where you are, where do you expect to find it?

-Dogen

If you need time to achieve something, it must be false. The real is always with you; you need not wait to be what you are.

-Nisargadatta Maharaj

TABLE of CONTENTS

Notes on the Text

This book is based on transcriptions of meetings I held between 2004 and 2006, mostly in Chicago, along with material from email exchanges, conversations and talks about nonduality from 2004 to the present. The material does not always appear in chronological order. In some cases I have edited and expanded upon the original material, often combining material from several different talks or exchanges. I have, of course, changed the names of anyone whose questions or comments are included and made other minor changes in their stories to protect their privacy.

I usually begin meetings with a period of silence before we begin talking, and I often say a few words to introduce this silent time. I don't think of this as meditation in any formal sense, but simply as an invitation to explore the timeless present moment. I've included a few of these "Invitations to Explore the Present Moment" in the text, but most of them have been omitted. After the silence, I typically give a talk, open the meeting up for questions and dialog, and finally end with another few minutes of silence.

Any comments I make in this book about the teachings or views of other teachers are my own impressions and may not reflect that person's intention or how anyone else sees and hears their teaching. Please look and listen for yourself.

Joan Tollifson
Ashland, Oregon
June 2010

The Simplicity of What Is

This book points to the simplicity of what is, just as it is. Traffic sounds, smell of coffee, the humming of the refrigerator, sensations in the body, these words unfolding in awareness – all of it the ever-changing, ever-present boundlessness of Here/Now from which nothing stands apart. This boundlessness never arises, never ceases, and never stays the same. No matter what is appearing Here/Now, in Reality, nothing is lacking and nothing is broken because no *thing* actually exists in the way we *think* it does. Reality is undivided – seamless and whole.

Naming this undivided wholeness (calling it wholeness, unicity, Consciousness, awareness, the Self, the True Self, the One Mind, presence, Buddha Nature, emptiness, or any other name) is always potentially misleading because names create the mirage-like appearance of *something* in particular (this but not that). And what we're talking about is not something. It is *everything* and no-thing. Emptiness is what remains when all our ideas, words and beliefs about life drop away. It is not nothing in a nihilistic sense. It is everything, just as it is.

This wholeness or emptiness is not some abstract idea or mystical state of consciousness, but simply the undeniable actuality of this moment – the sounds of traffic, the hum of machinery, the song of a bird, the knowingness that *this is* and that *you are here*. This bare being, this aware presence, this present experiencing requires no belief and cannot be doubted. It is undeniable and unavoidable. What *can* be doubted are all the ideas, interpretations, and stories *about* this. All our confusion and suffering is in this conceptual overlay, never in Reality itself. This book is about seeing through the imaginary problem.

Words such as "enlightenment" or "awakening" point not to a one-time event that happened yesterday or that might happen tomorrow. Enlightenment is only Here/Now. And it is not really an event in the usual sense, nor is it a personal achievement. It is the falling away (or transparency) of all beliefs and ideas, the popping of the imaginary (conceptual) bubble of encapsulation and separation, the recognition of oneself as no-thing and everything.

There is no way to achieve this boundlessness because it is all there is. Here/Now is ever-present *in spite* of whatever happens in the movie of waking life, never *because* of what happens. Here/Now is not any particular experience, but rather, it is the *experiencing* that is present as *every* experience. Boundlessness includes everything and depends on nothing. It is what remains when the whole universe dissolves – your face before your parents were born.

In case you might be tempted to imagine that I am in some way different from you, it is important that you know right from the outset that, as a person, I am absolutely and quintessentially human. I can be selfish, insensitive, controlling, opinionated, irritable, deluded, depressed, caught up in addictive habits, and generally flawed. In the dream-like movie of waking life, "Joan" has not stabilized permanently in any special awakened state or permanently lost all concern for her story, her self-image, or her survival. Unlike some who claim that a line in the sand was forever crossed on a particular date in time, no such final event has happened in Joan's story. And, in fact, true enlightenment is not concerned at all with "me" being enlightened. Enlightenment is not the absence or banishment of all those "negative" experiences (depression, anxiety, addiction, anger, and so on), but rather, it is the recognition that none of this is personal and that none of it could be any different, in this moment, from exactly how it is. Enlightenment is the absence of the mirage-like "me" who needs the appearance to be any different from how it is. Enlightenment sees *everything* as unicity, and this seeing is always Now.

What is meant by "Now"? Any answer is too late. Any experience you can remember or describe is too late. Any notion of "being in the

Now" or "not being in the Now" is too late. All experiences and states come and go, and all coming and going (and all staying) is too late. "Now" points to an immediacy that does not come and go, a presence that is equally present in (and as) every experience, the seeing that can never see itself, the *being here* that is impossible to deny. Think about it, and you immediately fall into confusion. *Try* not to think, and you seemingly confirm the imaginary problem. There is no way *not* to be here now. *This* is what you *are*. This is what *is*. This is *all* there is.

This (one, eternal, timeless) present moment is ever-present. What changes are the forms or the appearances that this formlessness takes (sensations, perceptions, experiences, thoughts, ideas, beliefs, stories – everything perceivable and conceivable – the whole movie of waking life – the tumbling shapes in the kaleidoscope). What never comes and never goes is the immediacy of Here/Now – *this* – the alive presence, the awareness, the boundless unicity that has no beginning and no end. The words are never quite right, and they can only point to a wordless reality that is right here, right now – immovable and all-inclusive.

Here/Now is not an idea or a concept, but a palpable reality. When we talk about "waking up" to it, or "being here now," it can sound as if it is a special experience that is absent in one moment and then present in the next moment – a particular state of consciousness that can be attained or lost, something that comes and goes, and in a sense, that *seems* to be true.

Whenever the focus of attention shifts from the mental story ("I'm a failure, I've wasted my life, this is miserable, what can I do to fix this?") to the aliveness of non-conceptual, present moment sensory awareness, there is an immediate sense of relief and freedom. Suffering disappears. Everything feels spacious and open, colors seem brighter, what is ordinary sparkles and reveals itself as extraordinary, beauty is visible everywhere, there is a felt-sense of love, joy and peace. But any *experience* of expansion and sparkle is always temporary. Thoughts, stories, neurochemical weather, unpleasant or contracted experiences inevitably show up. So at first it *seems* as if Here/Now is a special state or a particular experience that comes and goes. And *in* the story of coming and going, there seems to be this phantom "me" who goes back and forth between "being here now" and "not being here now," or between "getting it" and "losing it," or between "certainty" and "doubt."

But what actually comes and goes are the thoughts, stories, ideas, experiences, sensations, perceptions – the forms that appear and disappear Here/Now, including both the expanded experience of "being here now" and the contracted experience of being "lost in thoughts." Here/Now isn't actually an experience. It is the experienc*ing* that is equally present as *every* experience. Here/Now is beginningless and endless. And there is no one apart from this ever-present boundlessness who can find it or lose it – that "me" character is nothing but thoughts, stories, sensations, and images appearing Here/Now.

Yes, this boundlessness may *seem* invisible or absent, *apparently* obscured by the thoughts, stories, dramas and ideas that so easily capture the attention and fill the screen of awareness. Consciousness, by nature, seems to be a thinking, exploring, searching, wanting, grasping, story-telling, dreaming, drama-loving, imagination-producer. Again and again, thoughts spin their hypnotic webs, movies appear, attention becomes absorbed in drama. But this only seems problematic *within* the drama, from the perspective of the mirage-like separate self, and only if there is the mistaken idea that there should or could be a permanent *experience* of expansion.

From the vantage point of unicity, nothing is a problem. Only from the vantage point of the fragmentary (and always imaginary) separate self does the need arise to banish some experiences and acquire others. One of the more sophisticated dramas that consciousness produces is "me" trying to step out of "my story," the character trying to free itself from itself. This is like a mirage trying to eliminate a mirage, or a phantom trying to pull itself up by its own imaginary bootstraps, or a dog chasing its own tail.

But whenever resistance and the search for improvement stops, what remains is peace. When all belief and all grasping for answers ends, doubt and uncertainty vanish. When thought stops, all suffering ends. But this relative peace is always temporary. The suffering and the doubt may all come back a moment later if the grasping and the seeking resume, and there is no one who can control this coming and going of thoughts, movies and imaginary dramas. In fact, the attempt to control it only lends it a sense of reality and importance. *All* of this is bothersome only if there is a need for it to be otherwise or if it is taken personally. When it is recognized that *everything* is unicity, that unicity is all there is, then nothing is really a problem.

But if you reference unicity as a particular experience and then search for it, you immediately make it into an object and confirm the story of separation and lack. If you try to hold onto any particular state of consciousness, it immediately seems to vanish. It is like trying to hold onto a handful of water or air. Experiences come and go, clear ones and cloudy ones, but Here/Now is ever-present.

The mind typically imagines enlightenment to be some special state that a person attains. It is sometimes said that there is no coming back from enlightenment, and the mind interprets this to mean that a person one day crosses an imaginary finish line and enters a special "enlightened state" of infinite duration. This "enlightened person" is then imagined to be forever after permanently established in something called "unicity" or "oneness" or "the Now," and this is conceived of as a perpetual experience, a permanent state, or a final understanding that never again lapses or disappears for that person.

But actually, the word enlightenment points to recognizing the mirage-like nature of the separate person who would enter some special state and then stay there forever after. Enlightenment points to realizing that the only eternity is now, that time is only a way of conceptualizing. There is no such thing as "forever after" or an experience of infinite duration – there is only timeless presence. Nothing is excluded from unicity. Even seeking, doubting and pretending to be a separate person are all nothing but unicity. No one attains unicity because the one who would attain it is nothing but a mirage, and the mirage is nothing but the unicity it seeks. There is no person, in reality, who is enlightened or unenlightened. There is only this infinite, ever-present Here/Now, even if it *appears* otherwise. Sometimes enlightenment shows up and sometimes delusion shows up. None of it is personal. Unicity includes it all, the light *and* the dark. *Being* is undeniable and unavoidable even when thoughts are running wild and movies are playing in the mind.

What *seemingly* obscures this simple beingness is what the physicist David Bohm once beautifully called neurochemical smog. Hinduism calls it Maya, Buddhism calls it samsara, Christianity calls it sin (literally "missing the mark"). This smog is the dream-like drama centering around the imaginary "me" and "the story of my life" – the illusory sense of separation and encapsulation – all of it a kind of mirage created by unexamined thoughts, concepts, ideas, stories and beliefs, and also by neurochemistry, genetics, conditioning and who knows what forces of nature and nurture. It is this conceptual smog that Zen and Advaita and nonduality aim to expose and clear away, revealing the jewel that has actually never been absent.

The joke is that there is really nothing substantial to expose or clear away. The smog is a mirage, not a real obstacle. It is an imaginary problem. It has no actual substance. What solution is needed to an imaginary problem? The mind keeps desperately seeking solutions, but any solution it undertakes only confirms the apparent reality of both the imaginary problem and the mirage-like entity who seemingly has the problem.

Even the smog is revealed to be none other than the jewel. Boundless unicity shows up disguised as smog and mirages. Nirvana and samsara are not two, everything is one inseparable whole, and nothing can be pulled apart from everything else. Every relative experience always contains its opposite. Opposites appear together and define each other. Clarity and smog, expansion and contraction, enlightenment and delusion – you cannot have one polarity without the other. The manifestation requires contrast in order to appear at all. But nothing is actually *separate* from anything else. There is diversity and variation, but not separation. There are no independent parts and no individual owners.

Here/Now is the placeless place, the timeless presence, the formlessness appearing as ever-changing forms. This seamless unicity is not something complicated, exotic and hard to get. It is inescapable and impossible to avoid. What makes this so *apparently* hard to get is how simple it is, how obvious, how effortless. Here/Now is present *in spite* of whatever experience shows up, never *because of* any experience. This boundlessness is prior to every experience; it is what remains when every experience is gone; it is what every experience *is*. This boundless unicity is causeless and depends on nothing. It requires no shift, no transformation, no understanding, no figuring things out, no attainment, no special experience or state, no "being here now," no becoming in order to be.

There are many shifts that can happen *in* the story, *in* the dream-like movie of waking life, *in* the appearance. There is the shift from smog to clarity, from compulsive thinking to "being here now," from contraction to expansion, from tension to relaxation. There is the shift from the story of being a separate person encapsulated inside a bodymind to knowing oneself as the boundless awareness that includes the bodymind but is not bound by it. There is the ahh-ha moment when you see that clinging to the absolute is also duality. But it always takes thought, memory and imagination to conjure up the story of *something* or *someone* that is shifting and the story of before and after. Here/Now, there is no-*thing* to shift and nowhere to go. All shifts are conceptual stories that happen within the dream-like movie of waking life, and every movie is nothing other than unicity appearing as movement. There is no possibility of "you" shifting in or out of unicity because there is no "you" apart from unicity — there is *only* unicity. The jewel is never really lost.

In the simplicity of what is, there is inhaling and exhaling, expanding and contracting, dying and being born, dreaming and waking up, clearing and clouding, and there is no owner of any of this who could shift or stabilize or identify with one side of the gestalt and banish the other. The shifting tides are not personal. All of it is simply weather — the tumbling shapes in the kaleidoscope endlessly reforming.

Seeking wholeness (or enlightenment, or the present moment) "out there" in the future only makes it *seem* far away and elusive. The search seemingly confirms the illusion of separation and lack. And *trying* to stop seeking is only a new form of seeking, seeking the end of seeking. Trying to escape from the movie is only another scene *in* the movie, as is any apparent escape or any enlightenment event that appears to happen to the character. From the perspective of the character in the movie, this sounds like very bad news—a truly hopeless situation. But the whole situation is imaginary.

In reality, you are not this mirage character trapped in a movie. You are the boundless awareness beholding the movie, the beingness of the whole appearance, the unicity from which nothing stands apart. As awareness, as unicity, you are already free, regardless of what is appearing in the movie. The scenes in the movie are always changing; experiences and states come and go. Liberation is realizing that there is nothing outside unicity. Unicity is all there is. It includes *all* experiences, not just the ones we like. True freedom is not a constant *experience* of happiness and expansion, but rather, true freedom is not *needing* any particular experience to come or go. Of course, within the movie of waking life, the character has preferences and tries to find solutions for apparent problems—the character may meditate or stop meditating, it may take an anti-depressant or drink whiskey or watch television or go into therapy or rush off to another satsang—it may even appear to be writing or reading this book.

Unicity, appearing as Joan, is writing this book, which is nothing but unicity. This book is an ever-changing appearance, and unicity, appearing as you, is reading it. No two readers will read the same book, and no one reader can read the same book twice. A book (or a reader) is like a river. It doesn't hold still. This moment is utterly unique and will never be repeated. Already it is gone. And yet, Here/Now is ever-present.

Sometimes this play of life feels terrible. Sometimes it seems hysterically funny. Sometimes it is exquisitely beautiful. Sometimes it is heartbreaking. I've noticed that when the need to figure it all out drops away, beauty and joy emerge. There is a waking up to the miracle of green leaves dancing in the wind and sunlight glistening on wet pavement. It needs no explanation, no ultimate meaning, no larger purpose, no grand solution.

Whether there is clarity or smog, pain or pleasure, enlightenment or delusion, nothing real is ever being hurt, for every appearance is nothing but a momentary shape of unicity forming and dissolving.

Clarity and smog follow each other like night and day, and unicity includes it all. Everything *is* as it is, including the desire to change it! There seems to be a naturally arising interest here in seeing through the smog and recognizing the jewel. No one manufactured this interest. It is happening by itself, effortlessly, in the same way that everything is happening.

Clarity sees *everything* as the jewel, and this clear seeing is unconditional love or enlightenment. But unicity is ever-present with or without clarity. Unicity depends upon nothing and includes everything. The "you" who seems to shift between clarity and confusion is a mirage, and the dividing lines between enlightenment and delusion are porous and imaginary. The One Self, which is the boundlessness of Here/Now, has no other – no inside and no outside – no before and no after.

Whatever we say is never quite right. The writings and talks in this book sometimes point to a shift from conceptual thought to awareness, and sometimes they point beyond all shifts to what never needs any shift. Sometimes the perspective is radical and absolute, sometimes it is more relative and practical. What is said in one talk may seem to totally contradict what was said in another. You may be tempted to think that one is "right" and the other "wrong," or that one is a "higher" truth and the other a "lower" one. But unicity includes it all. Every moment offers a unique and totally new expression of boundlessness, and any place you land and try to set up camp is never the whole truth. Liberation is freedom from fixation.

It's very easy for the mind to make something out of nothing, to form new beliefs and then to identify with those beliefs and cling to them for a sense of security. This is what the mind habitually does. It's easy to become dogmatic, to stop listening or get defensive if we hear something that threatens or contradicts our beliefs. It's easy to fall into conflict over words, often without really even hearing what is being said. Buddhism, Advaita, and radical nonduality are not immune from this kind of dogmatism and fundamentalism. None of us are. I find it in myself. So, is it possible to hold all our ideas lightly and to be open to seeing something new and unexpected?

Words, analogies and pointers frequently get used in different ways by different authors, or even by the same author in different moments. This can lead to a great deal of confusion, misunderstanding and unnecessary disagreement. Words such as "awareness," "consciousness," "being," "I," and "emptiness," are especially vulnerable to this kind of confusion because what they point to can never be objectified, and on top of that, these words all get used in different (and even opposite) ways. In one place, we may read that Ultimate Reality is "prior to consciousness," and in another place, "consciousness" is used synonymously with Ultimate Reality. Are they saying different things, or are they saying exactly the same thing in different words? Likewise, common analogies such as mirrors, waves and movie screens can be used in different ways to clarify different aspects of reality.

In pointing to what is, I use many different words. Some of these same words (e.g., "consciousness," "I," or "here") may also be used to mean something much more limited. In one sentence, the words "I" or "you" may refer to Joan Tollifson or John Doe, and in another sentence, those same words might refer to boundless awareness or unicity, our True Nature. Likewise, the word "here" may sometimes refer to Chicago or my living room, and in another sentence, the same word may point to boundless awareness, impersonal presence – the One Reality. Sometimes, I use capital letters to convey the sense of Ultimate Reality, but not always.

Sometimes an author or a teacher speaks *as* the One Reality, and the word "I" then refers to this absolute boundlessness that has no opposite and no other. In the next sentence, the same author may speak as the personal self, and then the word "I" now refers to the person, Joe Blow or Jane Doe. "I" as unicity have no problem with anything, but "I" as Joan have a problem with all kinds of things. All of this can be quite confusing. *It is very helpful to remember that confusion is always about words and ideas, never about reality itself.* Reality is simple. It is what requires no belief, what cannot be doubted. The complication is *always* in thoughts and ideas *about* this undeniable presence. The problem is always imaginary.

Even though this book aims to expose the separate self as a kind of mirage, it is virtually impossible to speak or write fluidly and naturally without using personal pronouns or without at times sounding dualistic to the literal or dogmatic mind that wants to pick apart each sentence. So, if you can, when reading this or any other book, try not to get stuck on the words, or on arguing over different maps of the same territory. Any map is only a tentative abstraction of the territory. It is to the territory itself (what I call the actuality, *suchness*, or bare *fact* of the present moment) that the words in this book are always pointing.

These words are never intended as dogma or final truth, but rather, as invitations to look and listen, to question, to see and discover for oneself. Maybe in reading this book, the interest will arise to wonder what happens when all words and concepts and ideas fall away. What remains? *That* is where the juice and the aliveness is. And, of course, paradoxically, this aliveness is also present as words and concepts and ideas! We're not trying to banish all thinking and conceptualizing. Everything has its place.

In reality, no separate individuals actually exist in the way we think. Boundlessness is appearing as seemingly separate individuals like the ocean is appearing as waves. In everyone who attends my meetings, I meet only myself. There is no other. I don't think of myself – the Joan character, that is – as a teacher, but more as a friend and fellow-traveler. Even though Joan may be giving talks and responding to questions, there is only ever unicity exploring and realizing itself. This boundless unicity is the true "I" to which every apparent individual refers – the One Self. It is from this One Reality that this book (and every book) emerges, and it is to that One Reality that this book points. There is nowhere you can point that is not the One Reality. This One Reality is not other than the coffee cup in your hand, the cloud floating across the blue sky, or the biting of your fingernails.

The Movie of Waking Life

Invitation to Explore the Present Moment:

We'll start as always by sitting quietly. For those of you who are here for the first time, you can sit in any position that's comfortable. I'd recommend sitting in a way that feels relaxed and open and grounded, but any position is okay. If you prefer, you can lie on the floor or stand up. You can have your eyes open or closed or whatever you like. You can look around the room or out the window if you want. You don't have to sit motionlessly, you can move. We're not doing anything other than simply *being* here, present and aware. And actually, you can't *not* be present and aware, so this is absolutely effortless and simple.

Many of you have done some kind of meditation in the past, and maybe you still do. But for right now, I would invite you to drop all ideas about meditation and simply be here without a method or a practice of any kind, without any attempt to do something special. This silence is simply a space to enjoy and explore the ever-changing present moment, just as it is. Being silent isn't "better" or "more spiritual" than talking, it's just different. Silence may reveal things that words tend to conceal (and vice versa).

You don't need to get into any special state, or have some "spiritual" experience, or make something happen, or get rid of anything that shows up here. There's nothing to do but simply *being here*. Hearing the whooshing of the traffic, feeling sensations in the body, breathing... maybe *seeing* the thoughts that pop up *as* thoughts, noticing how they generate mental movies in the imagination...*seeing* how insubstantial these thoughts and stories are...seeing how insubstantial *everything* is – the whole movie of waking life – all of it a fleeting appearance without substance.

Here/Now accepts everything and sticks to nothing. Everything is allowed to be here in this vast space of awareness. *You* don't have to "do" this allowing – it's not some kind of spiritual practice. This allowing is the very nature of awareness. The bird song, the honking horn, the tightness in your jaw, the passing thoughts, a moment of resistance or restlessness, a moment of expansion or joy, the breathing – there's space here for everything. Nothing needs to be different in any way from exactly how it is. It's all one wondrous, ever-changing, ever-present whole.

The Talk:

This movie of waking life is a fascinating phenomenon. How every morning, mysteriously and unbidden, it appears – this movie with "me" as the main character. And then when we fall asleep at night, equally mysteriously, this whole world disappears, and for awhile we have other movies called dreams, and then there is deep sleep, where everything perceivable and conceivable disappears completely – including even any *sense* of awareness or presence. It all vanishes and no one is left to know or care that it has vanished. And out of this total absence, dreams appear, and then the movie of waking life.

Sometimes, when we wake up from sleep, we have to scramble for just a second (and sometimes more) to remember who we are, where we are, what we're doing. It happens every morning, but usually it goes by so quickly that we don't notice. But sometimes it takes awhile longer to remember. We wake up with no idea who or where we are, and we can feel the brain scrambling to get re-oriented. And then eventually it all comes back to us: Ah, yes, I'm So-and-So, I'm a doctor or a lawyer or a homeless drunk or whatever the role is, and this is my wife next to me, or my husband, or my lover, or my empty bed, and within a few seconds, we have reincarnated as this character in "the story of my life." Oh yes, I'm a failure, I'm miserable and depressed. Or, oh yes, I'm happily married and rolling in money. Or, my child is flunking out of school – what can I do? Or, oh my God, I'm devastated, my partner of forty years died three days ago. There's a brief moment before we remember these things, a moment when we are simply present as aware-ness itself. Impersonal awareness. But then we remember the partner who is absent and dead and gone for good, and grief floods the body. Tears well up in our eyes. The movie of waking life has begun.

And this movie seems to have layers. There is the simplest layer, which is pure perception: sounds, colors, shapes, sensations. This, too, is like a movie in the sense that it is an appearance in awareness that comes and goes. But pure perception is the least problematic layer, for it is without storyline or self. Pure nondual experiencing is the world that other animals and human babies presumably experience. It can include pain, but not suffering. It is nonconceptual sensory awareness and spontaneous action without fore-thought, after-thought or self-reflective commentary.

And then there are the other layers on top of this primary layer, movies inside of movies. Many times every day (or every hour, or every minute) during the movie of waking life, we seem to leave the world of pure perception and become absorbed in a secondary movie created by thinking, daydreaming, remembering, or fantasizing – this is the world of conceptualization and imagination. Actually, "we" don't leave one movie or become absorbed in another, that in itself is one of the conceptual imaginings. More accurately, this secondary movie appears in awareness and seems to obscure or overshadow the world of pure perception and sensation. That sensory world is still there, still being dimly registered, but the focus of attention shifts to this imaginary secondary layer.

This secondary layer involves suffering, by which I mean the sto-ries and ideas that are spun around simple pain. This suffering might include the fear of future pain or the memory of past pain, or something more psychological such as feeling "put down" or "unloved." Suddenly consciousness is lost in thoughts, memories, fantasies and projections, re-playing the memory of some past event or imagining some future event, going back over what happened yesterday, churning around in thoughts about world events, trying desperately to have some spiritual experience or figure out the nature of the universe. [the humidifier gurgles and Joan imitates the sound] *glug glug glug glug.* Back to the movie of pure perception!

The movie of waking life has yet another layer that happens when our character turns on the television, goes to the theater, or opens a novel. Suddenly, we find ourselves in a whole different drama, perhaps in another country, another galaxy, or another century. And then that movie ends, and we are back in the movie of "real life."

Movies inside movies inside movies. Basically, everything perceivable and conceivable is a movie—which means that *everything* (including you and me and this meeting) is a dream-like appearance in consciousness without objective or inherent reality. Nothing exists "out there" in some fixed and substantial way as we think it does.

The central underlying narrative running through all the "real life" movies is the story of "me," the main character, a fascinating story which is always being refined and revised. It's a story about how I was born into this world, how I grew up, the circumstances of my childhood, all the things that have happened to me, my various traits—positive and negative—and all the possible endings to this movie. Of course, we don't really want an ending! So we may have another movie about "what's next" after death. Heaven, hell, reincarnation, whatever it might be.

The smallest thing can set a new movie rolling that might play for hours, or days, or even years. You get a letter saying that your book has just been accepted for publication, and instantly you can be absorbed in a wonderful movie about success and happiness. Or you can get a very different letter saying that your book has been rejected—it's not what anybody needs to read. I did get a letter like that once. I got both of those letters actually. And it was fascinating to see on both occasions what was set in motion by simply looking at a sheet of paper with little black squiggles on it. A story of success and happiness and being somebody who was worth something in one case, and a story of failure and worthlessness in the other. Amazing! So it's "the story of me" movie with its ever-revising past and its various possible future continuations – some of them scary and some of them wonderful.

If we take up meditation or come to meetings like these, we may start to *notice* all these mental movies, these stories and fantasies. And then, before we know it, there's a new movie, in which our character is trying to wake up from movies. And yet any awakening that we can imagine, remember or experience turns out to be only another scene in another movie.

The meditation movie is all about "me" trying to "be present" and "be here now" and "be aware" and not get lost in thought. In this movie, the "me" character is seemingly going back and forth between spacious awareness and obsessive thinking. This "me" hopes to wake up from movies once and for all and become an enlightened "no-self."

The Advaita movie is rooted in the hope that "I" can realize myself as "pure awareness," or "the noumenon," or "the Self," or as that which is "prior to consciousness." In this movie, the "me" character hopes to realize that "everything is just a dream" and transcend this whole earthly mess once and for all, so that when that letter comes saying, "Nobody needs to read your stupid book," it won't bother "me" at all. "I" will be pure consciousness, undisturbed by anything.

This whole spiritual adventure of waking up from the movies may seem very real, very serious, very important. We may think that this me who is trying to wake up from the movies is the *real* me. We can see that the "me" who worries about getting my book published is an illusion – but this me who's trying to wake up from that illusion – *that* me, we imagine, is real.

But is it real, this mirage-like self who seems to be thinking my thoughts, making my choices, living my life, or else observing it all as a detached witness? How substantial are *any* of these movies, even the primary movie of non-conceptual perceptions and sensations? Even that bottom-line *sense* of awareness or impersonal presence, the bare *knowingness* that "I am" and "This is," even that vanishes every night in deep sleep. Could even *that* be an appearance in the movie? What is real? What is real in this moment here and now?

Let's consider the reality of this morning, say between 7 and 9 a.m., before we got to this meeting. Where is all of that now? Whatever was happening then, the whole world that seemed to exist so vividly at 8 a.m., the movie that was playing then – where is that now? There may be a memory trace that can be summoned up, but that memory seems rather vague and hazy compared to the vividness of this present reality right now. Memory is a kind of abstraction. It's not the same as the *actuality* of 8 a.m. – *that* is totally gone. And then, right now, where is that memory trace that was here just a second ago – where has *it* gone?

If we start to look closely into all the things that seem so solid, we don't find solidity. We don't find substance. We don't find continuity in any form. We know this scientifically. If we watched this table here with speeded-up, time-lapse photography over many centuries, we would see that the table is disintegrating in front of our eyes. We know that if we had a very powerful electron microscope, and we zeroed in on this table, we would find mostly empty space and no solid boundary line between the table and the objects on the table. We would find thoroughgoing flux and particles that magically turn into waves. No table has ever been found outside of consciousness, and physicists have discovered that the act of observation changes what is being observed. Nevertheless, the illusion that the table is separate and solid and "out there" as some kind of persisting and continuous objective reality is very convincing.

We may have some idea that if only we would have this great awakening experience, then this table would magically dissolve into thin air and we would see through the world of appearances. It would be like taking psychedelics or something. But that's another fantasy movie. We may even remember taking a mind-expanding drug or being on a meditation retreat in India and having some fantastic experience of Oneness. But where is that experience now? In retrospect, our whole trip to India and every magnificent or mundane experience were all a kind of movie, an appearance that has completely vanished.

Any form – whether it is a "person," a "chair," a "thought," a "movie," or anything else we can name – any apparent form is like a whirlpool or a river – it's not really a solid, separate, continuous *thing*. That appearance of solidity and continuity is an illusion, like a mirage. Any form is, in reality, an ever-changing process inseparable from everything else. There is diversity and variation in reality, but not separation. Reality is seamless and formless.

It's one thing to adopt a philosophical *belief* that there's no self, but we can *see* this for ourselves by giving close attention to the actuality of this present moment. When we do this, we discover that the solidity, the boundaries and the continuity aren't really there. No "me" apart from everything else can actually be found.

Meditation, in the best sense, is this kind of direct, firsthand exploration. Of course, once it gets called "meditation" and turned into a formal and methodical system, it can easily become a hindrance. But the heart of intelligent meditation is really nothing more than paying attention. It's simply a way of exploring the actuality of this present moment, as we do at the beginning of our meetings. The value of this kind of non-conceptual, meditative exploration is that, instead of just having an *idea* that "the table is not solid" or that "Buddhism and Advaita both say there's no self, so it must be true," instead of *believing* this stuff, meditative inquiry is a way of actually *investigating* – looking and listening and seeing directly for oneself.

I've heard that there's not a single cell in this body that was here a decade ago. They have all been replaced during that period of time. Subatomic particles are dancing around, energy is moving, forms are continuously breaking down and reforming – there's actually no-*thing* here now that was here when I was five years old. There's no "me" who went from being five to being fifty-six. And that five-year-old's world – where are the 1940s, the 1950s, the 1960s, the whole 20th century? There are some memory traces which are notoriously unreliable, mutable and vague, a few old photographs, but where is that five-year-old? She's completely *gone*, and her world is completely gone as well.

Impermanence is scary if we think that *things* (including this bodymind and everything I love) are impermanent. But when we see that impermanence is so complete and so thoroughgoing that no-thing forms in the first place to *be* impermanent, then there is no more impermanence. There is only unicity. Buddhism calls it emptiness. Advaita calls it the Self. We could also call it boundlessness, ground-lessness, seamlessness, no-*thing*-ness, or the present moment.

[sound of dog barking outside which Joan imitates] *woof-woof-woof!* Hearing that sound happens effortlessly. Once we get into some deliberate practice of "meditation," then we start thinking we have to *do* listening. We have to *do* awareness, but awareness is actually natu-ral – it's happening by itself the same way everything is happening, effortlessly. Even effort is happening effortlessly.

Is there somebody or something that hears the dog bark? Or is that "listener" a mental image, an idea? We have lots of *ideas* about what is hearing that sound – we can *think* that it's "me" or "the brain" or "the ears" or "consciousness." But in our immediate direct *experi-ence*, is there a listener apart from the listening, a hearer apart from the hearing? There's simply *woof-woof-woof*, isn't there? No separation – no subject, no object, just *woof-woof-woof*. Without words, there's really no separation between awareness and the content of awareness, or between form and emptiness. *Woof-woof-woof!* Just *this*.

To the mind, "nothing" sounds really scary, "There's *nothing*, oooo, scary…" [laughter] Or, "There's no me. Oh no! I'm nobody!" It doesn't sound good to the mind. But when there's simply *woof-woof-woof*, or the emptiness of deep sleep, it's very relaxing, a big relief, quite delightful.

Now, of course, as soon as I say that, it can set off another movie: "She says it's relaxing and delightful. Have I experienced that delight and relaxation? I'm not sure if I have. She's probably more delighted and relaxed than I am. I feel tense and unhappy. I must not be getting it yet." And then we start trying to get it, *trying* to be delighted, and *evaluating* whether we're as delighted or as relaxed as somebody else. Pretty soon we start building up this mythology about the person who said that – she's walking around delighted and relaxed and blissfully happy all the time. And if this person has been dead for a few decades or a few centuries, then these stories can get better and better. "She never had a bad moment. She was Pure Delight. One, long, happy, unwavering celebration."

Or maybe we have a glimpse of how simple and effortless it all is. But then a split second later the thinking mind takes delivery of this insight and personalizes it ("I am awake!"), or makes it into a new ideology ("Nothing exists!"), or *thinks* about it ("What exactly does this insight do for me? How can I be sure it's true?"), and then immediately, suffering re-appears. And we think, "I feel rotten. Where's the beef? Maybe I lost it. Maybe I didn't really get it after all."

It's amazing to see how these movies – stories, worlds, universes – appear out of nowhere. The other day, I was sitting in this living room, and I had earlier that day just finished cleaning out my mother's apartment, and there was a great sadness that came suddenly, that hollow, empty feeling, and a story about, "What's left? My mother is dead and gone forever. I'm all alone. I'm becoming an old woman." Accompanying the thoughts, there were mental pictures floating through the mind, pictures of my mother's empty apartment, my mother's face, the thought that I would never see that face again. Sadness and grief filled me. And then, out of the blue, there was a *seeing* of this whole story *as* a story, a waking up from the apparent reality and seriousness of it. Suddenly, there was the realization, "Oh, it's *nothing*! Nothing is missing, nothing is happening." I began laughing. There was a huge rush of joy and delight. I wasn't *trying* to have that shift; it happened spontaneously by itself.

And I'm not sharing this story – this movie – in order to suggest that delight could or should be our perpetual state of mind. Because there is no up without down. Nothing can appear without polarity and contrast. So if you are trying to be in *any* particular state "all of the time," it's a setup for disappointment because no state or experience lasts. What comes will go eventually. And what goes can always come again. *Whatever* state is showing up is only a scene in the movie of waking life. It's not happening *to* anybody, it's not anybody's fault. It has no inherent or fixed reality.

There's a very popular story that you are responsible for your life. If you are angry, that's your fault, and you have to *do* something about it. If you are depressed, there's something wrong with you, and you have to fix that. Depression *means something* about you – you're spiritually not very advanced, you're not meditating enough. That way of thinking has been conditioned into us. But more and more, science is finding that there is no executive in the brain, that "the self" is a process and not a thing, and that so many things that have been treated as psychological, spiritual or moral maladies and blamed on the phantom executive are actually the result of uncontrollable neurochemistry, genetics, brain patterns, injuries, hormones, social conditioning, and other factors of nature and nurture.

The movie of waking life includes every possible experience, and from our human point of view, there are definitely many, many troubling things that happen. Earthquakes, floods, tsunamis, genocides, rapes, crush videos, snuff films, children being sold into prostitution and slavery. The list goes on and on. But where is this all happening? If you say "in Africa" or "in Chicago," then where is Africa or Chicago happening? How real is any of it if you see it from the subatomic level or from a distant galaxy light years away – or maybe from the point of view of an earthworm or a virus? How real is the whole human drama then? Who or what is experiencing it all? Is it anything other than a momentary appearance? Is anything real ever being damaged or destroyed?

These questions may feel very threatening, and it's interesting to investigate what exactly is being threatened. If we really look closely at this present moment, we see that everything that happens is indeed very much like a movie or a dream, that it is all vanishing as soon as it appears, that it disappears whenever we stop paying attention to it or thinking about it. How real is it?

Something is here, yes. That's undeniable. But if you look, you can see how ephemeral it all is, how everything changes, including our opinions and our memories. Isn't it fascinating how different people look at what is supposedly "the same situation" or "the same person" or "the same movie" and see something completely and totally different from each other? Maybe that's because they're not really looking at "the same thing" at all – maybe there *is* no single objective reality "out there" behind the appearance. Maybe there are only infinite appearances, movies within movies, multiple movies all playing simultaneously, all of it happening Here/Now.

To see that it is all a dream-like appearance with no inherent reality is freedom. Not the freedom to do whatever you want, but the freedom that wants nothing other than exactly what is. Seeing how ephemeral it all is doesn't mean we won't act or respond to things that upset us. As a character in the movie, we do whatever we are moved by life to do. Some people meditate, some become aid workers, some commit murder. Some care deeply, some don't. We do what we do, and we cannot do otherwise. All our desires, inclinations, interests, abilities, actions, thoughts, and impulses come from the totality, not from some phantom individual agent. Our next breath, our next heartbeat, our next thought – where does it come from? Can you find a source? It simply appears – and none of it could be any other way than exactly how it is. Everything is one seamless whole.

When you think of the world as a collection of separate objects, and you think these objects actually exist "out there" separate from you, and you think that you have to figure it all out and control it – this is delusion. This is suffering.

When you see the world as it really is, as one seamless whole, this is unconditional love. You see perfection even in what appears to be imperfection. You see unicity and not separation. Every cloud, every flower, every leaf, every car, every piece of trash, every dictator, every bigot, every wife beater, every child molester – wherever you look, you see the One Self.

You're not at war with anything. You're not fighting desperately for your rights or your survival or feeling outraged by all the injustices of life, at least not in the same way. Even if you are doing aid work in Africa, running a shelter for battered women, marching for equality, or getting child molesters off the streets, it is all happening without the expectation of a cure. You see the wholeness that is ever-present. You know that the movie is a movie. You know that there is something prior to the movie, at the heart of every apparent form, that is boundless and seamless and causeless.

Participant (P): The "Me on My Way to Enlightenment" movie is pervasive in many spiritual groups. Lots of us in this room have been caught up in this story and some of us still are. I was duped by this story for years.

Joan (J): I'm sensing a new movie: "Poor Me, I Was Duped." [Humidifier gurgles and Joan imitates the sound] *glug glug glug* [laughter].

P: I've been duped. That might last for a few hours today.

J: It's an entertaining movie. Nothing wrong with it. But is there really *someone* who has been duped? Where is the whole past right now?

P: Thankfully gone. It's seems like when I was a child, I knew this. I would go out and play in the sun and ignore all the strategies to grow up. It seems like there was more presence then.

J: Yes, in childhood we haven't yet been —

P: Duped.

J: The conditioning hasn't gotten very far yet. Self-reflective, conceptual thought isn't that developed yet. When I was a little girl, my mother used to give me a pail of water and a paintbrush, so that I could paint on the sidewalk. I'd paint these paintings on the sidewalk with water, and they would disappear in a matter of minutes, but that didn't matter because what I was enjoying was the joy of doing it. And then at another point in my life, I was an art major — and I was seriously questioning whether it was worth going on as an artist given that I wasn't as good as Picasso or Michelangelo. It wasn't all about the joy of doing it anymore; that had been overlaid with something else having to do with evaluation, comparison, success, failure, identity, and so on.

One minute you're enjoying the feel of a brushstroke, the joy of water darkening the cement, the excitement of a shape, and then the next minute you've grown up and you're in a world where you're getting letters saying, "No one needs to read a book like this." And it starts when we're very little actually, when our parents are praising us or criticizing us. We begin working not for the pure joy of it, as we did originally, but now we do it in order to get approval and recognition and a gold star. And then it's a Pulitzer Prize or an Oscar. Or in spiritual circles, it might be dharma transmission or a certificate of enlightenment. That natural, childlike sense of playfulness and curiosity and enjoying the simplicity of being gets overshadowed by this attempt to make something out of "me," to make "me" into a successful me or an enlightened me.

All of this happens out of infinite causes and conditions. And in the moment it happens, it could not be otherwise. It's all a dream-like appearance, a story: "Me Seeking Approval," "Me Getting Dharma Transmission," "Me and My Big Awakening." But we begin to notice that it doesn't work. There's never enough approval or enough success.

P: Is it something to do with putting a result into the doing?

J: Yes, it's putting a result into the picture, and also putting a "me" into it. There is no "me" in painting the sidewalk with water – there's simply the joy of movement and shapes and dark cement and gesture. The pure joy of that. There's no thought about some final result or whether I'm as good as Picasso or whether my work will be shown in some prestigious art museum or approved by the critics or sold for millions of dollars. And there's no thought of wanting "my" painting (and "me") to endure forever. The fact that it all evaporates is no problem. There's only the joy of painting.

P: So does suffering imply a me?

J: I would say so. But the me is only a thought, a mirage. There *never* really *is* a me. It's always an illusion. And there is no "me" who *has* this illusion. That's part of the illusion. Thought inserts an agent into the picture who isn't really there, and then we have blame and shame and guilt and retribution and all that stuff that keeps us fighting wars and beating ourselves up.

If, by suffering, we simply mean things happening that are hurtful, then there can certainly be suffering without a "me." The tsunami or the earthquake will come whether there's a sense of me or not. And on a certain level you can call that suffering – people losing their children, their homes, their livelihoods. But if we say that suffering is what the mind does with all of that after the fact, then suffering requires the mirage of a sufferer. Animals have pain, but humans suffer from their pain in a whole different way, because humans can remember the past and imagine the future.

P: Right away I want to find out how to avoid that. Oh, man.

J: So, there was just a *seeing* of that desire to avoid suffering as it came up. Beautiful! But then instantly thought slips a sense of agency into the picture and passes judgment on the phantom agent it has just created. When you said, "Oh man," it was like "you" had screwed up by wanting to avoid suffering. It had a feel of despair and discouragement and self-blame. Right? [participant nods] But *all* of these thoughts happen automatically. The first layer: "How can I avoid suffering?" And then the secondary layer taking delivery of the first layer, taking it personally, and passing judgment on the phantom thinker: "Oh, man. I screwed up again. What a loser I am." It's *all* a bunch of conditioned, impersonal thoughts arising out of infinite causes and conditions, all of it nothing but a dream-like appearance, a scene in the movie of waking life, gone in an instant. But it *seems* personal because at the center of every story is the core idea that "I" am somehow doing all this. *I* am responsible for all this. It's happening *to me*. It's *my* problem. And it all seems very serious and real. People commit suicide over stories as flimsy as this.

P: This is why animals and children do not seem to suffer so much.

J: Yes, they recover much more quickly. A child will cry if you take his toy, but three minutes later, he's totally forgotten. Where an adult could nurse that story of "what you took from me" for decades! So, yes, animals and babies suffer much less. They are more in the moment, less absorbed in stories. They stick with the facts.

But there is a positive side, obviously, to our adult human capacity for complex thinking, memory and story-telling. It allows us to have empathy and compassion, it takes us to the moon and gives us great art, it puts us at the very top of the food chain. And maybe we're learning in the course of evolution to use these abilities more wisely. Who knows? That's another story, as is evolution, as is the Big Bang, all of it appearing in this dream-like movie of waking life that mysteriously started rolling this morning. Actually, even "this morning" is a story.

P: Staying with pain might help to diminish strategies because avoiding pain is a motive for strategies.

J: Yes, to the degree that we can stay with pain as pure sensation, there will be less suffering than if we get caught up in a story about "When will this end? What if it gets worse? This might kill me. I can't take it." But there's no "me" who can *make* that happen.

And, in fact, some strategizing is quite helpful and important. It's useful if you're feeling chest pain to be able to remember your history of heart disease and to have the thought that it might be a heart attack and to be able to strategize how to get help. It's only that there's no one at the helm actually *doing* all that. It's all arising out of the whole universe.

Meditation can offer certain strategies that may be helpful, like if you're feeling depressed, there's the possibility of fully being with the feelings and experiencing them as pure sensation, and seeing the thoughts as thoughts. And maybe that's a useful strategy within the dream. But what often gets missed in the meditation world is that there's no one doing any of that, and so the illusion gets reinforced that "I" have to do that, and "by gosh, I did it wrong again," and all of that. And if meditation is motivated by the desire for a future result, then instantly it becomes suffering again, because if you're paying attention to the sensations of depression or pain *so that they will go away,* then you're not really paying attention. You're actually focused on something else – an outcome – and you're engaged in trying to avoid the actuality. So it gets very subtle.

When the mirage of the "me" who seemingly *has* a problem is absent, then whatever happens is no longer problematic. It is simply sensations, appearances, passing forms, like the tumbling shapes in a kaleidoscope. None of it *means* anything. It may be unpleasant or painful, but the one who wants to control it or cure it or do something with it is absent.

When contracted experiences show up, I find there is no need anymore to do anything at all with them – they're part of the passing show. Whatever doing or undoing shows up in response to them (relaxing, sitting quietly, paying attention to the sensations, distracting myself, whatever it is) all happens by itself, effortlessly.

P: In Buddhism there's a lot of encouragement to try harder, at least the version I was in was that way, and that message is not useful for me. I end up just beating myself up a lot.

J: Yes, trying harder assumes that something is lacking, and it encourages you to take that imaginary lack personally.

P: I feel very stuck in the I-story. I know there's no self, but I still *feel* like there is. And I keep trying to see that there isn't.

J: There's no "I" who is stuck in the I-story, that's part of the story. There is a functional sense of being a particular body that you need in order to survive – proprioception or whatever. That won't go away. There are many misunderstandings floating around about what is meant by "no self," as if this were some special, magical experience to be had. "No self" is simply the ever-present Here/Now within which everything appears, including all the sensations, thoughts and stories that form the mirage of separation, encapsulation, and agency that we *think* of as the self. But if you simply notice your actual experience right now, where is this self? Isn't there simply a vast field of aware presence showing up as all kinds of sensations – visual, auditory, somatic, and so forth? Where are the boundaries? Where is the one in control? This is utterly simple. This ever-present Here/Now is so obvious, so clear, so all-encompassing, that it's easy to *seemingly* overlook. Actually, it's impossible to overlook. It's all there is.

P: How can you keep that mirage from happening? By getting drunk?

J: Yes, that works really well. Let me tell you. [laughter] I highly recommend that. It really clears everything right up. [laughter] Look, the mirage doesn't need to go away; it's only a mirage. The functional sense of being a particular bodymind appears when needed, but upon investigation, no separate, independent, continuous self is actually found. Nothing needs to be any different from how it is.

P: Investigating has been really helpful to me in dealing with my patterns that come up. But then I notice I want a result. It is still habitual for me to think of following a program to get someplace.

J: We can't really try not to try. Well, we *can*. It happens. Trying not to try. But it doesn't work. It's like you can't *make* yourself go to sleep, or you can't *make* yourself relax, so the only thing that can really happen is noticing how you are tensing up, *seeing* the strategies and seeing through them. But you can't even *make* this seeing happen. And whether this seeing happens or not, whether there is trying, or trying not to try, or totally relaxing, or whatever is happening, it's all a dream-like happening. It makes no difference for what you truly are – for unicity. It makes an apparent difference *in* the movie, from the perspective of the character, but from the perspective of unicity, it makes no difference. No one is in control of what movie plays or doesn't play or what happens in the movie. The character is not in control, thought is not in control, awareness is not in control, even unicity is not in control. The character is not in control because the character is a mirage. Thought is not in control because thought is an effect of causes and conditions. Awareness is not in control because awareness is like a mirror – it beholds and accepts everything just as it is, without judgment and without any desire to change it in any way. Unicity is not in control because control takes two, the controller and the controlled, and unicity is undivided. Control or the absence of control are both stories *in* the movie, and movies only seem to be a problem *in* the movies. In deep sleep, all our problems disappear completely.

P: There is a sense of progress, of improvement or becoming more awake over time. It seems that I am more aware, more awake, more present than I used to be.

J: Right, there's a story in this movie of waking life that this organism went from being a tiny microscopic thing to being a much larger thing that got a college degree and then found a job. Or it went from being drunk all the time to sobering up and getting into meditation. And all of that can be labeled "progress." And relatively speaking, maybe it is progress. But to come up with all that in the first place requires memory and imagination – thought has to conjure up this story with this mirage-like entity at the center of it who is progressing. It's like the whirlpool or the river again – there's really no "me" there who goes from being drunk to being sober. There's some pattern maybe, like the whirlpool or the river, that we're calling "Joan" or "Joan's life," but whether we call it progress or not is very relative to how we're looking at it, whether we think Joan is going in a good direction or a bad direction. And even though, in the story, I've been traveling along for fifty-some years, have I gotten anywhere? I am right Here. I've always been right here, not meaning in this living room, but Here/Now in this one eternal present moment. So have I gotten anywhere? Only by going into this movie story, this imaginary narrative, can we conjure up a story in which there is an enduring "somebody" who seems to have gotten somewhere. *Relatively* speaking, it may be a so-called "true story," but when we look closely, in the truest sense, it's all fiction. Nothing really happened.

P: Could you say, "I'm more here than I used to be" ?

J: [laughter] That's a good one!

P: So there's no possible way that progress makes any sense?

J: Well, it makes sense in the context of the story. Relatively speaking, in the context of the story, you can be dead drunk every day, and then you can sober up. You can become more awake to the present moment than you used to be, less hypnotized by ideas and beliefs. And you can call that progress. But you have to go into memory and imagination to conjure all that up, to separate out all the elements and give them continuity, to conceptualize cause and effect, to imagine the persisting entity at the center of it all evolving over time. Time itself is a mental construction. Our story of progress is like a painting in water on the cement — it evaporates in an instant.

So have I gotten anywhere? What are we actually talking about?

In this instant — without thought — where is the movie of progress or the one who seems to be progressing?

What is this "I" that seems to progress or regress? It's a bunch of sensations and mental images and memories and stories, isn't it? And what is seeing all of that? What is aware of the character and the drama? If we try to locate or see this undeniable awareness, what do we find?

[long silence]

We find nothing we can grasp. We find only an absence appearing as everything. When we turn attention backwards to see what is seeing, we find nothing and we find everything! The true "I" to which we all refer turns out to be another word for everything or nothing. This presence or absence is nothing objective that we can grasp. And yet, it is showing up as this whole appearance. But it is not limited to any particular thing, nor is it encapsulated inside the character in the movie of waking life. It is here prior to this appearance, and it is what remains when this appearance vanishes into thin air. It is what Here/Now *is*. The words are just words. But *this* [Joan gestures to include everything] is not a word or an idea.

P: Could you say something like, "Presence is more real than it used to be"?

J: That's a good book title. [laughter]

P: Presence happens more frequently.

J: Does presence happen more frequently, or does delusion happen less frequently or more transparently? And is there really a "before" and an "after" to be more or less? All of that requires the imagination of time – before and after – and the imagination of more or less, frequently or infrequently, but reality is timeless, always now. It never comes or goes.

P: If time is of the imagination, space is as well.

J: Right, exactly. It's a way of conceptualizing. In fact, everything appears right here at zero distance. But I have the *idea* that "you" are "over there" on the other side of the room and that the planet Jupiter is millions of miles away. It's like looking at a painting – the surface is actually flat, but we see (or imagine) depth. This instant (Here/Now) is timeless and spaceless. It has no duration and no location.

P: I'm working on getting rid of progress.

J: That should finally get you somewhere. [laughter] One of the wonderful things about having these meetings is that we can all see ourselves in everybody else. We have our different unique patterns, but the basic ingredients are very similar for all of us.

P: We are all whirl and pool. [laughter]

Another P: In Feldenkrais lessons, the instructions often include checking out where you are when you begin, and where you are when you end, and noting changes in order to help the brain process the change. We can use this information in some way.

J: Yes, nothing that is being said here is intended to deny the importance or usefulness of memory, thought, the ability to compare and contrast and evaluate, or anything else that we humans appear to do in the movie of waking life, including Feldenkrais lessons, yoga, meditation and coming to meetings like this one. It all is as it is – one seamless whole. This is definitely not about disparaging memory or thinking.

If we didn't have memory, we'd have a big problem. Alzheimer's can be quite terrifying and certainly disabling. So there is a functional importance to having memory, and it is undoubtedly crucial to any kind of learning, and that's fine. And relatively speaking, within the movie of waking life, we can learn to refine and improve our ability to do all kinds of things, from throwing a baseball, to speaking a foreign language, to seeing through thoughts and "being here now" – and that's all part of the show. But no one is in control of any of it.

Whatever happens is very ephemeral when you look closely. It's all like painting the sidewalk with water. In a moment, the painting evaporates. In a moment, a whole lifetime evaporates! To do Feldenkrais lessons and notice changes in the body is as delightful as painting the sidewalk with water. Both are fun. And both will evaporate. The body will evaporate. And that doesn't mean it wasn't worth playing the game. The worthiness is in the joy of the moment, the aliveness here and now, not some permanent or future result. Every result, every achievement evaporates.

And speaking of evaporating, we're at the end of our time, but before we end, let's take a couple of minutes to sit quietly in silence.

Where are the last two hours and everything that was said? It has all evaporated hasn't it? How real was it? What remains?

It's Hopeless

You are already awake. And by you I don't mean the imaginary separate individual. I mean this awake being that's here right now – the boundless unicity that includes everything, *everything*! The sunlight, the birds, the leaves, the traffic, the thoughts, the acid indigestion. *Everything* is the Holy Reality. There's no possibility of being separate from this boundless unicity or losing it or not having it yet, because there's no one apart from it to get it or lose it or find it or have it. The thought, "I'm not quite there yet," is only a thought. And that thought and the melodrama it creates are themselves nothing but unicity.

We only have to turn on the television to discover that consciousness loves playing. It enjoys melodramas, horror shows, crime dramas, happy love stories, tragic love stories, comedies, adventure stories, car chases, wars – and it also enjoys turning off the television. It enjoys silence. It enjoys waking up from stories. It enjoys playing hide and seek. It enjoys finding and being found, and then hiding again, and again being found. It enjoys going to sleep; it enjoys waking up. It enjoys the play of birth and death, creation and destruction, appearing and disappearing, expanding and contracting.

Sometimes there's clear, sunny weather – the wonderful feeling of joy and aliveness where everything is glowing and sparkling and bright and beautiful – and then other times the experience is one of flatness, agitation or upset – cloudy, stormy, overcast weather. And each of these sensations, thoughts and experiences is nothing but unicity. Even the thought, "This can't be it," is it.

There's nothing to find. There's only *this* [Joan gestures to indicate everything].

There's no you that has to fall away or be dissolved. There are different patterns of energy that we call Joan or Ted or chair or rug or tree. But there's no solid *thing* there, there's no solid *self* inside these ever-changing patterns, there's no separate, persisting *object* anywhere. It's all one energy, one seamless flux.

There are preferences — we'd rather eat ice cream than cockroaches, we'd rather see peace on earth than the holocaust (or so we like to believe). Those preferences are also this same seamless flux appearing as cockroaches, as ice cream, as the holocaust, as preferences. If the mind is busy saying, *"Yes, but... What if? Yes, but wait...What about...?"* — that, too, is the same energy, questioning itself, exploring itself, discovering itself, unfolding and enfolding itself, forming and informing itself, tricking itself, enjoying itself. This entire appearance that we call "the world" or "the universe" has no substance. Try to find the thought that you had five seconds ago — it's completely gone. Vanished. Earlier this morning is completely gone. Everything about it is gone. You might *think* that the kitchen table where you had your morning coffee is still there, but it is not the same table or the same kitchen or the same you from one instant to the next. It's all a disappearing subatomic dance, a display in consciousness. Does "your kitchen" even exist when no one is conscious of it? Your whole life up until this second [Joan snaps her fingers repeatedly] is completely gone! Vanished. How real was it?

What is real Here/Now? This is a wonderful inquiry.

Everything is happening effortlessly on its own. The sunlight is happening, the seeing is happening, the hearing is happening, breathing is happening, movements of the hands are happening, these words are happening. And all of it is *nothing* at all. Every night in deep sleep, and actually, second by second, it all vanishes completely into thin air.

P: I find a restlessness with no particular content — it doesn't want anything, but there is a restlessness that doesn't want to stay there.

J: Stay where?

P: Here. With what is.

J: But there's no way to leave here. What you're calling "restlessness" is actually some mix of ever-changing neurochemistry, thoughts and sensations that gets labeled "restlessness," and the label already has a judgmental, pejorative feel to it. And then a thought (posing as "me") pops up and takes ownership of the restlessness ("This is *my* restlessness, *my* problem."). That thought "takes delivery" as Nisargadatta used to say, it takes this "restlessness" personally. And that labeling and taking delivery and taking-it-personally also happens by itself, impersonally! And then there's more thinking – comparing, contrasting, judging, strategizing: "This restlessness is not enlightened behavior…it feels terrible…I want that other experience I was having before, that blissful feeling of empty space – *that* was spiritual. I have to get rid of this restlessness because it's taking me away from 'here,' where I'm supposed to be." It's *all* thinking, which comes out of infinite causes and conditions, and the whole picture it paints is completely insubstantial. There's no "you" to do anything about any of this. It's truly hopeless, which is bad news only to the mind that wants to do something about it. The problem is completely imaginary.

P: When restlessness arises, would you say to address it by just letting it –

J: Just see that right now the mind is looking for a strategy. There's the assumption that this restlessness is a problem and we have to find a way to deal with it.

P: It's hopeless! I am going to write that on the wall in big letters. It's hopeless. That's everything! If I would just stay with that.

J: But see, there it is again – the thought, "If I would just stay with that I'd be okay. I'm going to write it on the wall in big letters so then maybe I'll remember that." And even this strategizing is it, there is no escape from unicity.

Another P: What does it mean, "It's hopeless?"

J: I mean that there's no one who can do anything about this waking dream. There's the thought that I want to get to someplace that I've heard about, imagined, or been to before, and there's a strategy for how to get there. There's a thought that, "If I just try hard enough, I can do it." That's hope. But the one who wants to do that is a mirage and the destination is imaginary. Hopelessness is only bad news if you imagine that something is missing or that something needs to be eliminated. Hope is all about wanting something other than what is. Hope is rooted in the notion that some things are "it" and some things are "not it." Hope is a mirage chasing a mirage. Don't take my word for it, but look and see.

P: I always have trouble with seeing that there's just one whole and all of us individually don't exist.

J: Well, there are different patterns here, different colors and shapes, different sensations. There's no denying that. But what *doesn't* exist is the solidity, autonomy, continuity and separateness of apparent forms. *That* is a mirage-like appearance created by conceptual thought. You can't see the whole. Seeing can't see itself anymore than the eye can see itself. Nonduality or unicity doesn't mean same-ness. It means no separation, no autonomous parts. There is clearly diversity and variation here, but it's one seamless whole. We've learned to draw boundary lines, to see and distinguish separate objects, and we've learned to identify one of those conceptualized objects as "me." And then we *think* we're inside that object looking out. But there's a *seeing* that is bigger than *all* the objects. Awareness contains and beholds all the objects including "me," doesn't it? And in deep sleep, every object vanishes. Do the dream objects really exist outside of the dream? The senseless, objectless presence that remains in deep sleep is here now. It cannot be seen or known or possessed. It appears as people and trees and pencil sharpeners and bombs and flowers and thoughts and words and sensations and distant galaxies and black holes. This wholeness or emptiness is all there is. Nothing is separate from this.

Every object we can name is a mental concept, an abstraction, a reification of what is actually seamless flux. The boundary lines that apparently divide "me" from "you" are quite fluid and porous and arbitrary and notional if you look closely.

Objects (not just tables and chairs, but thoughts and emotions and "you" and "me" and "my mind" and "your mind") don't actually have the solidity that the conceptualizing mind gives to them. This is obvious when we look closely. Only in *thinking* about them do they *seem* to persist as solid, enduring, separate, independent things. But actually, you're not the same person you were ten years ago or even ten seconds ago. Your chemistry has changed, your cells have changed, your blood has moved around, your thoughts have changed. And "your mind" is full of thoughts and ideas from "other minds," and all of us in this room are breathing in and out, exchanging air and chemicals and subatomic particles and thoughts and vibrations of one kind or another. Where are the boundaries?

Relatively speaking, we can say we exist as separate individuals – that's how it appears (if you don't look too closely). And it's not like that appearance is going to vanish and we're going to forget our names and see some kind of psychedelic monicolor formless mush instead. No. But do you ever *actually* find anything apart from everything else that it is not? Does Joan *ever* exist or appear separately from everything that is not-Joan? Isn't she *defined* and *made visible* only by contrast to everything else that she supposedly is not, and isn't she actually, in fact, *made up* of everything else – air, water, space? Isn't everything appearing here all together at once as one whole indivisible picture? If you look closely, where does inside or outside begin and end? Can you actually find this boundary line? Right now, in your actual direct experience, is my voice inside of you or outside of you?

P: But I can move my arm and not your arm. I can feel the headache in my head, but not the headache in your head.

J: "My arm," "your arm," "my head," and "your head," are conceptual ideas. The actual experience is of shapes, colors, movements and sensations appearing right here. No distance or separation at all. Right? This moving of my arm is something that happens here, but if we hadn't learned to describe this happening as, "I move my arm," then would it still seem that some phantom "I" is initiating it? I can't move or feel the blood cells in my legs, and yet I've still learned to think of them as "my blood cells," in "my legs." So why should the fact that I can't move your arm or feel your headache mean that your arm or your head is any less "me" than my blood cells? See, it's all thinking, isn't it?

The way we describe things, and think about them, and conceptualize them gets overlaid on top of the actual direct experience. It's very, very subtle. These conceptual overlays are so familiar, so deeply conditioned, so ubiquitous, that it's quite difficult to even *realize* we're conceptualizing. And of course, *we're* not conceptualizing – conceptualizing is happening. Again, the language creates confusion.

So of course, we're not going to stop seeing what we call "you" and "me," or stop being able to distinguish one from the other, or start imagining that "I" can move "your" arm. But can it be realized that "you" and "me" are images and abstractions that appear *here* in this vast undivided wholeness that has no owner and no location?

Don't take this on belief, but if it is of interest, investigate it, not with analytical thought, but with awareness. Look deeply. Look carefully. See for yourself. It's really quite effortless and simple. Simply be aware of your actual experience right now before you think about it. I'm not talking about anything mystical. This is obvious, right in front of your nose (so to speak), impossible to miss. Everything is appearing right here all at once, seamlessly. Everything is exactly the way it is and could not be otherwise in this moment.

Participant *(to the other participant who was having trouble seeing that everything is One)*: I found that by staying with my doubt something totally shifted and opened up for me. You stay with your doubt until you break through.

J: I don't think she has to do anything. Nothing needs to be changed in order to be what you are. This is unicity right now. Experiences come and go. Unicity is present regardless of what shape experience is taking. There is nothing you need to do, nothing you need to break through, nothing you need to achieve or get beyond. You are the perfect expression of totality exactly as you are right now.

Participant who was offering advice: You're right. Thank you. It's amazing – that subtlety.

J: Everything is beautiful just exactly the way it is. *Everything* is the perfect expression, the *only possible expression* at this moment. It could not be otherwise. And *all* of it is empty of substance. It has no objective or inherent reality. It's a dream-like appearance. It has no existence outside the dream.

P: How do you know that? How do we know our perceptions are accurate? How can we know things are as we think them to be?

Joan: Nothing is the way we think it is! And what do we mean by wondering if our perceptions are "accurate"? We assume that there's some separate and substantial objective reality "out there" that we're standing apart from and perceiving either correctly or incorrectly. That's how we *imagine* and *think* of it. But our actual *experience* is simply undivided *perceiving*. Each of us apparently sees a totally unique world. No two are identical. And yet, like a hologram or the jewels in Indra's Net, every part contains the whole. Your world contains me, and my world contains you. So when I point to the undeniable *fact* of pure perceiving, I don't mean that the *content* of what is perceived matches some external objective reality, or that any kind of *story* or *interpretation* overlaid on top of that pure perception is true. I'm pointing to the undeniable *fact* of perceiving. *That* is undeniable, regardless of whether we *think* what is being perceived is a dream or material reality or a brain creation – those are all *interpretations* after the fact, and they can each be doubted – but the *perceiving itself* cannot be doubted. This present appearance, *as it appears,* cannot be doubted – the simple, bare *fact* of it, as it is.

All the words can do is try to undermine or demolish anything we *think* is true, any place where the mind is trying to land or get a grip. The words point to what is beyond words.

P: When things are speedy, I get more of a sense that I've lost it than when things are quiet. When things are speeding along and I'm resisting the way it is, that's when I seem to get into more trouble.

J: All of that is what *is,* the speeding along, the so-called resisting, the so-called trouble, the quiet that comes after the trouble. It all appears Here/Now. One fluid, seamless whole.

Another P: With this approach there's no room for judgment.

J: There *is* room for judgment, actually. There's room for everything. [laughter]

P: There seems to be a coming back, though, a remembering.

J: Well, there are different experiences that appear. Sometimes there's the experience of speeding and resisting and being angry and upset and sometimes there's the experience of spacious, open, empty, quiet. And then there's the *thought* that one experience is "it" and the other experience is "not it." And thought claims that there's "me" who is going back and forth between them, "me" who has to remember to come back to the "spiritually correct" experience and who hopes to someday be fully stabilized there, forever rid of the "bad" experience. But it's truly hopeless. [laughter] There's no one *having* any of these experiences. And no experience is permanent.

P: Sometimes that cuts it; sometimes it doesn't.

J: What exactly is there to cut?

P: A resistance.

J: Is there resistance right now?

P: A little probably. Right then there wasn't but then it started again. There was a millisecond of no resistance.

J: Well, if you work really hard, you may be able to expand that millisecond into a longer period of time. [laughter] *This is it! This.* Even the mind churning and resisting is nothing but unicity appearing as churning and resisting.

P: Is there any way to get there from here? There isn't, is there? The only way is here. That's the sense I get reading Krishnamurti and others, that there's no way to get there from here.

J: There's no *there.* Any *there* is in the mind. There's *only* here. There's *only* this. So any *there* that you are trying to get to, or any *idea* of "here" that you're trying to get to in the future is hopeless, because it doesn't exist and the one who would go there doesn't exist. There's always *only* this. It's inescapable. You can't *not* be Here/Now.

P: I think I can. [laughter]

J: That thinking appears Here/Now. It's only a thought. See the absurdity of the story it tells – that somehow there would be this one little stray piece, Bob Jones, who somehow broke off from the totality.

Another P: As soon as I see "this is it," my mind says, "What's next?" I want to get away from this.

J: That's part of what the mind does, it asks, "What's next?" It plans and organizes and wonders, "What's next?" That's its job. It's a survival function. And that movement of thought is the same emptiness, the same wholeness, the beingness. If there is an *idea* that what we are looking for is a place where the thought, "What's next?" would never again arise, that's a setup for disappointment and frustration. That's giving that thought more power and weight than it actually has, as if that thought ("What's next?") is something alien and terrible that must be banished, something that's not allowed to be. But if it pops up, then obviously it *is* allowed to be. It's here! And then instantly, it's over! Gone! Vanished! So if there's a thought, "What's next?" – so what? It's not like the goal is to be sitting down motionlessly in a state of thoughtless emptiness for the rest of your life.

P: My mind says that the emptiness movie should always be playing in the background of whatever form is appearing. Would you care to demolish that?

J: "The emptiness movie should always be playing in the background of whatever form is appearing." That sounds like a complicated, effortful thing to work on.

P: Always to remember emptiness.

J: Emptiness is inescapable. There's no need to remember it. Any "emptiness" you can remember is only another object. *This* right here now is emptiness. Emptiness is all there ever is. Emptiness is not some special experience or special state that has to be remembered and then played in the background of every other experience. *Every* experience *is* emptiness. These words are emptiness. You are emptiness. There is *only* emptiness.

P: I don't see that right now. The metaphor I use is figure and ground. I am all caught up with something going on and then I remember –

J: But there's no "you" apart from "the ground" who is all caught up in "the figure" and has to get back to "the ground." *Those are all just concepts.* It may have been a helpful conceptualization at one moment, a helpful map, but now it's become a burden.

Let's try a different map. You *are* the ground. The groundless ground. There's *only* the ground, appearing as all the figures. The ground is inescapable. There's nothing separate from the ground that has to achieve the ground. The ground is not a special experience that needs to be remembered and maintained. This present moment *is* the ground. Even the attempt to "get the ground to play in the background" is itself the ground, doing this funny little dance, playing tricks on itself. That's a story, of course. Don't take it too literally. The point is, the ground is not a separate *something*. It's not a state or an experience. It's not "out there" apart from you. The ground is all there is. You are That.

Another P: It seems that meditation brings about a sense of peace.

J: Meditation may bring about a sense of peace. It is also possible to meditate and get agitated. And it's possible to be in a traffic jam or at the office and suddenly have that experience of peace that you might be associating with meditation, which is really simply a waking up from the dream world of thought into the simplicity of presence. But yes, there may be a relationship between meditation and peace or insight or clarity. But true peace is not actually the result of a cause. It is the natural state, the ever-present groundless ground of being, and maybe what meditation helps with sometimes is the dissolving of the cloud cover that makes it *seem* otherwise. But that dissolving can happen in or out of meditation, and even the clouds are nothing other than boundlessness showing up as clouds.

There may be a preference for an *experience* of peace over an *experience* of agitation, and a belief that the cloud cover is something alien that needs to be banished. There is nothing wrong with sitting down and meditating if you enjoy meditating, and if it seemingly brings about a certain calmness in the organism, or a certain insight into the nature of reality, that's lovely. But the idea that calmness is the true spiritual state and that agitation or restlessness is unspiritual and off the track – and that there's "me" who has fallen off the track – and if only "I" would be good and meditate more often, then "I" could be always calm and spiritual and on track – all of that is agitation! Which is perfectly fine. Nothing wrong with agitation. It's an aspect of what is.

P: This approach of awareness results in peace and calm—

J: I'm not talking about an *approach* of "being aware" in order to get results in the future. I'm saying that awareness is the very substance of Here/Now, and that there is *only* this one eternal present moment. It is inescapable. You can't achieve it because it is all there is. And in this one present moment, many things appear including both calmness and agitation. Certain activities *appear* to bring about calm in the story of cause and effect, and certain other activities *appear* to bring about agitation, but this kind of relative cause and effect relationship, if you look closely, is a conceptual overlay imposed after the fact. Reality itself is undivided. You can't really isolate things out that way except conceptually.

P: It's like putting one foot in front of the other, it just happens.

J: One foot automatically goes in front of the other, yes. It's not like you have to make that happen – there's no "you" to do that. It may *seem* that you have to do it if you're in physical therapy after a stroke re-learning the art of walking, or if you're a toddler learning it for the first time, but each action in this learning process happens effortlessly out of the whole universe. And it's all a momentary scene in a movie or a dream. It has no substance, no continuity, except *in* the story.

P: How can you say that seeing is always happening? When you are caught up in an emotion, you're not seeing it, right? Can there be different levels of seeing?

J: If there weren't the seeing of what you are calling "caught-up-ness" as it was happening, it couldn't even be reported afterwards. Without awareness, it wouldn't even register at all.

P: But before that seeing one is caught up.

J: In that moment, caughtupness is what is appearing in awareness. Without awareness, it couldn't appear at all. But, I know what you mean – there is that moment of waking up from some story or train of thought, realizing it's a mental movie, *seeing* the story *as* a story, recognizing it as nothing more than thought and imagination, no longer taking it seriously, no longer being entranced by it. You're using the word "seeing" to point to that moment of seeing through the illusion and waking up from the entrancement, right? But that shift, that waking up happens on its own. No one does it. There is no "you" who wakes up. There's simply a shift in attention, waking up from a dream. It happens. A split second later, the thinking mind takes credit ("I woke up"), and begins strategizing about how to keep this expanded state of consciousness and repeat this waking up. The mind wants to divide everything up (good experience, bad experience) and take it all personally (my attention, my inattention), but it's truly impersonal and undivided. And *all* of it, everything we can imagine and describe and remember and talk about, *everything* perceivable and conceivable, *all* the shifts and all the changes, *all* the awakenings and *all* the entrancements, *all* of it appears in awareness, which is another word for Here/Now. Without awareness, nothing can appear.

First P: What I tend to have to do is keep saying, "Just this, just this, just this, just this." It would be good to have a tape recording in the background saying that.

J: That sounds really good. Maybe you could wear a little implanted headphone. [laughter]

P: It seems like I need that.

J: In order not to fall from grace?

P: Yes. [laughter] This is probably one of the steps to solving the illusory problem.

J: It is, because there is no "you" to fall and no where to fall. There's only Here/Now.

P: I do need that.

J: The thought, "just this" may keep arising. The "I" that thinks it's doing that is illusory.

P: Then what's doing that?

J: What's doing everything?

P: It seems like it's a process, a short process, but a process.

J: It *seems* like a process in the memory, when the thinking mind constructs a story about it after the fact. What's *actually* happening though, is that there is some sort of sensation going on that we call agitation, and then a thought arises, "Just this." And then, as you say, sometimes that thought "works" and what arises next is a spacious calm feeling, and sometimes it "doesn't work" and then there's still the agitation. And then there may be another thought, "Damn, it's not working. I'll try again. JUST THIS!"

And then there's even more agitation! And then at some point, the agitation is gone, maybe because there was some kind of waking up, seeing the agitation as just a bunch of thoughts, or maybe because your neurochemistry and hormone balance shifted, or maybe because you suddenly looked out the window and saw a beautiful bird fly past, but somehow, that shift happens, and then there's an experience of calm for a moment, feeling the breathing and hearing the traffic or the birds without thinking about anything.

And then maybe the thought, "Oh, this is it! This is presence-awareness. This is emptiness. This is the ground. This is what I have to maintain. I have to hold onto this. I have to keep the ground behind the figure!" And immediately thought is off and running, wondering, "Have I really got the ground? Is this really it? How can I be sure? What *is* the ground anyway?" And then after awhile there is a noticing of agitation again, and again the thought pops up, "Just this!"

And in all of this, there's an underlying thought-story that, "*I* am doing all this. *I* am the one who keeps slipping into agitation. *I* am the one who has to keep reminding myself to be aware. *I* am the one who has to get the ground behind the figure. *I* am the one who has to make the waking up happen. *I* am the one who has to manage and control all of this, and *I* could botch it and ruin *my* whole life. And it appears that I *am* botching it some of the time. *I* am the one who is failing, the one who is unenlightened. But *I* have hope that if *I* keep trying, it will get better. Someday, *I* will be permanently established as the ground."

P: You have the movie right. [laughs]

J: So it's a movie and where is it all coming from? All the movies, all the thoughts, all the actions, all the trees, the leaves, the sun, the wind—

P: I want to turn off that movie.

J: Good luck. [laughter] Groundlessness has no problem with that movie. Only the phantom "me" *in* the movie has a problem with the movie. The movie character wants to escape from the movie. It's another scene in the movie. Can you see the joke? There is nothing that needs to be liberated. To *see* that is liberation. And if it is not seen, then maybe there is agitation and drama. So what? It's nothing but sensations and thoughts, all of it a momentary dream-like appearance, a scene in a movie, and then it's over. The ground is always here, movie or no movie.

P: Social interaction can be distracting. Right away it sets up questions of who I am, who am I trying to impress.
J: When you say distracting, distracting from what?

Another P: From the ground. [laughter]

P: That structure builds up, though, and that is illusory.

J: Yes, it is illusory. It has no reality. Look closely at it, and nothing is there.

P: But I lose awareness of the present moment and become more and more obsessed with ego and thought and interrelationships.

J: Yes, and it's very useful to see that, but then see that you can't get any closer to Here/Now than you always already are. You *are* Here/Now. *Everything* appears Here/Now, including this so-called obsession with ego. Everything that appears disappears instantly, every moment. There's no "you" doing any of it. There are simply sensations and thoughts, and all of it is unicity. Unicity is all there is.

P: Right, and that's okay unless there's a lot of contraction.

J: What's wrong with contraction? It's natural. It's part of organic life. "Okay" and "not okay" are evaluations after the fact. You used the word "distraction," and it's interesting how we *think* of something as a "distraction." If you have the *idea* that you want to be in a state of complete quiet, for example, and all of a sudden the lawn maintenance crew arrives and turns on their giant weed whackers and leaf blowers, then the mind says, "This is a distraction and it's upsetting me." And it is definitely a different and less pleasant neurological experience, but the idea that it's a distraction comes from this underlying picture of how I want this moment to be and now it's deviated. Something is getting in the way of my fantasy.

P: And then that idea of it being a distraction becomes more of a distraction than the sound. Sometimes I feel I will become really upset and I start worrying about that.

J: There are different experiences. There was calm and then there's upset. That's part of being alive; that's part of organic life.

P: But it shouldn't be this way.

J: Ohhhhhhhhhhh... [laughter]

Another P: But how do you know it *should* be this way? Because it is?

J: I am not saying it *should* be this way, but rather, it *is* this way.

P: Tomorrow I could experience some real fear. Where do I go with that?

J: First of all, right now, it's a total fantasy. But *if* that happens, then it will be happening now. It will simply be what is appearing now, and you'll see how it unfolds.

P: But who wants that?

J: Nobody. I would rather feel peace than fear, just as I would rather eat ice cream than cockroaches, but the fact of the matter is that that sometimes I do feel intense unpleasant emotions of one kind of another.

P: I could suggest some techniques.

J: I'm sure everyone in this room already has a repertoire of things to do. And it's all happening by itself, including using techniques or not using techniques. There is no one who can control this movie of waking life and there's nothing inherently wrong with any of it. It may be painful or uncomfortable. Fear or anxiety may even lead to the death of this organism if it gets really bad, but even that is simply what's happening. And truly, nothing is happening. What we truly are is deathless and unborn, beginningless and endless, infinite and ever-present.

P: The fear will eventually go away.

J: And you actually have no choice in the matter. If the impulse arises to apply one of your techniques, then that will happen. And if the impulse arises to do nothing, then the techniques won't be used.

But notice how the mind is looking for a strategy, a way to deal with this thing that might happen tomorrow morning. It's hopeless. When I say it's hopeless, I don't mean to say that this fear is going to be here for the rest of your life. I mean that there's nobody apart from it to do anything about it. No one is in control of what appears.

And it only *seems* to matter *within the context of the appearance.* Hopelessness is actually very liberating. If we think, "I *wish* there were hope but, Oh God, there isn't," that's despair, but to actually *see* that there's no hope, that there's no *need* for hope, that the ground is all there is, that there's no way that you could ever lose it because you *are* it, *that* is very liberating.

P: But it is better to look at the disturbance rather than to look away from it, and that is hard because pain is painful.

J: There is no "you" to control what response to a disturbance happens. Sometimes looking at it and being completely open to it happens, and sometimes looking away and resisting it happens. There's no you who can choose one or the other. It's true that if the urge to open up to it arises, then the suffering may very well dissipate in that open acceptance, as opposed to what may happen if the urge to escape arises and you rush in and start eating lots of comfort food or drinking scotch. Then chances are you will experience indigestion and a hangover and a lot of other suffering. But there is no you who can manufacture one or the other of those experiences. And even the overeating and the hangover and the indigestion is all equally the ground. It is simply a different pattern of energy, a different appearance, a different shape, a different sensation. It's less desirable to the mind in the same way that we prefer ice cream over cockroaches. We prefer peace over agitation. Although, interestingly enough, we do seem to have some interest in agitation. Hang around in peace long enough and the mind wants to turn on some crime drama or watch the News and experience a bit of agitation.

P: I want to be open to what's here and not escaping from it.

J: Right now, what is arising is that thought, "I want to be open to what's here and not escaping from it." But tonight, a very different impulse and train of thought may arise. I find that sometimes I want to be open and sometimes I want to escape and close down, and I find no one at the helm inside of me who can choose what I want or what action will follow from that wanting. Whatever has the most energy in any given moment is what wins out in that moment. Every happening, opening or closing, is equally the ground, and all of it is a dream-like appearance. So I find that I'm not really that *concerned* any more with whether I am opening up or closing down. Yes, there is an interest in opening up that can arise here, and if the closing down is taking forms that feel harmful, a concern may arise and perhaps an interest in exploring the situation and uncovering what's going on. But *all* of that comes unbidden.

Brain experiments show that the thought that appears to choose or intend an action occurs a split-second after the action has already been initiated in the body. "I'm going to bring my attention to the present moment" is an after-thought, describing what is already happening, initiated by no one, or we could say, initiated by the whole universe.

For a long time I was very focused on trying to "be present" and "open up fully" to the bodily sensations of fear and anger, and I was trying very hard to see the thoughts as thoughts and come back to the present moment and all of that. And that movement from thoughts to present moment awareness still happens, but without it being a big deal either way. It happens by itself. Actually, it always did. But it's not seen anymore as this burdensome task that "I" must do to be a spiritual success. That overlay is gone. Opening up happens or it doesn't.

And I notice that actually awareness is present either way. Everything perceivable and conceivable happens in awareness including thoughts and so-called distractions. What is prior to everything perceivable and conceivable is here now, inescapable and impossible to lose.

P: So how do you get there from here?

J: By seeing how that question is creating the imaginary problem it is pretending to solve. By recognizing that you can't ever step out of Here/Now. Let this moment be exactly as it is. Notice that you have no choice. It *is* as it is. Always. Even this absurd and hopeless search for "there" is nothing but thoughts and sensations appearing Here/Now. It's just a passing show, gone in an instant. It has no owner.

Our time is almost up. So have we gotten anywhere? Have we improved? Are we closer to unicity now than we were before? Have we slipped further away? [laughter] There's simply *this*, the *rummmmmmm* of that truck. That's the Holy Reality, the Absolute Truth, no-thing at all. *rummmmmmmm*.

You Can't Not Be It

It takes no effort to hear the traffic, to breathe, to see whatever images are appearing if the eyes are open, to feel the breeze. This present moment is so simple, so obvious, so unavoidable.

Thoughts such as "there must be more than this," or "I don't get it," if they are believed, may be accompanied by sensations of tension or contraction, and those sensations may seem to confirm what the thoughts are saying: "This can't be it, this isn't enough, because if this *were* it, the sensations would be more pleasant and I'd feel better than this."

But all of these things like contraction and depression and tension and agitation are fleeting appearances. If you try to find a sensation, if you really give total attention to a single sensation, you discover that it's not solid at all — it's moving and pulsating and changing and, "Whoa, it's gone," and then it's back again, but it's different, and now it's changed again, and at the very core of it, there seems to be nothing at all. Empty space! When you look closely and deeply, you discover there's nothing solid in this whole manifestation. *Nothing!*

As babies we have no problem. We may be hungry or afraid, we may have diaper rash or a fever, but we're not lost in thought about all this in the way an adult would be. We're more like other animals at that stage of our development. There's simply whatever *is* in the moment.

We don't really know exactly what babies experience or how the adult consciousness develops, although there are many theories about all of this. From very early on there may be some rudimentary sense of separation that is beginning to develop. The mother or father or caretaker does not come when we cry, or they do something we don't want them to do. They're not there when we want them, or they're too invasive or maybe even abusive. So there may be some sense of separation that occurs very early. And there *is* apparent separation – the baby is *apparently* a separate body, independent of the mother. But in fact, they are both aspects of one seamless whole that includes the entire universe.

As the baby moves around, it begins to discover the ability to move arms and legs and roll over and things like that. You can watch babies discovering these things. We are not born with the ability to walk into the kitchen and get a glass of water if we're thirsty. It develops slowly over time. There is a discovery, a learning that occurs, a discovery that I can reach out and grab that object and bring it to my mouth. But the baby doesn't conceptualize it that way. The baby simply reaches out. That ability is discovered and enjoyed. There is no "I" in the picture yet. That whole developmental process is all arising on its own – the ability to reach out, the discovery of that ability, the reaching out and grabbing – it's all arising out of infinite causes and conditions. And eventually, along with language and the ability to conceptualize and abstract – which is also arising out of infinite causes and conditions – a descriptive narrative takes shape: "*I* am grasping the object and bringing it to my mouth." That is a conceptualization of something that is actually not divided up into subject, verb and object – the actuality is undivided, seamless, flowing wholeness. But thought divides it up and then gets lost in its own description. It thinks, "*I* did this," and with that thought, the mirage of the independent executive at the helm is born.

And this sense of agency grows bigger because, "Whoa! If 'I' can do that, then maybe 'I' can do a lot of other things. 'I' can decide to be hard-working and successful, or 'I' can decide to stop smoking." And we're told that this is true. We're told, "You are responsible for your life. You have to make something of yourself. You have to use your talents. You have to make the right choices." And we're told that certain people are failing to do that – the bum on the street, Uncle Al who beats his wife and gambles away his money – these people are *choosing* to screw up. They are not being responsible. They are failing. They are evil or sick or weak or sinful or irresponsible or whatever our belief system tells us they are – but whatever it is, it's not good. And you want to make sure you don't do that. Or, maybe you are a rebel, and you *do* want to do that. But whatever you want arises unbidden, the result of infinite causes and conditions, and how it plays itself out also arises unbidden. Every desire, every choice, every action comes out of the whole universe and could not be otherwise. And all of it is one seamlessly flowing whole that can only be broken into bits conceptually.

But once we get lost in thought, then it *seems* as if we are each a separate part – an independent individual with free will. That idea is also arising unbidden. We're given a name and we're told what it means to be a boy or a girl, what it means to be a member of our particular family and social class. We learn, often in very covert ways, what it means to be black or white or gay or straight or fat or disabled or smart or stupid. We are taught to see boundary lines that we don't see when we're first born. We learn where "the rug" begins and ends, and where "I" supposedly begin and end, and what "I" am like, and what my part is in the play of life.

And if we believe that we are in charge of being this person we've learned we are, then of course there will be anxiety, because at any moment we might slip up. No matter how well we seem to be doing, it's never very secure. It's never enough. There is guilt and shame when "my story" doesn't seem to be going well, and blame when the others don't behave as I think they should. And the ultimate, bottom-line fear is that if *I* make the wrong choice, then *I* will die. So it is part of our survival system – this anxiety – part of what insures that we don't eat the poisonous food or wander into dangerous places full of predators. But sooner or later, no matter how good the choices are that we appear to be making, the body does die.

Although actually, there isn't even a body here that could die. "The body" is an idea. If we close our eyes, we can't find the body. Nor can we find any separate soul, or any independent executive, or any "me" who could end or be reborn. Is that a scary thought? When you really see it, it's actually immensely freeing! There is no death anymore.

There is only this boundless emptiness reincarnating every instant as everything. This wholeness is deathless and birthless. It is appearing as you, me, the carpet, the lamp, the chair, the whole universe. The apparent forms are continuously breaking down and reforming, but the emptiness is ever-present.

We hear that, and then we start *looking for* this boundless emptiness. "What *is* it?" we wonder. "Have I got it? Has she got it? Let's find it!" The very act of looking for it implies that we are separate from it, that we could actually *find* it, that it is some particular "thing" – some object "out there" that we could see and experience and understand and grasp and take home and put on our altar or something. But boundless emptiness is not a *thing* – it's *everything* and no-thing. But it's not any *particular* thing.

So you may say, "Well, yes, but your experience is different from my experience, so doesn't that prove that we really are separate people?" There's this line from a Zen koan coming into mind: "Eyes and hands throughout the body." What it suggests is that this whole bodymind *is* seeing and doing and being from head to toe. Millions of cells, sensory organs and nerve receptors are all doing their little jobs – eyes and hands throughout the body – all functioning together as one seamless whole, even when they appear to malfunction or come into conflict. There are no little independent agents in there at any point. It's all one functioning, one intelligence, one whole system.

Similarly, we could say that all the billions of apparently separate individuals on this planet are the eyes and hands of the totality, that each person is an eye and a hand in this boundless unicity. It's all happening out of one vast intelligence, and all of it is one process, one energy, one being. It's the same functioning that is growing the trees and blowing the clouds across the sky and rotating the earth around the sun. It is the same intelligence, the same energy that initiated the Big Bang and that grew these bodies and these brains out of little cells. It's the same intelligence that is seeing and talking and listening and breathing with all these apparently different hands and eyes and ears and mouths. Totality is dreaming infinite dreams simultaneously – universes being born and dying, galaxies spinning through infinite space – all of it one whole.

Unicity is realizing itself from infinite points of view, functioning with infinite eyes and hands. So it seems that we are separate individuals each living in our own unique movie world, but all the movies go together. It's like, if you look out of your left eye, you see a different picture than if you look out of your right eye. There are certain things in the left eye picture that are not in the right eye picture, and vice versa. But when you put them together, they are what we call our whole vision. Likewise, when you put together all of the eyes in this room or in this world, there's a whole vision, you could say.

So there are different experiences – every individual has a completely unique experience. But it is all one energy, one whole seeing, one whole being. Unicity is all there is, and unicity does not belong to me or you. We belong to it. It is what "we" are.

We try to zero in on "unicity" as an experience. And we feel very frustrated because we keep seeing chairs and tables and different people, and so we wonder, where's the unicity, where's the boundless emptiness? All we're seeing is chairs and tables. Unicity shouldn't look like this! Or maybe we think we've got it, but as you may have noticed, that thought leads almost instantly to the opposite thought, "Oh, no! I've lost it." [laughter] Any *experience* that we identify as unicity will go. If it came, it will go. It may stay for a minute, for an hour, or for a decade. But it *will* go. And then suddenly there's a different experience, that pesky dualistic "me" experience again. And then the thought, "I've lost unicity. I've fallen out of the Now. My spiritual ship has sunk!" Very disappointing, very humiliating.

The mind can get very confused trying to *think* its way through all this and figure it out, but what's here right now is utterly simple. This present moment can't be lost and it can't be found, and there's nothing apart from it. Even the thought, "I'm apart from it," is nothing other than this present moment.

P: Even the thought that this isn't it, is it. Can you say more about that?

J: Well, what is that thought if you examine it?

P: It's empty, it's immediately gone.

J: Yes, and where did it come from?

P: The anxiety at the pit of my stomach.

J: The anxiety at the pit of your stomach thought that thought?

P: It might be a co-indicator of it.

J: That might be a story. If you actually look, where does any thought come from?

P: Nowhere.

J: Yes. There can be a story based on what we've learned that tells us thought comes from our conditioning, or from the brain, or from the pit of our stomach, and these stories may be relatively more or less accurate. But ultimately, these are all conceptual overlays. The actual *experience* is that thoughts simply pop up out of nowhere. Thoughts appear here in the same way the traffic noise appears. In a way, thought is also a form of sensation – a kind of energetic vibration that shows up as ideas, mental pictures, images, stories. It's another appearance in consciousness like the colors and shapes of this room and the sounds of the crickets and the street traffic.

P: I can see that this thought comes from nothing, but how can it also be a manifestation of intelligence or unicity? I can see it as neutral or nothing, but I can't see it as positive.

J: Ah, well, perhaps it's a manifestation of the Evil Force? [laughter]

P: ...which also has to be unicity.

J: What is the mind doing right now? Rather than coming to a logically believable philosophical conclusion, let's stick with direct experience. Philosophies can all be doubted, but the bare actuality Here/Now is impossible to doubt and requires no belief. In your actual experience right now, everything appears Here/Now, yes? It all shows up as one seamless picture, right? All the different shapes and colors and sounds and sensations go together in a remarkable way – the stars, the galaxies, the ecosystem, the thoughts, the whole show. Thought divides, labels, categorizes, evaluates, and judges everything that appears. That's its job. It's a survival function. But sometimes it gets far removed from actual survival. It becomes confused and seems to create problems rather than solving them.

Thought comes up with the *idea* of good and evil, and then it sorts everything into those two categories based on our point of view, our conditioning, our judgment of whether something is good or evil in reference to us. If a million people are exterminated, that's evil. If the smallpox virus is exterminated, that's good. Of course, the smallpox virus might see it differently! We overlay our human judgment, and then our personal point of view, on whether something is good or bad.

We can notice that certain thoughts may not be useful or intelligent, that they only bring suffering. This noticing happens by itself, just as the thinking happens by itself. We can speculate that human beings are learning to use our complex brains in ever more intelligent ways, that we are learning to discern the difference between the map and the territory, learning to see through and not to be entranced by dysfunctional thoughts. We can say that such learning is part of an evolutionary development or an awakening process. This is all a story, the evolutionary story, and maybe it's true and maybe it isn't. But *all* of this (human evolution, the trials and errors, the mistakes, the corrections, the learning process) is happening spontaneously as an appearance in consciousness. No one is directing the show. No one is in control.

P: But there seems to be some idea that unicity is good. Why do we always say things like "God is good" or "everything is perfect as it is"? Why not bad? Why not imperfect? Why is everything fundamentally okay or good? That seems like a belief to me.

J: All those words like good and evil, perfect and imperfect, are conceptual labels and judgments. I would say the more accurate thing is to simply say that what is, *is*. Relatively speaking, we can call something a mistake, but in the larger sense, we can say there are no mistakes. It does seem to be a theme in all religion that Ultimate Reality is somehow good or perfect, as opposed to bad or imperfect, and that the devil (evil or illusion) is somehow an aspect or creation of God, and not the other way around. We could attribute this recurring theme to our desire for a happy and reassuring fairytale, and that may be part of it.

But don't we all have a deep intuition, a deep *knowing* that everything is whole and complete and okay? Maybe we don't feel that way all the time, or even most of the time. But in those moments that we feel are clearest and most true, isn't that what we sense, that wholeness and unconditional love? And when we have conflict, anger, war, confusion, doubt, hatred, addiction and that kind of thing going on, don't we intuitively sense that this is rooted in some kind of delusion? Which feels clearest and most true – the moments when we are angry and upset at everything, or the moments when we feel love and equanimity?

I suspect this deep intuition of wholeness is what gives rise to putting labels like "perfection" and "goodness" on unicity. There's a deep sense that the fundamental ground of being is love, not hate. Unicity sees unicity everywhere, and that seeing is love. Delusion imagines separation, and that imagination gives rise to fear, anger, hatred, envy, jealousy, addiction and so on. When we see clearly, we understand that these "negative" behaviors and states of mind are the result of infinite causes and conditions. They may be deluded, destructive and painful, but they are no more "evil" than an earthquake or a hurricane. When there is clarity about all this, there is love and compassion. We know in our deepest heart of hearts that unconditional love is somehow more true – more fundamental, more real, more radical (at the root) – than hate, which always seems to be confused, deluded, reactive, divisive and false. Love breeds love, and hate breeds hate. We all experience this.

The problem with words is that as soon as you use any word, it immediately implies its opposite, and then we get all confused trying to figure out *why* God created the devil in the first place, or why we have evil in the world, and how to reconcile the existence of evil with God being all-powerful and good. Human beings have jumped through some pretty contorted hoops trying to square all of that, including the invention of free will, and it never quite seems to line up as long as the basic idea of separation is taken to be real – the separation between good and evil, between me and God, between awareness and content, between subject and object. But these separations are always notional, not real.

The confusion is always in thinking. So if you notice your mind getting all knotted up and stuck and confused, it's a clue. Thought is spinning its wheels trying to solve some imaginary problem. Return to the simplicity of [Joan slaps her leg – *whack!*] – *that* is not confusing in any way. *That* is not a thought or a word or an idea. [Joan slaps her leg again – *whack!*] *That* is utterly simple and undeniable. If we try to talk or think *about* it, then we have to use words, and words are always abstractions, always limited, always functioning in duality. But *[Whack!]* is beyond belief, beyond doubt, beyond words – it just *is*.

P: Why is slapping your leg beyond belief? I don't get it. This is one of those Zen riddles that totally baffle me.

J: "Slapping my leg" is an abstract verbal description, and that's way too far removed! I'm pointing to [*whack!* – Joan slaps her leg again]. *Just that!* Any verbal description is too late. There's no way to put the bare actuality of that sound into words. The word "whack," or the phrase "Joan slaps her leg," is not the nondual *immediacy* of hearing that sound. The sound and the hearing are one whole happening. No separation. You don't need any belief to hear that sound. This only seems like a riddle because it's too simple and you're looking for something much, much more complicated. This moment is not complicated. No words can contain the actuality of *what is*. It speaks for itself.

Another P: I find a huge gap between the spacious experience that arises here in these meetings and my everyday life.

J: Experiences come and go. What happens in these meetings, I suspect, is that the mental overlay falls away to a large degree and the ever-present ground of awareness becomes more obvious. Awareness becomes aware of awareness, we could say. You become aware of simply being present, aware of the simplicity of what is. The complication created by thought melts away or becomes more transparent. The so-called "spacious experience" that you have in these meetings is simply a recognition of the ever-present Here/Now that is actually *always* present.

Here/Now is not an *experience*, per se, but rather, it is the experien*cing* of everything – watching television, going to work, seeking enlightenment, asking questions – it is the common factor in all these diverse experiences. They all appear Here/Now. This aware presence, this undeniable immediacy is your True Nature.

So this story that you're not experiencing it, or you're experiencing less of it, when you are not at these meetings – when you are at your job or watching television – that story is based on referencing unicity or spaciousness to a *particular* experience, rather than recognizing unicity as the presence that is equally present as *every* experience. This space of Here/Now is big enough to include everything, even an experience of contraction or upset.

Referencing unicity to a *particular* experience is suffering, because any *particular* experience will come and go. There is no way out of unicity. But the experience of a meeting will be different from that of the office. The common factor in all those different experiences is the undeniable fact of being present. The screen is present in every scene of the movie, and you cannot *not* see the screen, even if you are not consciously aware of it when your attention is absorbed in the movie images. The character you pretend to be is a character *in* the movie. The experience of spaciousness that comes and goes is a scene *in* the movie. But Here/Now does not come and go. Here/Now is the ever-present ground of being, the unicity that includes both the movie and the screen, awareness and the content of awareness, sound and hearing. Only thought draws dividing lines. Unicity is undivided.

P: But I don't want suffering, and I can't see how evil is good. I still can't see how genocide or racism or child abuse is God. I see spirituality as being about ending suffering and overcoming evil.

J: In a way, we could say that nonduality or Buddhism or Advaita is about exploring our suffering and seeing whether the obstacles and problems we think we have are real, and whether the one who seems to have them is real. We are exploring the root of our suffering, what generates suffering, how it happens, what it is. What is at the root of genocide or racism or child abuse? How do things like this happen? How do we respond to such things? (Not how *should* we respond, but how *do* we respond?). And instead of trying to solve suffering "out there," this approach is more about solving it right here, right now. In a sense, you could say that nonduality (or Buddhism or Advaita) is about waking up from suffering and *realizing* unconditional love and liberation. But nonduality is also about seeing through all feel-good ideas about what we're doing. Nonduality comes back to the simplicity of what is, as it is, not as we *think* it is. It comes back to silence, to what *is* before the movie of waking life. It erases every idea and leaves nothing at all.

Nonduality is about seeing that the things we call "evil" happen out of infinite causes and conditions and not through individual free will — no one is behind them. They could be called unskillful ways of trying to relieve suffering or erroneous ways of trying to find happiness and peace. People fight wars for peace and take heroin to avoid suffering. No other animal gets this confused, because no other animal is capable of such complex thinking. The folks who flew planes into the Twin Towers thought they were doing a good thing for humanity. So did Hitler. So does George Bush. These people do what they do because that is the only possible thing they *can* do at that moment given their nature and nurture. And in a larger context, all the errors and mistakes and corrections are part of a bigger picture where all is well.

When we see everyone and everything as unicity rather than as "the enemy," that seeing is unconditional love. That is the love Jesus talked about when he said to love your enemies, turn the other cheek, remove the speck in your own eye first. This is enlightenment. It doesn't mean you won't act to change things, but you'll act differently when you act from love rather than from hate – when you recognize that the enemy is not "out there" somewhere, when you see that nobody can behave any differently in this moment from how they are behaving. One of the most powerful embodiments of this kind of love that I've seen in my lifetime was Martin Luther King Jr., the great civil rights leader. He faced vicious bigotry and violence, constant threats on his life, all the worst horrors of racism – and he came from love, not from hatred.

Right now, as we speak, terrible things are happening. People are being raped and tortured and murdered and blown up. Like it or not, this seems to be part of life, part of the show. And chances are, no matter how spiritually evolved we get, horrible things will always happen. And in the end, no matter how much progress we appear to make, *nothing* will have happened – that is the beautiful message of death. Everything is a dream. Nothing lasts. It all gets erased. But that which is real is never destroyed. I'm quite sure that Martin Luther King knew this intuitively in his heart or he wouldn't have been able to do what he did. You can kill a person, but there is something you can't kill.

P: Do you always feel that kind of love now that you are enlightened?

J: Joan is not enlightened. Nor is Joan unenlightened. Enlightenment isn't a personal possession, and there is no "person" here with substance and continuity except as a thought-form. Here/Now is ever-present. Sometimes there is enlightenment here and sometimes there is delusion here. Speaking as Joan, no I don't always feel that kind of love. Sometimes I feel rage and hatred and fear and all of those emotions. Sometimes I'd like to strangle George Bush. Not literally, of course, I'm not that crazy, but that's the feeling that shows up here sometimes – anger and outrage. But I know that this feeling is suffering, that it is a form of self-destruction, and that expressing this kind of feeling only pours gasoline on the fires of bigotry, ignorance and hatred. I can *feel* that it's a delusion even as it is happening.

There are no perfect people. Martin Luther King probably had some very dark moments. Apparently he struggled with depression and infidelity to his wife, and maybe he felt anger and hatred sometimes as well. I've heard Thich Nhat Hanh, the gentle Vietnamese Buddhist monk, talk openly about being overwhelmed with anger at times. Nisargadatta had a very fiery temper. So as always, I would caution against idealizing and idolizing people or seeking perfection. We all contain the whole universe. We all contain Hitler and George Bush and Martin Luther King and Ramana Maharshi. The whole spectrum is present in all of us. We are the world. The problem is not "out there." It's right here. And the problem can only be resolved here and now, not in the future, not somewhere else.

P: I have had the sense that there is a kind of global awakening going on, that more and more people are waking up and getting interested in realizing their true nature. But now I'm wondering, if everyone gained this nondual perspective, you couldn't really say that no one would hurt anyone else, because there is no morality at that level, no right or wrong, right?

J: When we are awake, when the nature of reality is truly clear to us, we don't behave like Hitler. Behaving as he did requires tremendous confusion and delusion. We don't need *ideas* of right and wrong to know that. It's obvious. Morality is a conceptual abstraction that reflects our natural inclinations as well as our cultural beliefs. But we don't need a moral code to tell us that murdering our neighbor is wrong. We know this intuitively. And if we are not awake, if we are driven by nature and nurture to commit murder or genocide, no moral code will stop us.

This so-called global awakening you speak of can only happen now – right here, right now. In you. Not "out there" somewhere. The only real awakening is Here/Now. Wake up now and then the rest of this question dissolves. This question is the mind spinning imaginary problems and then wanting to discuss them.

Once we begin to spin these stories about the dream-like world "out there," these stories are endless. Yes, in this dream-like appearance, there seems to be a growing interest in nonduality and meditative inquiry and present moment awareness and seeing through stories and beliefs – that does seem to be happening more and more. But it seems to be equally true that the fastest growing religion in this dream-world is Islam, not Advaita or Zen or radical nonduality. Humans, with our incredible technological abilities, are operating much of the time out of our primitive lizard brain while seeing everything through the lens of delusional thoughts and ideas that are (mis)taken for reality. That wasn't so dangerous back when we were armed with clubs and spears. But now we are armed with weapons of mass destruction, and these weapons are falling into the hands of more and more people. We have fueled this catastrophic climate change, which no one seems able to stop; the population is exploding; our whole economic system is predicated on continuous growth – like a cancer that is consuming the planet. The insanity of it all seems to have snowballed into a giant self-perpetuating system that no one has the ability to stop. If the economy collapses, as I suspect it will, and if climate change brings more and more catastrophic weather – floods, famines, water shortages – and if we have more wars and terrorist attacks, maybe with nuclear and biological weapons – as things melt down, maybe masses of people will wake up, but an equally likely scenario is that people may just become more and more frightened – and then we will have repressive fascism instead of some progressive utopia. Right-wing and left-wing, war and peace – these things come and go in waves, in cycles.

To be honest, I'm not all that optimistic about human survival. It looks pretty dicey right now. And I don't feel that humanity *must* survive, that our survival is imperative. We're so terrified of death, but everything dies eventually. And whatever happens, it's all a dream-like appearance. Within the appearance, humans have been a pretty destructive species. Maybe the earth and the rest of its inhabitants will be relieved to see us go. I wouldn't be surprised. But who knows, anything could happen. There might be some huge evolutionary leap in consciousness, a global awakening, as you said. Humans have a beautiful side, too. We can be amazingly wonderful. But if we don't wake up to our True Nature, if we keep going on our present suicidal course, it seems pretty likely that we will destroy ourselves.

And even if there *is* some global awakening, even then, one day the sun will explode and the show will be over, as it is every night in deep sleep, and actually every moment. The show is always changing – sometimes it looks beautiful and sometimes it looks horrible – sometimes it seems to be expanding, sometimes contracting. But right now, can we notice that this is all happening in the mind, in the imagination? What are we actually even talking about? Can we wake up *right now* from these stories about the world, the scary stories and the hopeful stories? Can we discover the aliveness, the possibility, the love, the immensity Here/Now?

What is going on when people hurt other people in the ways we consider immoral or evil? In the case of a serial killer, it may be some kind of brain condition or childhood abuse or who knows what. In the case of the holocaust, to take everyone's favorite example of catastrophic evil, in order for that to happen, there had to be tremendous caught-up-ness in some kind of a story, some kind of delusion. In order to decide that an entire race of people needs to be exterminated to save the nation, there has to be a tremendous lack of clarity – that kind of action doesn't come out of clear seeing or the recognition of unicity. It comes out of identifying oneself as a fragment – a separate self, a separate nation, a separate and superior race. When you really *see* someone, you don't put them in a gas chamber.

That kind of confusion, that kind of entrancement, is an aspect of the seamless unicity that includes everything. But it is not enlightenment. Enlightenment is realizing unicity. When you see everything as unicity, as your own Self, then you don't want to go to war with it or torture it. Unicity is unconditional love. It accepts everything.

So hypothetically, if there were nothing but clear seeing, then we wouldn't have things like the holocaust or George Bush bombing Iraq. But that's very hypothetical, and even if there were that kind of global awakening, then we'd have some new problem. Aliens from another galaxy would land and start colonizing us and raising us for food or something. Because the appearance always involves contrasts and polarities. It can't show up without them.

But *all* of this is like a dream, including the six or seven billion people who are supposedly living on planet earth who might or might not recognize unicity. There are actually no separate people here to wake up or to recognize unicity, because all of these apparent people are nothing *but* unicity in thin disguise. And even *that* is a story. In reality, there is only this moment – this boundless presence Here/Now. *This* is the peace that remains when all stories fall away, the space that accepts everything and holds to nothing. *This* can't be killed even if the whole universe goes up in flames.

P: So you can create a good story or a bad story.

J: Stories arise in the mind. And stories are very contagious and mesmerizing, like viruses or memes. One moment I turn on the television, and several newscasters tell me there is nuclear material floating around, and that there is strong evidence of a possible terrorist attack in Chicago, so instantly a scary movie arises momentarily in this bodymind. And the neurochemistry sings along. Muscles tighten, adrenalin surges. And then another moment, I'm looking out the window, and there are these nice birds, and they're chirping and singing, and there's a feeling that everything is peaceful and fine. Endorphins or whatever the happy chemicals are flood through the system. Muscles relax. So different movies arise, and any attempt to make one movie stay on the screen all the time, in my experience, doesn't work. There is no one in control of what movie plays. The one who *wants* to control all this is a character *in* the movie.

P: If everyone saw this, and saw that all is one, would everything disappear?

J: The world as we *think* of it disappears every time thinking stops! When we *see* how everything is created, moment by moment, in the mind, we discover true freedom.

P: I feel like I've been in the ultimate state experiencing this total bliss so many times and then always falling out of it, over and over.

J: Bliss comes and goes, as does despair. But ultimate reality is not an experience or a state that "you" can enter or leave. All experiences come and go. No experience is permanent. But that in which every experience appears, that which *is* every experience, *that* is impossible to gain or lose. The experience you call "being in the ultimate state" is appearing Here/Now in the same way the experience you call "falling out of it" is appearing. Ultimate Reality is being and beholding every appearance, and it is prior to all appearances. It is the common factor in every experience, and it is what remains when all appearances end. Liberation isn't about being permanently blissful and expanded. That will never happen.

P: There is the appearance of this space of nonduality and then the sense of helplessness in getting to that place.

J: But it's not a place that you get to. That's all part of the story. Nonduality is always right here. In the story created by thinking and imagining, there *seems* to be duality and separation, and in the movie of waking life, there may be a relative lessening of suffering at times, but what goes away can always come back. Night and day follow each other in endless cycles, just like enlightenment and delusion, and like progressive and repressive governments. Unicity includes it all. You are absolutely helpless, and that is only troublesome from the vantage point of the imaginary phantom self. Unicity accepts everything.

P: But there's still a sense that there's a "beyond the story."

J: Well, there is. What's beyond the story is the *seeing* of the story, the awareness in which the story appears, the space of Here/Now that is present before and after the story and *as* the story.

The simple *beingness* of the story – the bare *fact* of it as sensation, the registering of it – *that* is prior to the plotline and the involvement in the content – and even that plotline and that content and that involvement is nothing other than unicity. Even that is nothing but sensations and images and consciousness appearing Here/Now. There are differences that can be discerned, distinctions that can be drawn, but what is illusory is the idea of separate, independent "things." The absence of that separation is what we mean by oneness or emptiness or unicity or the Self. What is beyond the story is what is being and beholding the story – *that* is prior to the story and *that* remains when the story is gone.

And one of the stories is that there is "me" who gets caught up in stories and who longs to be free of them. "Beyond the story" then becomes an idea *within* the story, a destination – like Hawaii – that unfolds in the imagination like a travel brochure. But Here/Now is not a destination. It is not "out there" somewhere.

In deep sleep, there is no concern anymore with waking up from the story of my life. There is no one to wake up. That is the emptiness, the silence to which we are always pointing.

P: But it seems like there are my good movies and my bad movies, and there is a sense of abiding more in the movie than in the seeing. I want to abide more in awareness and not be taken in by the movie.

J: Well, if you truly don't want to be taken in, then you won't be taken in. But chances are, at least some of the time, you *will* want to be taken in. Consciousness enjoys movies! Apparently it enjoys being seduced and ravished, tricked and fooled, absorbed and entertained. Have you noticed? We experience that mesmerizing absorption and the delight of it when we go to the movie theater or when we read a good novel or watch the daily news. We get entranced. We love it! We pay money for it! Our attention gets drawn into the movie and the spell of the story and the characters, and we feel like this drama is really happening. Maybe unicity has some interest in exploring every possibility. It seems that way, doesn't it? And what fun would it be if we didn't get absorbed, if we didn't care?

It's the same with an addiction or a compulsion – if we really want to stop, we will stop. But the catch is that there is no one in control of what desire arises. Sometimes we want to take one more puff, and in that moment, that desire for one more puff is stronger than the desire to stop. So we postpone stopping for later, and we take another puff. No one is in control. It happens. We cannot control whether the desire to stop smoking is stronger in this moment than the desire to have a cigarette.

This "I" who wants to not be taken in, who wants to abide in one state but not in another, who wants to be in control, that "I" is a mirage. The real you, which is unicity, cannot help abiding everywhere, for it *is* everywhere and everywhen, everything and everyone. Unicity is all there is.

P: When the movie is too painful, there will suddenly be a movement back into seeing.

J: The seeing is happening even when there's a painful movie. Otherwise you wouldn't even be able to report that there had been a painful movie.

P: Yes, but that's a small seeing –

J: It's not small. It's boundless. It contains the entire universe.

P: It feels like it's a very contracted seeing –

J: Is the seeing contracted, or is the contraction something that's being seen? The lens of attention may be narrowed down to focus intently on my big toe or it may be absorbed in the plot of a movie. It may open up and expand into a spacious, clear awareness that has no focal point at all. But is the awareness itself really narrowed down or opened up? Or is it simply the lens of attention that opens and closes and moves from one spot to another? Of course, it depends on how we are using words, and different people may use them differently. But I would say that Here/Now is absolutely open and all-inclusive. And *everything* appears Here/Now, whether it is my big toe or a movie or the solar system, and all of it disappears instant by instant. What remains cannot be perceived or conceptualized.

P: We are all just like camcorders...

J: Not just camcorders. That's a little bit too detached, one step removed. You aren't just watching the movie, you *are* the movie. No separation. Being and beholding, as I like to say. Hands and eyes throughout the body. But there's no agent, big or small, no "one" apart from all of this who is seeing or doing it. There is simply seeing and doing.

P: How can we overcome losing ourselves in the story?

J: There's no "you" to get lost. But what you're describing is what a lot of meditation practices are built on – seeing through the story and resting in thoughtless awareness. And that's great. Coming back to the present moment, as they say, being awake to nonconceptual actuality, being aware of awareness.

But now we're seeing that this waking up and falling asleep happens by itself. No one is in control of it. The thoughts and the stories are also unicity. When that is realized, there is no more concern with trying to manage this "coming back to the present moment." It happens effortlessly by itself, as it always has, this alternation between movies and no movies. Whatever appears or disappears, Here/Now is ever-present. It doesn't need to be maintained. It can't be lost.

P: Is human life then just a story of "welcome to contraction"? Is the universe set up so we are stuck with this contraction?

J: Well, the notion that the universe is "set up" in some way is only an idea. But the manifestation certainly seems to inescapably include everything. There is a quote from the songwriter Leonard Cohen that I really like. He says something like, this world is not perfectible, and it always presents you with a sense of something undone, something missing, something hurting. He talks about a wound that never heals, and he says that true wisdom is learning to live with the wound. There is no escape. We like to imagine that spirituality will heal our wound, free us from pain and suffering, take away all ambiguity, and make us forever happy and blissful. But it doesn't work that way. My old Zen teacher Joko Beck used to say that our suffering is our mistaken belief that there is a cure. But when you finally dissolve into that hopelessness of no escape, there is a surprising sense of relief and freedom. The problems are still there, but they're not problematic anymore. A habit such as compulsive fingerbiting is still unpleasant, but it is no longer seen as an obstacle to freedom that must be removed if "I" am to be free. There is no such "I," no such separation.

P: We judge everything as well.

J: Judgment can arise in awareness. But awareness is free. Awareness has no judgments.

P: But what I am seeing is filtered in some way. How do you get away from filtering?

J: Well, *you* can't get away from filtering. As a conditioned organism, your perceptions and interpretations of those perceptions are always going to be filtered through the particular conditioning and make-up of your organism. No two people are ever seeing the same movie. No two people are having the same experience right now in this room. There is no way to get away from that uniqueness. In that sense, you are absolutely alone. But all these multiple viewpoints are the eyes and ears of one seamless totality, and the filtering is part of how that totality is functioning (or maybe malfunctioning at times, relatively speaking).

P: But I want to see everything clearly without imposing my own filtering.

J: You can't! And apparently, the universe needs your unique viewpoint. Obviously, since you're here! And although the relative world – the appearance – is always conditioned, the absolute is unconditioned and uncaused. In the absolute sense, there is nothing separate from anything else to condition or cause it, or to be caused or conditioned *by* it. The absolute is unicity or emptiness. This is our True Nature. It has no outside, no inside, no before, no after, no cause and no effect. The relative world is only an appearance – and even this *description* and *conceptualization* of unicity is part of that appearance. The absolute has no such word as "unicity." It has no *need* of any such word.

In awakening, the conditioned, relative world of appearances is revealed to be a kind of mirage and not a substantial reality. All limitations are seen to be entirely imaginary. And yet, paradoxically, true freedom is realized *in* limitation, and there is no longer a *problem* with limitation. We no longer need to walk on water or get rid of all our neurosis. The alternation between contraction and expansion is no longer a problem. So there are relative differences in the apparent world, but for unicity, they make no difference.

Awareness itself is not filtered. But the conditioned perceptions and the conceptual interpretations that we call the movie of waking life – *that* is always filtered. The filter is like the film that the pure light passes through to project a movie – what appears on the empty screen of awareness is light conditioned by the filter of the film. The light and the screen represent the unicity that is unconditioned. You are the unconditioned light behind every perception – the perceiv*ing* itself – the bare screen of awareness – and at the same time, the conditioned perceptions and ideations that make up your unique movie of waking life continue to appear. These appearances (the movie) are nothing solid or substantial – they are ever-changing, thoroughgoing flux. And they are not actually in any way ever *separate* from the screen or the light. There *is* no "screen," there *is* no "light," there *is* no "movie" – these only exist as thought-forms in relative reality, as appearances *in* the movie.

That's the trouble with analogies. They can be helpful, or they can add to the confusion. The mind can get itself really wound up: "Okay there's the conditioned and the unconditioned, and if it's all one then why does it seem different all the time, and is this the screen or the light or the film or the movie or the projector or what the hell is it?" [laughter] We get all tangled up in our words and thoughts and analogies. So to come back to the simplicity that's right here, right now, the simplicity of this moment, just the way it is. Everybody saying exactly what they're saying, feeling exactly whatever feelings are being felt, thinking whatever thoughts are being thought, seeing exactly what is being seen – just *this*, exactly as it is. *This* is effortless.

P: It's too simple. [laughter]

J: That's the problem, it's too simple for the mind because the mind loves complexity. It wants to grasp everything and package it up. But life can't be grasped, so all attempts to grasp and package it are ultimately unsatisfying. Even if there's mental knotting or grasping happening right now, that too is unicity appearing as knotting and grasping. It's not a problem that needs to be fixed. It's nothing personal. No one is doing it. It is nothing more than an appearance. It isn't even real.

Well, our timeless time is almost up. The movie of this meeting is coming to an end. So let's sit quietly for the last little while. Notice that our entire meeting is completely gone. Our entire past is completely gone. *All* of it! Memory can dredge up some abstraction or story of it, but the thing itself is completely gone. And right here, there's an aliveness. We wonder what it all means, and we get very serious trying to sort it all out, but for just this moment now, can we simply appreciate the whole show, just exactly as it is?

Maybe, maybe not.

Is Anyone Directing the Show?

Invitation to Explore the Present Moment:

Notice that *everything*, as it is, is effortlessly present. The sound of the train whistle, the cars, the birds, the sensations of breathing – it all happens effortlessly by itself – hearing, seeing, sensing, breathing. "You" don't have to *do* any of it.

When thoughts come, as they almost certainly will, is it possible to simply notice that they *are* thoughts, and to notice how they very quickly spin a whole movie-world in the imagination, a story full of emotions, ideas and beliefs?

Notice how these thoughts and mental movies arise on their own seemingly out of nowhere. Can you find anyone who is actually choosing or authoring these thoughts? Or do they simply *happen*, spontaneously, by themselves? You may discover that the "thinker," the "author," the "chooser" is only an image, an idea, another thought.

Notice that waking up from these thoughts and stories and mental movies also happens spontaneously by itself. One moment there is thinking or dreaming, a whole plotline unfolding in the imagination, and then suddenly – *poof!* – like a bubble popping, there is waking up from that story and being back here in Joan's living room. It happens by itself, naturally. Dreaming and waking up. And whatever happens, dreaming or waking up, it's always happening Here/Now in awareness.

Awareness is the ever-present ground, the common factor in every experience, the undeniable presence that you cannot doubt. But don't start looking for awareness. You'll never find it. Awareness is what you *are*. So just *be* aware. Actually, you can't *not* be aware. *Being aware* is effortless.

If there is tension or seeking or thinking going on, there's no need to judge it or take it personally. You don't need to overcome it or go to war with it. It's just something that's appearing here like the train whistle and the clouds in the sky. It's all an impersonal happening, like weather. And if judgment or resistance *does* arise, this, too, is simply one more cloud formation. *Nothing* needs to be any different than exactly how it is. Nothing *can* be any different than exactly how it is. This is absolutely simple. Being here. Being aware. Being present. Hearing *these* sounds, feeling *these* sensations, being *this* moment, just as it is.

The Talk:

Thought divides the present moment up into separate things, labels everything it has created, and then invents stories about how it all works. Thought tells us, "That is a bird cheeping out there. I am in here hearing it." By describing what's appearing in that way, thought creates the illusion that there is an "out there" and an "in here." It suggests that "the bird" is some *thing* separate from "me," that there's an "I" separate from "the hearing" who is "doing" the hearing, that there's "a bird" separate from "the cheep," and "a sound" separate from "the hearing." By the way that it describes and labels things, thought literally creates a mirage world of separate *things*, a world that comes to *seem* completely believable and real, just as a movie or a dream or a mirage seems real and believable. But this world created by thought is conceptual. It's not what we actually *perceive*, but rather, it is what we've learned to *think* we are perceiving.

Thought evaluates and judges everything, has all kinds of ideas about how things should be, how they could or should be differ-ent—how I should be different, how the others should be different, how the world should be different. Thought creates stories about where we think we're going and where we think we've been.

The root thought is the "I" thought – the idea that there is "me" *having* all these thoughts and authoring them, "me" who is steering my ship down the waterway of life, "me" who hopes to one day "drop the self" and become an enlightened me.

But does this "me" really exist? *Something* is here, an undeniable presence that I identify as myself. I know beyond a shadow of a doubt that I am here without having to look in a mirror, without having any-one tell me, without having to think about it, I *know* I am here. *Being here* is undeniable. But *what* is it that is undeniably here? Is it the image in the mirror, the character in the story? Or is it the awareness in which all the images and stories appear, the presence that has no boundaries and no limits?

This undeniable aware presence has been erroneously conflated with the character we've learned to think of as "me." We have come to *think* and *believe* that this undeniable presence-awareness is located or encapsulated *inside* the bodymind. But is this true? And what *is* the so-called "person" or the "bodymind"? Is it anything more substantial than a collection of mental images, thoughts, sensations, memories, stories? Is all of that what you truly are?

Isn't it obvious that all of that is something that is appearing here, just like the colors, shapes and sounds in this room? Everything that appears – every sensation, every perception, every thought, every memory, every fantasy, every form, every apparently solid object, every apparently real event – if we look at it very closely, we find only thoroughgoing flux. There is no solid, enduring *thing* at all. We can also notice that Here/Now is equally present everywhere we look. Whatever time of day or night it is, regardless of whether we are remembering the past or imagining the future, it is always Now. Wherever we travel in the movie of waking life, we are always Here in this placeless place, this immediacy. This timeless presence is the substance of every appearance and it is what remains in deep sleep and after death. This presence has no owner, no location, no before and after, no birth and death, no cause, no boundaries, no other. There is nothing outside of it. It is all there is.

The story that we have learned to believe is that we are encap-sulated inside the bodymind looking out through the windows of our senses at an objective world that exists independently of awareness, "out there" somewhere, a world that is full of separate "things," including millions of other people, each of them with free will, each freely choosing what to do and what not to do. But does any such objective, external, material world really exist? Are we actually encapsulated inside an object gazing out at a bunch of other objects?

We have absolutely no doubt about *being here*, and yet, when we look closely to see what this "I" is that is doubtlessly present, what do we find? Any particular object we find – such as a sensation in the chest, an image of "the bodymind," or a story about "my life" – that object is being perceived. What is perceiving?

We look for what is perceiving all of this, and we find nothing at all. And yet this absence is vibrantly alive. It *is* everything – this whole show. This aware presence, this aliveness, this beingness is the ground and substance of everything, but it isn't really a substance in the usual sense, because no one can take hold of awareness or presence or being. It has no location, no boundaries, no color, no shape, no form. And yet, it is *every* location, *every* color, *every* shape, *every* form. It is the aliveness of this moment, that which distinguishes present reality from a memory or a fantasy. This boundless, seamless presence is the true "I" in "I am."

The world that we *think* is "out there" is not really "out there" at all when we look closely at our actual present moment experience. Everything is appearing *right here*, isn't it? No separation at all. No inside and outside. No boundary. The boundary is only an idea, a conceptual dividing line. The present moment appears as one seamless unicity. Only thought divides it up.

How solid is anything perceivable or conceivable? Where is this morning before you got here? Or last night? Or September 11th? Any of those supposed events can be conjured up, they can play in the mind as a movie would play, and of course there are infinite versions of each of those events. Even our own version seems to change from one minute to the next. So how solid is any of it? How solid is this bodymind? How solid is this room? These words that are emerging out of I don't know where, these sounds or vibrations are here for an instant and then they're gone – or we could say, they continue forever, endlessly morphing into something else, like ripples in a pond. And likewise, the breathing and the beating of the heart and the traffic and the breeze and the thoughts that try to make sense of it all – all of it is one seamless ever-changing flow.

When we investigate this whole appearance closely, either with meditation or with science, we find that it is utterly insubstantial. Everything is vanishing into thin air. Thus, it has sometimes been said that everything is a dream, or everything is Mind or spirit or Consciousness. But words are tricky – they make something out of nothing and divide up what is actually indivisible. "Mind" and "matter" are two different words for whatever this is Here/Now. Look deeply into matter and you find nothing solid. No matter ever appears outside of consciousness. Where is the boundary between mind and matter? Form is emptiness and emptiness is form. Whatever this is – Here/Now – it cannot be grasped by any word or any concept.

We want to grasp it with the thinking mind, but we cannot grasp life. This urge to make sense of everything, to nail it down, to get a grip, is undoubtedly a survival function, an evolutionary impulse, part of our human nature. We're not trying to eliminate this urge to make sense of the sensations, or to find meaning and construct stories. This is an aspect of life that can be functional and beautiful. We're not condemning it or trying to get rid of it. But is there an aspect of this urgency to "get a grip" and "make sense" of everything that comes from a false idea of separation and encapsulation? Once we have the idea that we are a fragment located inside a bodymind looking out at a hostile world, we live in fear. There is even a fear of awakening from this illusion, a fear of boundlessness, a fear of "being nobody." Because from the perspective of a separate me, dissolving into boundlessness sounds like death. But what exactly *is* this "me" who could seemingly dissolve or die? What *is* this phantom "somebody" who seems to be forever incomplete, never quite good enough, always lacking something, separate from the whole?

Does this separate me really exist or is it only a bunch of stories overlaid on top of certain sensations and perceptions – a habitual mistaking of a conceptual object, "the bodymind," for the subject, the aware presence that is beyond doubt?

As soon as we label this presence, as soon as we call it "presence" or "awareness" or "boundlessness" or "unicity" or "Here/Now" or "the Self," then instantly it seems to become *something* – another object. Words create the appearance of objective things. Words draw boundary lines where none really exist. They create the mirage of separation, the mirage of solid entities with continuity. So be aware that words are only pointers. There is no such *thing* as "awareness" or "unicity." There is only *this* [Joan gestures to include everything].

Is there anyone inside this bodymind who is *doing* the talking, doing the hearing, doing the thinking, making the choices, performing the actions? Is there anyone directing the show? Is there anyone in control of what is arising and appearing? Is there an owner of the so-called internal weather, someone who is responsible for it? Is there any fundamental difference between a thunderstorm and an outburst of anger, or between a cloudy day and a wave of depression or a moment of anxiety? When it's the weather outside, when it's the thunderstorm or the haze or the clouds, it's clear that no one owns it. We don't take it personally. But when it's the internal weather, then there's a very old story that someone owns it, that there's a "me" who *has* it, who is responsible for it, who needs to figure out what to do about it and how to fix it. It *seems* personal.

And in this movie of waking life, there are many things to do: bodywork, meditation, coming to meetings like this, reading books. But is there anyone doing any of this? And after all the fixing and evolving and transforming and all the experiences of a lifetime, has anything *fundamental* really changed? Where has it all gone? Has anything substantial even happened or was it all like a dream? Doesn't your childhood seem like a dream? Where has it gone? If it has vanished into thin air, then how real was it?

Is there even anything here right now that can be grasped? Or is there only thoroughgoing flux and change? That sounds scary, maybe, to the mind – and yet when we really *see* that, we realize that thoroughgoing flux is unbroken wholeness or seamless unicity, and in that realization, there is no more fear of death, no more concern with personal failure, no more urgency to fix things and achieve something, for we realize that nothing is ever missing. This unbroken wholeness is here right now. It is the one thing that is completely trustworthy and impossible to doubt. We can't get hold of it for we are not outside of it. We *are* it. It is what Here/Now *is*.

Right now, in this moment, is there really a problem that needs to be solved or is there only this ever-changing appearance, endlessly solving and dissolving itself, effortlessly, naturally? Right now, is there anything that needs to be different in this moment, or is the idea of a problem and the search for a solution all nothing more than a bunch of passing thoughts, no more substantial than last night's dreams?

P: With the storm analogy, I feel that when the storm is outside, then you can get out of the way, but if it's inside, you can't get out of the way. So there's a big difference to me.

J: Yes. In some sense, that's very true. Relatively speaking, as an apparent person in the movie of waking life, as the bodymind organism, I can get out of the rain or take shelter from the wind. But who is it who would need to get out of the way of the inner storm and where would they go to escape?

P: I know you'd say there is no one.

J: Well, let's explore. We may discover that the so-called "inner storm" and the so-called "outer storm" are both happening inside you – inside awareness – and that both storms are made up of changing sensations, and in the case of the inner storm, also thoughts and stories – all of it a momentary, changing appearance.

We may discover that both the "inner storm" and the "outer storm" are something observable and that you are the awareness that is undisturbed by the storm, like the screen that is untouched by the weather in the movie. We may discover that the one who apparently needs to get out of the way of the inner storm is nothing but a mirage, a *part* of the inner storm, and that *all* storms are nothing but unicity appearing as stormy weather.

Let's bring it down to earth. Let's say there is an internal storm of anger. What's actually going on? When we look closely at this thing we call "anger," what do we find? Thoughts, stories, sensations, right? Thoughts such as: *"I can't believe he did that to me! He doesn't respect me. I don't deserve this. Screw him!"* Every thought generates neurochemistry, and neurochemistry generates thought, like the chicken and the egg. So there are thoughts and sensations – maybe a churning in the stomach, a tightening of the jaw, blood rushing up to the head, the face flushing, sensations of heat, maybe a clench in the gut or a contraction in the shoulder or a quiver in the lip – all kinds of sensations and movements in the body. That's actually all that's happening. Thoughts, neurochemistry, sensations. No one is doing any of it. No one is in control of it. It's simply happening out of the infinite causes and conditions of nature and nurture. And one of the thoughts is, "I need to get away from this. This is hurting me. But I can't get away. I'm trapped in my anger."

Thoughts have a way of seeming like an objective report on reality. If thought says I'm trapped, then I must be trapped. And if thought posits an "I" who is trapped, then this "I" must exist. But let's really look and see if what thought tells us is true.

Can we see that there is nothing personal about any of this? The thoughts, the sensations, the neurochemistry, the genetic predispositions toward particular inner weather patterns, the infinite causes and conditions of this moment – it's not personal. No one is *doing* any of it on purpose. It may *seem* that there is a doer, but if you really look carefully, you'll see that it all simply happens. This stormy weather arises out of the whole universe, and in a way, even that is another story, another conceptual overlay. Our actual *experience* is that it simply appears. It shows up. It's here. And then a moment later, it isn't!

And the root thought in this inner storm is the I-thought: "I" was not respected; "I" was slighted; "I" was hurt. And then a secondary layer of thinking in which this I-thought claims ownership of all these earlier thoughts: "These are *my* thoughts. This is *my* anger. *I* am angry." Taking it personally, inserting a nonexistent owner/author/thinker into the picture who is seemingly responsible for this anger, and who is seemingly trapped in it, and who could or should be doing a better job of handling this. This is the "I" who wants to get control and get out of the way of the inner storm.

And of course, there is also the complimentary idea that there is an owner/author at the controls inside the other person as well, someone who freely *chose* to say something insulting, who *could* have been nicer: "*You* made me angry, *you* hurt my feelings, *you* should have been nicer."

And sometimes, the anger erupts into action and we yell nasty things at the other person or slam doors or give icy looks. And then maybe there are more thoughts, judging the anger, judging "me" (or "you") for having it and not controlling it. After all, we've been told all our lives that we are or should be in control. So thought says: "I'm a real jerk. I lost my temper. Anger is not spiritually correct. I'm obviously not very enlightened if I feel this much anger, or if I yelled the way I just did. This is not good for my self-image or my karma or my blood pressure. I have to make this stop. I have to get away from this anger. How can I do that?"

And then thought suggests a strategy, something to do in order to get away: "smoke a cigarette," or "eat some potato chips," or "have a beer," or "turn on the television," or "go for a run," it might suggest. Or, if we're on a spiritual path, maybe thought suggests turning *toward* the anger rather than trying to escape or distract oneself: "Pay attention to the present moment, feel the sensations, be aware of your breathing, see the story as a story and let it go." And briefly, maybe the attention focuses on the breathing and on sensations in the body, the so-called "present moment." But then a memory arises (unbidden) of the apparent insult, and again the bodymind is instantly full of thoughts and sensations, stories, chemistry, stormy weather. Feeling self-righteous, wounded, defensive, wronged.

And *all* of that is simply arising on its own, unbidden: the neurochemistry, the thoughts, the escape strategy or the meditation strategy, the memories of the perceived insult, the thoughts about the thoughts, the whole thing. No one is doing *any* of it, although thought keeps suggesting otherwise.

And in the swirl of all that emotion, we may even discover that there is a certain enjoyment in being angry, in thinking that "I'm right," in feeling victimized and righteously indignant and a little bit sorry for myself. The whole story and the strong sensations all reinforce the sense of "me" as *somebody*. Somebody who is superior and separate and *right*. But perhaps there's also an uncomfortable glimmer of recognition that this whole drama is in some way make-believe, that my position isn't entirely solid or true. And besides, anger is not spiritual (or so I've been told), and therefore, I can't totally revel in it. And besides that, it hurts. Anger is suffering. It's enjoyable in some way, it's alluring, and yet, it's also painful.

So now there is this mental conflict between the desire to go on being angry and the desire to get away from the anger, between the "spiritual me" (the enlightened one, the Good Girl, the mature adult, the neocortex) and the "pissed off me" (the unenlightened one, the Bad Girl, the two-year-old who gets off on throwing a tantrum, the lizard brain). And that whole inner conflict is composed of conflicting thoughts and impulses. First: "This isn't spiritual. I shouldn't be angry." And then: "How could he have done that to me? Who does he think I am? I don't deserve this. Of course I should be angry!" That's all that's happening. Inner weather made up of conflicting thoughts, stories, sensations and neurochemistry. It's *all* happening on it's own, unbidden. It all simply appears. No one is at the controls. Don't accept that on faith, but watch and see. Even if we *seem* to get control, even that appearance is happening by itself. The ability to "take a time out" and pause before speaking when feeling angry may *seem* like "me" being in control and *choosing* to do this – but it all happens by itself. In another moment, the idea of "taking a time out" doesn't even come up, or if it does, it fails miserably. But thought inserts the notion of this "I" who can seemingly "choose" to "take a time out" rather than yelling – this phantom executive who seems to be in control, or who *should* be in control, or so we think.

This "I" is a mirage. The True Self, or the true "I," is the undeniable presence being and beholding the whole show that is appearing. The false "I" is the mistaken identification of this undeniable aware presence with a particular object – the bodymind – and the idea that "I" am encapsulated inside this bodymind. Thought (posing as "me") claims it is running the show, when actually, thought is conditioned and powerless. It happens automatically out of ten million causes and conditions. There is no independent author deciding what to think. Thoughts happen, like secretions of the brain and the nervous system.

But we have the mistaken belief that a thought, such as "I am never going to get angry again," actually has the power to prevent future anger, and we have the idea that there is a thinker behind the thought, a ghost in the machine freely authoring our thoughts and steering the ship. So we imagine that this "I" *chose* to think this thought, and that this "I" has the power to make it come true. And then we wonder why it doesn't work.

Thought and imagination have this magical ability to create the mirage of "someplace else" other than Here/Now – a better state of mind, a better experience, a better future, a better "me." Thought imagines that we can separate time and space from each other and "me" from both of them – as if we *could* be somewhere else right now. But is that really possible? Do these "things" (time, space, me) really come apart that way? Or is it all one inseparable whole that could not, at this moment, be other than exactly how it is? Is there really anywhere else to go? Wherever you appear to go, have you ever left Here/Now? The scenery changes, but you (presence-awareness) remain!

P: Can't we get out away from the inner storm by observing it? It seems like we can, but it doesn't always seem to work. I got really angry at my wife last week, and I was trying to be detached and just observe it all, but it didn't really work. I was still angry.

J: Because thought has no power. The one who was trying to be detached doesn't exist. Awareness is *never* caught up or involved in the storm – like the screen that is untouched by the storm in the movie. Awareness accepts everything, the way the screen accepts the movie, without being damaged in any way. The storm is composed of thoughts and sensations. Awareness is seeing the storm, registering the storm, experiencing the storm, but it is simultaneously free from the storm. It is prior to the storm. It is what remains when the storm has passed. So yes, there is a freedom in being consciously aware rather than being hypnotized by thoughts and lost in the story–this is often called observing or witnessing or "being here now," and it is sometimes spoken of as a shift in identification from imagining oneself as the character, encapsulated inside the bodymind and trapped in the story, to recognizing oneself as the boundless awareness in which the character and the bodymind and the story appear. This shift from encapsulation to boundlessness, this observing presence, this clear awareness is what meditation often aims to cultivate. But actually, this boundlessness, this awareness is never absent. What meditation is really doing is seeing through the false ideas that seem to obscure this and thereby revealing what is always already present.

But as you have noticed, this isn't always how it appears. *As a strategy,* "witnessing" or "being here now" doesn't always work, because the strategy (and the desired outcome) is *in* the story. It's a bunch of thoughts and ideas. In the situation that you describe with your wife, there is a story that there's this spiritual "me" who *should be* watching the weather and not being affected by it or getting involved in it. And there is an idea or a belief that this observing process should have a certain result. It should "work." I should no longer be angry. There is an illusion that "I" exist as *something* that can either be misidentified as the character and then lost in the story, or else correctly identified as awareness and then free of the story.

But is there really any such entity? Is awareness actually *separate* from whatever is appearing *in* awareness? We speak of it that way sometimes to draw attention to awareness, which is otherwise easily overlooked, but you can't really find a boundary between "awareness" and "content" anymore than you can find a boundary between "inside" and "outside." These are only conceptual boundaries. Reality is seamless. The present moment is seamless. There are different shapes and colors and sensations, yes, but the idea that these are separate, independent things that can be pulled apart from each other is always a construction of thought. Nothing is really separate from anything else.

In one moment, the desire and the intention not to be angry at your wife arises. In another moment, uncontrollable anger arises. Both arise spontaneously out of infinite causes and conditions just like the weather outside. And I'm not saying you shouldn't take an anger management class or do meditation or that you shouldn't "take a time out" or "pay attention" when you are angry, *if you can, if that happens* – I'm saying that there is no "you" who can *make* any of that happen at will or on command.

P: When it's seen, there is spaciousness. But when it isn't, there is anger and a sense of failure and caughtupness in the little me.

J: So?

P: I want to be in spaciousness all the time!

J: "I" want to be in spaciousness all the time. The "I" who wants to be in a special state "all the time" is a phantom. There is no owner of these different experiences going from spaciousness to caughtupness. That's another subtle thought, part of the caughtupness. And the notion of "all the time" is only an idea. The only eternity is Now. Eternity is not duration, it is timeless presence. Any "spaciousness" that can be experienced is always fleeting. The real spaciousness is what Here/Now *is*. It is ever-present and accepts everything, even contraction, anger and unhappiness. Nothing is left out.

Sometimes the thought-sense of me is appearing Here/Now, and when it is, then maybe the spaciousness *seems* to disappear and narrow down. This apparent narrowing down is only a dream-like appearance. Boundlessness or unicity doesn't ever really narrow down or go away. The image in a movie can change from a vast open sky to a narrow dark tunnel. But the screen itself is not expanding or contracting. Here/Now is without any size or shape. Expansion and contraction is an optical illusion created by rapidly moving pictures.

There can be the *thought*, "The space has gone away. I've left the present moment!" There can be the *sensations* that go along with that thought—tightness, contraction, agitation—but, so what? If thought identifies boundlessness as a *particular* experience that comes and goes, then there is immediately a sense of lack when this experience disappears, as it always will. And then there is wanting and fearing, and the imagination of gain and loss. When this thought-story becomes transparent as a story, what happens to wanting and fearing, gain and loss?

P: The me is sometimes present and sometimes absent and I want to be without the me.

J: "I" want to be without the "me"—can you see the joke there? Actually the me is never present. The me is only a thought, a sensation, a mirage, right? It's a mental image which sometimes appears and sometimes doesn't appear. Who cares if it appears or disappears?

P: So I'm trying to watch the thoughts and catch the thoughts, but—

J: Who is trying to do that?

P: There is a me who is in relationship to thoughts.

J: Isn't that another thought, that there's a me in relationship to the thoughts, a me who has to watch and observe "myself" and be detached? Isn't it simply one train of thought apparently monitoring and trying to control another train of thought, and all of it simply an appearance that is spontaneously arising in awareness?

P: Yes, and there are times when there is no me.

J: There is *never* a me. You mean there are times when there is no *sense* of a me or no *thought* of a me.

P: Sometimes there is just awareness.

J: Without any thought that there is *someone* being aware.

P: Yes.

J: That's the truth. There is no one being aware, there is simply awareness. That is *always* the actual fact of how it is. There is no one thinking the thoughts. There is just thinking. And one of the thoughts is that there is me thinking the thoughts or me being aware.

P: But sometimes I get totally lost in some train of thought.

J: "I" get lost in some train of thought. That "I" is itself a thought, and "getting lost" is a story, a mental narrative. That sentence – "I get totally lost in some train of thought" – is a thought-story. Can you see that? Yes, movies can appear and attention can be absorbed for awhile in the plot of a movie. It happens. It's entertaining (or not). And then there's a waking up. The movie or the train of thought ends. That also happens. It all happens naturally by itself. And it all happens in awareness.

Thinking depends on awareness. It can't happen without awareness being here first, but awareness doesn't depend on thinking. Awareness underlies everything perceivable and conceivable in the same way that the screen underlies every scene in the movie. As you watch the movie, you're always seeing the screen, you just don't consciously notice it. And in the same way, whatever appears, you're always seeing awareness. Without awareness, nothing would appear at all.

Thoughts create a mental movie, and then there's a waking up. The movie is over. It happens naturally. And a millisecond later, thought takes credit for the waking up ("I woke up"), and starts strategizing about how to stay awake forever, how to stop thinking and "stay in the now," how to identify as awareness instead of as "me," all of which is a new thought-train, a new movie, again starring "me," the one who could either screw up my life or else get enlightened and cross the imaginary finish line. Dreaming and waking up. No one is in control of *any* of it. The "me" is *never* really there.

P: Does meditation help to expose the illusion?

J: What is behind this question? Isn't the very question of whether something will help to expose the illusion itself part of the illusion? I'm not saying meditation *doesn't* help. I'm only questioning the question. The mind loves these mental discussions – is meditation helpful or unhelpful? – let's try to figure that out – round and round the mind spins. But where does the question come from in the first place? Isn't it rooted in the story of a problem that needs to be solved? Right now, without thinking, where is this imaginary problem?

What we call meditation (paying attention deliberately) happens naturally, and within the dream-like movie of waking life, intelligent meditation can sometimes be a very useful tool for seeing thought as thought, recognizing mental movies as imagination, questioning beliefs, seeing through the conceptual mirage, and waking up to the nondual actuality of sounds, sensations, shapes, textures – pure perception, bare being.

But paradoxically, as soon as we call it meditation and make it into something special and try to *use it* as a tool to achieve a result, it begins to reinforce the very illusion it set out to expose. As soon as it becomes a deliberate, intentional, formal activity, it begins to reinforce the idea that there is *somebody* who is paying attention, somebody who is caught in the thoughts, somebody who is *doing* the meditating, somebody who is becoming more and more aware, somebody who is meditating in order to get to a better place in the future.

The clearest meditation teachers will tell you that meditation is not about improving, that it is about seeing through the desire for improvement and seeing through the meditator. They will tell you that this seeing gets subtler and subtler. They may even tell you that meditation is useless, that it is about not doing anything, that wherever you go, here you are. But then many of them go on to tell you how important it is to meditate regularly, and they show you all the correct postures and hand positions. There's nothing wrong with any of this, but there's no necessity to it either.

Meditation happens for some. For some, it doesn't. If it happens, then it is necessary. Whatever happens is unavoidable. In my case, there was meditation. But was meditation any more important to the process of waking up than being a drunk, which also happened in my story? Whatever we say, however we answer that question, it's all a story. If meditation arises, then it arises. But it only happens *in* the movie of waking life. In deep sleep, the one who needs to meditate vanishes completely along with the whole practice of meditation and this question of whether or not meditation is helpful. It all disappears! What a relief, eh? What remains is the groundlessness that needs no solution and that has no questions.

P: I keep trying to tell myself that this is all a dream and that my anger is just a story. I keep trying to see through my thoughts and be detached, but I keep failing. I keep forgetting it's all a story. I keep taking it all very seriously. I keep getting involved.

J: There is no "you" doing any of this. The attempt to remember that this is all a dream is part of the dream. Sometimes this dream-like appearance is messy and painful. Sometimes life hurts. Stormy weather is part of the show, part of the texture of life. There's no way to avoid it. But when *trying* to avoid it, or *needing* to avoid it, or taking it personally as "my" problem falls away, then it's clear that whatever is happening is simply weather, like a thunderstorm or a cloudy day. There's no resistance left. Pain still hurts, sadness is still sad, but the suffering disappears. And when I speak of all this falling away, don't imagine some dramatic final event after which you will feel only peace and equanimity forever after. That's the dream again. The falling away that I'm pointing to can only happen now. I mean that very literally. *Right now.* Any thoughts about "a moment from now," or "yesterday," or "forever after," are just thoughts, dreams, fantasies, forms of avoidance and postponement, forms of suffering. And you can't *make* these thoughts go away. *Simply see them for what they are.* You can't even *do* that, but it can happen.

"How dare he treat me that way!" is a thought. "My anger is just a story," is another thought. But *seeing* these *as* thoughts is not thinking; it is awareness. Awareness is what *sees through* and dissolves old habits and fixations. But awareness isn't a technique that "you" can use to achieve "your" goals – that's thought again, strategizing and trying to get somewhere. Awareness has no goals, no strategies. It seeks nothing and goes nowhere. It simply illuminates what is. Awareness is our True Nature – the groundless ground that is always Here/Now. The strategies and goals are thoughts. Thought happens by itself. Even a thought such as "stop thinking" or "think positively" that *appears* to be about "me" taking control of "my" thinking is itself only another conditioned thought. There is no one at the controls who can choose to want what we want in any given moment, or to think what we think, or to do what we do. Again, don't take my word for that, but watch closely and see for yourself.

Definitely if the thought arises to put attention on the breathing, and if that's what happens, if attention *does* go to the breathing, there will be less suffering than if thought says, "I am going to shoot this person I'm angry at," and if that thought is followed by shooting the other person, which in some cases it is. And in those cases where it is, there is no choice – pulling the trigger becomes an overwhelming urge, the way we have all experienced on a smaller scale when suddenly we find ourselves saying or doing something that we later regret. At the moment that it was happening, there was no stopping it. In a more extreme case, maybe you pick up a gun and actually shoot ten people. And definitely (at least in the short run, at least apparently) that causes more suffering than if the thought arises to focus on the breathing, and if that thought is followed by awareness of breathing. Ultimately, since everything is one seamless whole in which everything is the cause and the effect of everything else, we can't really say that focusing on the breathing causes less suffering than shooting ten people. It *seems* that way from our limited viewpoint. But we can't really know how everything goes together.

The central illusion is that there is a me in there who is in control of this, a me who decides what thoughts to think and which thoughts to act on, a me who can decide, "I am not going to shoot ten people, I am going to meditate instead." In fact, you could not shoot ten people (or meditate) if that wasn't what was already arising.

In recent brain experiments, they've discovered that the thought that proposes an action ("I'm going to shoot that guy" or "I'm going to meditate") actually comes a split-second *after* the action is already being initiated in the body. The thought is an explanatory commentary after the fact that only *looks like* a decision or a command. Other brain experiments have shown that an action (such as going to get a drink of water) can be stimulated by a probe in the brain or by flashcards that are seen only by one side of the brain, and the brain will then produce a rational explanation for the action (such as, "I was thirsty, so I went to get a drink"), an explanation that sounds perfectly convincing and reasonable, but it is entirely untrue and fabricated because the action was actually induced by the probe or the flashcard. And the person who is the subject of the experiment fully believes the explanation that their brain has produced! They believe that they "decided" to get a drink of water because they were thirsty. As such experiments demonstrate, the decider is an illusion and the so-called decision is nothing more than a way of describing what happened, a kind of fictitious commentary after the fact. So, it *seems* that we can decide whether to pay attention to the present moment or daydream instead. Is it true?

The illusion is that there is *somebody* here who decides to be one way or the other. Thought paints the picture that there is *somebody* who decides to be Jack the Ripper and *somebody else* who decides to be Mother Theresa. We imagine that Jack the Ripper could have behaved like Mother Teresa but *chose* not to. And when that power of choice or that mirage of agency is called into question, we may feel very frightened. If we imagine we're separate from everything and in control, then being out of control sounds nightmarish. It sounds like we're just robots. It sounds really dangerous, like we'll all go around being totally licentious and immoral, killing and raping and plundering. But I don't think so. I don't feel any compulsion to run out and start behaving like Jack the Ripper. It's not that I'm restraining myself. The urge simply isn't there. And as for being a robot, I'd say that a living organism is not a machine, but it's not an autonomous, independent agent in the way we imagine it is. The functioning of thought, like the functioning of genes and chemicals, is in some ways quite robotic and mechanical.

But to whom is that frightening? And what *sees* the robotic aspect of nature? Is awareness robotic, mechanical or conditioned?

We want to have a perpetual *experience* of clarity, peace, love, bliss – up without down – eternally sunny skies. And that's a fantasy. It won't ever happen. What *can* happen is that the *need* for that falls away. The sense of personal ownership falls away. The thought that "I" am contracted and deluded, or "I" am expanded and enlightened becomes transparent as just another passing thought happening to no one. Awareness is beholding it all. Awareness is *always* open, accepting everything, clinging to nothing. Awareness is the openness that is so open that it is open to being closed. Awareness is the solvent that dissolves illusion. You don't have to go looking for awareness; awareness is ever-present and inescapable. But you can't *use* awareness. That's thought again, conjuring up "you," conjuring up the future, conjuring up a strategy, looking for a result. Awareness is the light that exposes all of this for what it is. Awareness is the seeing that sees the false as false. Awareness sees through and dissolves the mirage of separation. Awareness is the wholeness that is borderless, seamless and ownerless. Awareness is another word for Here/Now.

Anger, anxiety, depression and other weather patterns may appear more frequently for some people than for others because of different genes, different neurochemistry, different conditioning. If somebody is sexually, emotionally, physically abused as a child every day, they are going to have a different experience as an adult than somebody who grows up in a relatively safe and happy home with loving parents. If you're born black, female and gay in a society that is racist, sexist, and heterosexist, well, you're going to have very different experiences from someone who grows up white, male and heterosexual in that same society. That is conditioned stuff, different weather. Chicago has more stormy weather than Oakland. There's nothing personal or ultimately meaningful about it.

One of my teachers, Toni Packer, grew up in Nazi Germany, and she was half Jewish, so you can imagine the undercurrent of paranoia and anxiety that was part of the fabric of her childhood. The city where she lived, Leipzig, was being bombed repeatedly. That was part of her growing up experience – bombs dropping, explosions, fires everywhere, never knowing when it might be her house that would be hit next, seeing her father, whom she revered, huddled in the corner in terror. Imagine what that would be like. To this day, if Toni hears an unexpected, loud noise, she's told me that it triggers a momentary panic in her bodymind. It's no big deal, but it happens, whereas when I hear the same noise, I don't feel the same panic, because I grew up in a peaceful situation where no bombs were falling on my neighborhood and no war was raging around me. Our different reactions to sudden, loud noises certainly don't mean that I am more enlightened than Toni. It is simply that different conditioning has produced different reactions in these bodyminds, different weather systems. There is no owner, no doer of either one of these experiences. None of it *means* anything. The weather is not personal.

Some people are naturally good-natured, even-tempered and easy-going, not because they've meditated a lot or because they're enlightened, but because they were born with that temperament. Other people are naturally high strung, sensitive, moody and temperamental, and they tend to be that way even after years of meditation and enlightenment. The easy-going people probably receive more approval and affection from the world around them throughout their lives than the temperamental people, and this input further reinforces and conditions each of them. Some bodymind organisms have a genetic, neurochemical or hormonal inclination toward depression or anxiety. Some people have a more fiery temper, more sadness, a better sense of humor, more energy or greater resiliency than others. All of that is simply the result of nature and nurture – different conditions. It is impersonal weather, like Chicago having more thunderstorms and more cloudy days than Oakland. But thought wants to take it all personally: "It's *my* weather, *my* anger, *my* clarity, *my* depression, *my* restlessness, *my* enlightenment, *my* delusion." But where is this mysterious owner?

We think we can control all of this. When a thought such as, "I am not going to be angry anymore," is followed by anger dissolving, then we think we did it. But what about all the times we had that thought and then got angry again?

P: So we are just the witness, not the actor.

J: There's nobody being either a witness or an actor. There's simply witnessing and acting. I have never liked that term, "the witness" because to me it conjures up the image of some kind of detached thing off in the background witnessing everything. It implies separation. The term is used a lot in spiritual circles, but I find it a very misleading word. There is seeing and acting and hearing and breathing and being and awaring and talking and listening and singing and dancing, but there is no one doing any of it. Who is witnessing what? There can be a *thought* that "I" am doing the witnessing, or "the witness" is doing it, or "God" is doing it, or "consciousness" is doing it, or "awareness" is doing it, but is there actually *anyone* or any-*thing* doing this witnessing? Where is the separation between seer and seen? Isn't *seeing* the actual reality? The "seer" and the "seen" are conceptualizations. Undivided *seeing* is our actual experience. Likewise, where is the separation between seeing and acting? It's one whole movement.

P: So who paints a picture? Who writes a book?

J: My actual experience in writing a book is that it writes itself, it really does. And then afterwards thought says, "I wrote this book," and our name is on the jacket, and people call us "a writer," and all of this confirms the idea that "I" wrote the book. But when I look closely, the whole universe wrote the book. Yes, this bodymind sat at the computer and typed the words, but where do the words come from? Where does everything come from? Where does that urge and that ability come from to write a book? Some people have the urge and the ability to write a book and some people don't. Some people stop after ten pages while other people keep going. Some people send the manuscript off to a publisher; some people put it in the closet. Of the manuscripts that go to the publisher, some get accepted and some don't, and it often has nothing to do with real merit. Where do the words and the urges and the abilities and the "decisions" come from? No one is running the show. Investigate this for yourself. As you are writing a letter or talking on the phone or driving the car or fixing breakfast or whatever it is, look closely and carefully, not with analytical thinking but with bare attention, and see if you can find the writer, the talker, the driver, the doer, the author, or the investigator. See if there's a "you" in control of these things, a "you" that is making them happen (including the inquiring and the seeing). See if you actually know *how* "you" do any of these activities. How exactly do you drive the car? Or compose a letter? Or raise your arm? Or breathe? Or beat your heart? Or digest your food? Or hear and understand these words right now? Look closely. Who is in charge? Is anyone directing the show?

P: What are we here for? If there's nothing we can do, then why are we coming to these meetings?

J: We can speculate and come up with answers, but is it possible to simply be awake to this amazing aliveness that's right here, right now? In this aliveness, what would it even mean to have a purpose, to be here *for* something?

Doesn't it take conceptual thought and imagination to conjure up a "purpose" for this gathering? No tiny child or baby would worry about the purpose of being here now. They'd simply be full of curiosity and amazement and wonder and playfulness, enjoying the colors and shapes and sounds and the warm patch of sunlight and the fun of moving their arms and legs. And if they suddenly got hungry or wet, they'd start to cry, without for a moment worrying that this might be an unenlightened thing to do. And a moment later, they'd be laughing and gurgling again, their tears completely forgotten.

Of course, we can't become babies again. But maybe we can discover that our thoughts and ideas are not as serious as we think, and that the actuality of what's right here is very simple, very immediate, and really, quite delightful and free.

Why Sit Quietly?

Why do we begin by sitting quietly?

The deepest truth is, I don't know. I enjoy it. I'm drawn to it.

But maybe I can say a little bit more than that.

No matter how many times we hear that "this is it," and "there's nothing to attain," and "there's only now," and "there's no self" – no matter how many times we hear all this stuff, there's a very persistent habit of *thinking* otherwise – thinking that there is a "me" in the driver's seat, thinking that this isn't it, working very hard to get rid of something that's here or trying to achieve something that isn't here, feeling a sense of lack. The belief that something is missing is quite strong, quite tenacious, as is the idea of "me," this seemingly solid entity encapsulated in a separate bodymind, adrift in an alien world, trying to get control. There seems to be a big gap between the things we read and hear about nonduality and our everyday experiences of unhappiness, doubt and uncertainty.

So sitting quietly is a way of stopping our usual activity (all the talking and doing) and simply being present to the bare actuality of what is going on in this moment. We can call it meditation, but that word has so much baggage attached to it and means so many different things to different people, that I prefer to call it nothing at all. What I'm talking about is nothing more than a simplified space where there can be careful attention given to what we usually overlook, overlay, ignore or avoid. And as we explore the present moment in depth, we can discover firsthand for ourselves how suffering happens, how the mirage of separation is created, how decisions and choices actually unfold (as opposed to how we *think* they unfold), and we can *see* directly how the idea of "me" and the story of "my life" are created by thought and imagination. We can discover that true joy, true happiness, true love, and true freedom are here in this simple presence that is right here, right now.

Otherwise, if we only read about this and hear talks about this, we often tend to take it in on a purely conceptual level as a new set of ideas – a philosophy or a belief system. But true freedom is all about seeing through all our beliefs and ideas, seeing through the mirage-world that thought creates, and recognizing what cannot be doubted, what is beyond belief, what is most obvious. Being in silence and doing nothing is one way of seeing through beliefs, stories, thoughts, concepts and ideas, and discovering the truth directly.

In simply being here in silence, one of the things that we notice is that the mind is not silent, it rattles on. So we can sit here in silence and actually spend the whole time talking to ourselves in our heads or watching mental movies – thinking about our upcoming vacation or some pressing problem, going over and over what happened to us this morning, trying to get into some special state or have some experience that we remember having four years ago on a retreat. We can sit here in silence and the whole time be absorbed in some kind of mental activity. And there's nothing wrong with that, it's not bad, and it's not personal. I often say it's just weather, it's what's appearing – the same way a thunderstorm or a cloudy day is appearing. No one is *doing* it.

But the more caught-up-ness there is in obsessive mental spinning, the more unhappiness and suffering there is. So in sitting quietly in silence, one of the things that can happen is *seeing* this mental spinning, *seeing* it for what it is, becoming *aware* of it without being totally absorbed in it and mesmerized by it, and noticing how alluring and also how unsatisfying it is, how it is often a form of suffering. We could say that sitting quietly is a way of giving attention to what actually *is*, seeing what's really happening underneath all our ideas and stories about what's going on. Not so that we can finally get to someplace better, but rather to *see through* the whole fixation on getting to someplace better, to *see* that habitual thought pattern as it arises again and again in so many different ways – that thought of somehow transcending, escaping, controlling, or getting beyond what's here now.

In seeing that thought pattern for what it is, it loses its credibility. It becomes increasingly transparent. It's easy to say spiritually correct things – these Advaita or Zen or nondual teachings are easy to talk about, at least in one sense. In fact, nonduality is utterly impossible to talk about, but what I mean is that it is easy to *say* things like, "There's no separation, there's no self, there's no time, there's only now, unicity is all there is." But if it's just words, then it's ultimately unsatisfying. So sitting quietly is a way of making it real, actualizing it, embodying it.

As soon as I put any of this into words, no matter what words I use, it's off in some way. If I talk about "making it real" and "embodying it," immediately it sounds like another process for "me" to undertake, another accomplishment, another goal. So the words are always off in one direction or another. If you can, take them very lightly, because words can't really capture what happens in silently being here – the actuality of simple, bare being. The words can only describe it in some way. The actuality – the *suchness* – of hearing, seeing, breathing is absolutely indescribable and impossible to grasp, and yet it is effortlessly and undeniably present, just as it is.

There's no separation anywhere except in thought. Thought can *think* about dividing lines. That's what thought does. It draws imaginary lines around things, like on a map, and then labels them. It fractures unicity into pieces like a jigsaw puzzle. Thought says that "my skin" divides "me" from "the room." But if you tune into non-conceptual sensing and perceiving, you discover that this boundary line doesn't really exist, it can't actually be found. Meditation, as I mean it, is that kind of tuning in to direct, present moment, non-conceptual experiencing and seeing through the conceptual overlay.

Of course we need those relative boundary lines in order to function. We need to be able to distinguish between me and the chair. Waking up is not about getting to some state where we walk around having some constant mystical experience that there is no difference between me and you, or between people and carpets. But as we begin to *see* how all separations are created in thought, they lose their absolute solidity. They become more like tentative functional appearances instead of absolutely solid facts. We fight wars over absolutely solid facts, or what we *think* are absolutely solid facts – big wars on the international scene and little wars in our daily lives or in our heads. We fight over the illusion of solidity and separation when it isn't really there. And all of our suffering is generated by these illusions of separation and solidity.

Being silent is a space to look and listen and to begin to appreciate and enjoy the wonder of simple things like the breeze and the chirping of a bird and the sound of traffic, and to discover and see through subtler and subtler layers of conceptualization.

Seeing is not thinking. It's *seeing* the thinking *as* thinking, being *aware* of the thinking. Awareness is upstream from thinking. A thought pops up like, "There's got to be more to life than listening to the traffic." That's a thought. It tells a story, delivers a message, or draws a conclusion, and the truth of that story or that message or that conclusion can be questioned. There's also an *awareness* of that thought, a *seeing* of the thought *as* a thought. That awareness is outside the thought-realm, prior to thought. Awareness is not bound or limited by the imaginary map-world that thought creates. Awareness is unconditioned, unbound, free. There could be a second thought commenting on the first thought, such as, "I shouldn't be thinking," or something like that. Awareness is *seeing* that thought as a thought. Awareness is always without judgment or preferences. Judgments are always thoughts, and preferences are impulses rooted in hereditary or conditioned tendencies of the organism. Awareness *sees* judgments and preferences.

True meditation as I mean it is simply awareness. It's not about thinking and trying to work all this out conceptually with analysis and rumination. That doesn't mean we try not to think, or that we aim to banish thought completely. It simply means that meditation is an invitation to be aware, to be still, to be present. To stop, look, and listen. To be what we always already are – aware being. Meditation is not about *thinking* our way to clarity. It's about seeing the false as false and waking up to the simplicity of what is. In silence and stillness, we begin to notice this ever-present Here/Now and we become consciously aware of being aware. Eventually the boundary between meditation and the rest of life melts away and we see that awareness is always present. Meditation isn't about correcting what is showing up, or fixing it, or manipulating it, or changing it, but simply beholding it, as it is. Meditation is a way of being awake to present moment actuality. Simply *this*, as it is.

Instead of our habitual attempt to get what we want or to get rid of what we don't like, meditation is an invitation to not move toward anything or away from anything, but simply to discover what actually *is* – even if it's something we find unpleasant or painful or something we think is "not very spiritual." Instead of trying to get away from it and get to something better, what if instead there is complete openness to what is? Openness is the heart of true meditation. This isn't some grueling task I'm talking about. It's the opposite of a task. It's not doing anything at all. It's not seeking a result. It's what Here/Now *is* – the open space of awareness beholding everything just as it is.

So I would recommend sitting quietly *if* this invites you, if it interests you. You don't have to be sitting, you can be lying down – sitting is not the essence of it. And you certainly don't need to in any special posture. You can be in a recliner or on a park bench or on an airplane or anywhere at all. You can move when you feel like it – you don't need to be motionless, rigid or bolt upright. There is a natural stillness that occurs by itself, and a naturally open, relaxed and grounded posture that the body finds. There are no special hand positions. You don't have to close your eyes or open them or keep them half closed or anything in particular. This isn't about forcing your mind to stop thinking and focus instead on your breathing. It isn't about visualizing deities or repeating a mantra. It's nothing more or less than being silently present, doing nothing other than being here. And if this attracts you, as it does me, then I encourage you to take time and make space to be still, to do nothing, to simply be aware, to explore and enjoy the present moment, exactly as it is.

Suggesting this is a kind of heresy in some corners of the non-dual world these days, but something quite wonderful can happen in stopping our busy activities and being quiet. And, as I said, we don't need to call it meditation, and it's probably better if we don't. All I'm talking about is being present, giving attention to what *is* – hearing, feeling, sensing – seeing thoughts as thoughts, being here without judgment, without an effort to get somewhere else. And if judgment or effort comes up, seeing that. Nothing needs to be eliminated. That, to me, is meditation. Nothing fancy. No bells and whistles. No correct or incorrect hand or eye positions. No lotus posture or meditation cushion required. Simply present moment awareness.

This can happen anywhere, anytime. You can set aside a time and space for it, but it can also happen spontaneously – in your car while stopped in a traffic jam, at the office between clients, on the bus as you ride to and from work, at home as you drink your morning coffee or while you fold the laundry. Whenever it invites you.

Eventually, you notice that awareness is always here, even when you are talking or working on the computer or watching a movie. Awareness always has been here. It is what "Here" *is*. It is what you *are*. It is never absent.

But when you're talking to somebody, dealing with screaming children, working on the computer, or watching a movie, it's much easier to lose sight of that and to become absorbed in and entranced by the ideas, stories, narratives and beliefs that thought, language and imagination create, and especially the story of "me." As we interact with others, so many conditioned patterns and emotions can easily get triggered. We can so easily feel hurt or threatened or belittled, we can get angry or defensive, envious or jealous – all those human reactions that we all know so well. Human interactions can get messy and murky very quickly. That's why it can be very helpful to make time and space in your life on a daily basis for being in silence, doing nothing, simply being present, aware, awake to what is. It can be just ten minutes or five minutes.

And you may find that there are many, many situations in daily life, such as being on a bus or a train or a plane, or in a waiting room, when we habitually busy ourselves with magazines, books, ipods, snack food we don't really want, and so on. But maybe, if it interests you, you might explore what it's like to simply *be*, doing nothing, simply being present. At first this may seem scary, like being naked in some way, but you may find that it is quite enjoyable. And you may discover that there are many moments in the midst of an ordinary busy day when it's possible to stop all outward activity and be still. Instead of checking your email one more time or filling that time with some kind of busyness, what happens if for one moment you simply stop and do nothing? Breathing, hearing the traffic sounds, watching the clouds in the sky or the shadows on the carpet, simply *being*.

Not because it's "better" to sit silently than to check your email, not in order to improve or get enlightened, but for no reason at all. Without seeking any result. You may find that there is tremendous beauty in the most ordinary sights and sounds, and you may discover that in doing nothing, all your problems and doubts and all your confusion disappear.

P: What is the nondual view of meditation? You mentioned it was seen as heresy.

J: There are some teachers today who hold to a very uncompromising insistence that meditation presumes the existence of a separate self who can choose to meditate. These teachers would say that meditation reinforces that illusion, and that meditating is absurd because "everything is already it" and "there is nothing to attain," so what would be the point of meditating? Unicity is always already the case. These teachers consider meditation dualistic because it suggests that one state of consciousness (being here now) is somehow closer to the truth than another state of consciousness (being lost in thought or daydreaming). They claim that meditation necessarily perpetuates the illusion of "someone" who can choose to move from one state to the other. I often speak from this radical and uncompromising nondual place myself, but occasionally, like this morning, I slip into heresy. [Joan smiles].

Nisargadatta and Ramana, two of the most revered figures in the Advaita world, often told people to give attention to how they lived, to observe what was arising, to inquire. Many contemporary satsang teachers begin their satsangs or meetings with silence as I do. Many who would not use the word meditation do, in fact, encourage or invite a direct exploration of the present moment in one way or another. I've even seen Tony Parsons, one of the most uncompromising radical nondualists, invite everyone to close their eyes and then offer what could be described as a kind of guided meditation, much as I do at the beginning of my meetings, bringing people's attention to the simplicity of what is — although, of course, Tony would never call it a guided meditation and neither would I, but in a sense, that's exactly what it is.

Some radical nondualists are more open-minded and less dogmatic about this than others, and I appreciate the ones who are uncompromising as much as I appreciate the more eclectic ones. That utterly uncompromising, radical message can be wonderfully liberating if you're stuck in the idea of "practicing meditation" in some effortful or goal-oriented way driven by an underlying sense of lack and unworthiness. It totally stops you in your tracks and offers no way out.

But I personally think that the total dismissal of meditation as dualistic is a misunderstanding of meditation. The kind of meditation that I have encountered in Zen and with Toni Packer, and the only meditation that I ever suggest, is all about *seeing through* the illusion of a separate self and being awake to *whatever* state of consciousness presents itself. It has *nothing* to do with sitting bolt upright in the lotus position, counting your breath. And I'm not saying any of that is wrong, just that it isn't what I'm talking about. I'm not pointing to any kind of deliberate methodical "practice," but rather, to something much more open and spacious that is in no way separate from the whole of life. It is simply listening and being awake here now.

For me, formal meditation in the way we usually think of it has almost entirely fallen away. Occasionally, I find myself sitting on a cushion at home, or going on a silent retreat someplace where they have timed sitting periods and all that, but this is pretty rare. For the most part, all of that has disappeared from my life. However, I do still sit quietly every day in my armchair or on a bench in the park. I do it simply because I love it, because it interests me, because it happens, not because I think I "should," and not because I'm trying to get somewhere or improve myself or save the world by meditating. I have no such ideas or motivations at all. It's simply something that happens. I find that there is something infinitely precious and deeply joyful about silence and simply being present. It goes right to the heart of life.

Of course, there are many traditional forms of meditation that are very methodical and often quite oppressive. Some forms of meditation aim at producing exotic transcendental states, or developing intense, one-pointed concentration, or bringing about relaxation and stress reduction, or drawing you closer to Jesus and the Virgin Mary. There are forms of meditation that employ techniques such as mantras, labeling practices, breath-counting, koan work, visualizations and all kinds of mental activity. Some meditation may even involve deliberately thinking certain thoughts, as in Centering Prayer. Some meditation encourages you to shut the world out – to *ignore* sounds and sensations rather than being openly aware of them as I talk about. So the m-word means many different things to different people, but what I mean by it is simply present moment awareness, giving attention to what is, in a very open and spacious way.

The wonder of life is in presence, it's not in the scenery that happens to be showing up. That's why you can be looking at the Grand Canyon and feel miserable, or you can be looking at trash blowing down the street and feel ecstasy. The wonder, the ecstasy, the joy, the beauty is in the quality of the looking. It's in the presence. If you're looking at the Grand Canyon and thinking that you've wasted your whole life, you'll probably feel miserable. If you're looking at trash in the gutter and you're totally present and open and not caught up in thinking, you'll feel wonderfully alive.

Of course, meditation isn't about feeling wonderful all the time either. Anything we say can always be misunderstood. And there are some nondualists who would say that because of the way I am talking here today, I have become a dualistic heretic hopelessly mired in illusion. But I'd say, who are they talking about and why do they care?

P: I think of meditation as more of a doing and what you are saying is not that, it is just being with whatever is there.

J: Yes, and of course, even if meditation is being talked about in the way I have been talking about it, as simply being here and seeing what is, even then, the perfectionistic, achievement-oriented mind can mis-hear this and turn even *that* into a program with a goal and ideas of success and failure. If I say, "Can those thoughts about trying to get somewhere be seen as thoughts?" – immediately the thinking mind can translate that question into an injunction or a command: "Don't have any thoughts of trying to get somewhere, those thoughts are bad, get rid of them, you shouldn't have them. Your goal is to eliminate them." Which of course isn't what I said at all! A gentle, inviting question can be mis-heard as a shouted command: "Pay attention! Don't daydream!" So it's very subtle how the mind operates.

In my experience, being quiet and doing nothing is like creating a simplified space where you have temporarily put aside a lot of the clutter and noise and demands of life, and in that simplified space, the antics of the thinking mind can come to light and be exposed and seen through. It's much harder for this to happen in the midst of fast-paced verbal interaction and the chaos of daily life. Of course, the more you take time to be quiet and do nothing, the more it permeates every moment of daily life. And eventually, as I said, there is the realization that "being present" never really comes and goes, that awareness is ever-present. The separation between "meditation" and "the rest of life" melts away.

Then you don't have to rush into a special room to meditate. Meditation is every moment. It's simply hearing the sounds of traffic and birds, feeling the sensations of cool air or heat, seeing the thoughts coming and going, breathing, fully enjoying a cup of tea or the sounds of rain. And if you notice that the mind is trying to turn this into a new project designed to achieve results, some endeavor you're try-ing to succeed at, then just to *see* those thoughts as they arise. If you hear shouted commands like "Pay attention!" or "Don't fantasize!" playing in your mind, simply to hear them, and to recognize them as conditioned thoughts. That is meditation.

P: I feel stuck in thoughts. I look at someone like Ramana Maharshi, and I can see he was in a totally different place than I am. And I just feel stuck.

J: So is it possible to really explore that stuckness? What *is* that experience we call feeling stuck? What is actually going on? "Stuck" is a label, and "I am stuck" is a thought-story. But what does this stuckness actually feel like in the body? In giving attention to the actual sensations, how solid is this stuckness? What thoughts accompany it, or give rise to it, or keep it going? The thought-story *seems* to be a kind of objective report on reality that's telling you how it really is – you're stuck. But is this true? Is there really a "you" and are you really "stuck"? If you are paying attention to stuckness so that you can get rid of stuckness, that's not the kind of attention I'm talking about. That's paying attention with a motive. I'm talking about exploring stuckness without any motive, without seeking a result.

And the idea that Ramana Maharshi was in some totally different place from you is imagination rooted in illusion. There's only ever this placeless place, Here/Now, and as presence-awareness, there is no difference at all between you and Ramana. Any differences are in the appearance, the scenery, the momentary forms, but that which is being and beholding it all is undivided and boundless. You and Ramana are different names for Here/Now, the One Self.

P: It can be a motivation or an inspiration, seeing that what Ramana found is possible.

J: It can be tremendous suffering, if you keep thinking of yourself as a fragment and then comparing yourself to some other fragment that you've idealized – contrasting your experience to what you imagine his experience was. Ramana is all about waking you up from this dream and pointing you to Here/Now – what you cannot not be.

P: It doesn't feel like suffering; it feels like it gives me a sense of hope.

J: Hope is suffering, isn't it? Hope is all about ignoring or rejecting what's here now and hoping for something better in the future. It leads us away from the only place where true freedom, true peace, true love is ever found.

P: Can't hope be somewhat positive?

J: We've been taught that it is. But is it?

P: Isn't hope akin to faith and trust? Don't we need faith and trust and hope?

J: What is truly trustworthy? The only "thing" (and it isn't a thing) that I've found to be truly trustworthy is Here/Now, this alive presence that cannot be denied or lost. My experience with trust in anything else – trust in some deity, some ideology, some belief, some authority figure, some theory, some system – that kind of trust is ultimately disappointing and unsatisfying. Any of these things may be relatively trustworthy up to a point, but none of them are absolutely trustworthy.

It might feel good for a moment to believe (or trust) that "everything is perfect," for example, but as an idea or a belief, there's something that doesn't feel very certain about it. As a belief, it always comes with a shadow, the shadow of doubt. Pretty soon the opposite possibility starts to come up: "Maybe everything isn't perfect. Maybe I'm really just a brain in a jar in some laboratory somewhere on a planet of vampires. Maybe it's not so good after all." [laughter]. So what can I really trust? *Just this.* The bare fact of *being here.* That is beyond doubt; it requires no belief. I'm pointing to the *here-ness* of Here, the *now-ness* of Now, the aliveness of this moment, that which remains when all beliefs fall away, that presence or absence in which all the movies appear and disappear, including this meeting and Ramana Maharshi and the planet of vampires and the brain in a jar. The appearance is ever-changing, but the beingness is ever-present. That alone is trustworthy.

P: But isn't it helpful to have an idea that maybe it's all good, to aspire to see that and realize that, the way someone like Ramana seems to have done? Isn't that a happier and better way to live?

J: Is it? In my experience, *believing* all of that is very uncertain, very doubtful. Only *realizing* it for ourselves is truly liberating, and that realization can only be real Here/Now. We can't postpone this realization. If that realization is imagined to be some fabulous experience that we aspire to attain in the future, that aspiration is the very obstacle that prevents us from seeing that Here/Now *is* what we are seeking. That hopeful aspiration is simply a thought telling us that we are not here yet. How absurd! Ramana often said that this was the last obstacle – imagining that we're not here yet. When all that thought about Ramana falls away, when all our ideas and fantasies and hopes and fears fall away, when the thought of a better future falls away, when *all* that is absent and there's simply *this*, the simplicity of the breeze on the skin and the sounds of wind in the leaves and this vast presence being and beholding it all, that is peace.

Ramana is pointing you to Here/Now – not to the future. He is inviting you to discover what you already are, what you can't not be.

P: I enjoy the hope that things might be better. I go there in my mind and it brings me some peace.

J: Well, if it works for you, that's great. But does it really work? I would question that.

P: Thinking that there's hope feels good. Thinking that it's hopeless doesn't feel so good.

J: Well, I'm not suggesting the opposite thought as a better alternative! They are both thoughts, hope and hopelessness. Neither of them is true.

P: I cannot stop myself from having thoughts, so why not thoughts that make me feel better?

J: Well, actually, you can't control what kinds of thoughts you have anymore than you can stop yourself from thinking. But I am questioning whether these feel-good thoughts are really that satisfying. "I hope there is not a nuclear war" is a hopeful thought. "There probably will be a nuclear war," is a pessimistic or negative thought. They are both thoughts. "I hope there isn't a nuclear war," may feel better than "there probably will be one," but it doesn't really assure me that there's not going to be a nuclear war. Because underneath that hopeful thought is doubt and fear: "I am afraid there might be a nuclear war, but I hope there won't be." And what if there is one? Then that's what *is*. So what happens then if we've planted all our hopes on the other outcome? Of course, in the case of a nuclear war, all these problems will probably be dissolved quite quickly! [laughter]

Thoughts pop up out of conditioned habit, sometimes one type of thought, sometimes another. Some organisms are conditioned by nature and nurture to think the glass is half full and others are conditioned to think it's half empty, and both inclinations probably serve a different evolutionary function – one is more likely to take risks and be adventurous and the other is more likely to be cautious and avoid danger, and both tendencies are needed for survival. So none of this is bad or wrong. But if it interests you, I would invite you to watch closely and to see whether those hopeful thoughts are truly bringing you peace of mind or not. Not that we should get rid of these thoughts, because we can't get rid of them by any act of will, but to see that they are only thoughts. And to see if they are really bringing you peace.

P: But are you saying there's really no difference between all of us and Ramana Maharshi, that we are all as deeply realized as he was, that there's nothing better to hope for?

J: I'm pointing out that this question is a form of suffering, rooted in delusion. It assumes that Ramana and you are separate, bounded entities, rather than different waves in a single fluid ocean. Both waves are equally water, equally ocean. It was to this wholeness, this emptiness, this nondual reality that Ramana was always pointing. No one owns wholeness. Wholeness appears as everything, including me and you and Ramana.

I'm not denying that *within* the movie of waking life, there are relative differences between different waves and different people. I'm not denying that *in* the movie, Ramana was a remarkably clear, awake, deeply realized being – a Bach, a Mozart, a Leonardo da Vinci, a Babe Ruth, an Einstein of nonduality. And of course, *within* the movie, I wouldn't put everyone else, myself included, into that same exceptional category. I'm not trying to deny or erase all relative distinctions.

But I see that these distinctions are dream-distinctions, that the boundaries between categories and individuals are notional, arbitrary and ultimately illusory. I see that the ice cream vendor in the park is being who he is as perfectly as Bach was being Bach, and Ramana was being Ramana. I see that no wave is any wetter or any closer to the ocean than any other wave. I recognize the Self to which Ramana was pointing Here/Now. I recognize the dream-like nature of the whole movie of waking life, in which it appears that there was once some guy named Ramana sitting at the foot of a mountain over in India back in the 20th century and a bunch of other folks presently sitting in a living room in Chicago. *It's all a dream. Ramana was pointing to waking up from this dream, this story in the mind.*

This ranking and categorizing that the mind loves to do has its uses. But it also has its misuses whereby it only creates suffering and confusion. Focusing on Ramana as an idealized historical figure "out there" apart from you, feeling inferior to him, and then hoping to one day attain what he had, is completely antithetical to what Ramana was trying to express. It is a form of idolatry and a way of overlooking the *living* Ramana, Here/Now, your own True Self. That to which Ramana pointed and which he so beautifully embodied is not outside of you. It is not somewhere else.

If the mind starts to argue and say "yes, but," then perhaps Ramana will appear in your dream disguised as a middle-aged woman with one arm and invite you to question that argument, to wake up now, to see what you truly are, what everything is, what cannot be lost, what is impossible to divide up and rank. Ramana is always pointing only to this one seamless and boundless reality that is ever-present. Don't waste time on hope. Hope is a form of postponement, a form of denial.

Another P: I experience meditation as a whole body experience. Feldenkrais [awareness through movement bodywork] is a form of meditation for me. I feel like openness is the best description of meditation.

J: Openness is a very good word for meditation, yes. And you're absolutely right, it is being aware of the whole body – sensing everything – and in opening to pure sensation, we discover that there are no boundaries anywhere to be found, that the whole body includes the whole universe.

P: Years ago, I had a very bad drug experience. I felt like I lost who I was, and I was totally panicked. I've heard many people talk about the fear they have about losing the "I" thought and it sounds similar.

J: Yes, there can be a fear that comes up – a sense of losing control. This fear of losing control and being overwhelmed is at bottom a fear of death, and it always involves some kind of thought-image-story about "me" coming to an end or being lost in the void. To some extent, this may be a survival mechanism – the job of the thinking mind is to stay oriented and know where I am and what's safe and what's not safe, and if I take a powerful drug and suddenly lose all my moorings, it may be a kind of knee-jerk reaction of the survival system. But as those of us who took psychedelic drugs discovered, when you resist the trip, it turns into a nightmare very quickly. When you relax into it, it's okay. Because it is the *thought* of dying that is scary, not the reality, just as it is the *thought* of being nobody that is scary, not the reality.

The fear of losing control and being overwhelmed rests on the illusory idea of a "me" who could lose control or be killed. But it's only a thought! In fact, there is nothing here to be lost or destroyed, to be born or to die.

P: Even though "I" is just a thought, everyone operates that way.

J: Well, it *seems* that way if you don't look too closely. But often when we're doing something without thinking about it, there's no sense of personal doership at all. In sports or in the arts, we call that being in the zone. But it might be a very ordinary moment, doing the dishes or vacuuming the floor or driving down the freeway, and for a moment (whether it is a second or a minute or an hour) there is no thought of "me" at all. It's so ordinary, we don't even notice. But when we *think* or *talk* about doing the dishes or vacuuming the floor or driving down the freeway or anything else, language inserts a subject – the phantom "I" that we come to believe is the author, the doer, the thinker, the experiencer, the chooser, the controller – the executive at the helm of our ship. We're not born thinking that way. We *learn* to think that way. But when we actually examine any kind of doing, whether its washing the dishes or writing books, we don't actually find this phantom executive.

P: But we do tend to own what happens and take credit for it somehow.

J: Yes, and that is our suffering. On a practical or functional level, it's no problem. The publisher knows where to send the royalty checks – no problem. But at a deeper level, if we really believe we are the author of our lives or our books, that is suffering. I remember one reviewer wrote this horrible review of my first book. She said, "This is the dreary, solipsistic tale of a narcissistic, self-absorbed, middle-aged, handicapped lesbian." [laughter] Hearing that, there might be a moment of terror, identifying as Joan and identifying my book as myself, and then taking this review very personally: "Oh my God, *I'm* a dreary, self-absorbed, narcissistic, handicapped lesbian." [laughter] It doesn't sound good! Actually, that one was so far over the top that I think I actually laughed and thought about putting it on the book jacket.

P: I'm intrigued that you seem to have an ego around criticism of your book, that you are not immune to that.

J: Oh, I can certainly get my feelings hurt or feel miffed and get defensive. I have yet to meet anybody who never experiences those kinds of reactions ever. But there is an interest here in seeing how it all works, the thought that "she has insulted *my* book, therefore, she has insulted *me*, therefore, 'I' have been threatened and diminished." So interesting to see all that, to see how it works, to see firsthand how we humans get upset over stuff like this! And not to take this upset personally. Wanting to be somebody who never gets upset is just more concern about *my* self-image rooted in the illusion that there is a separate self. So whatever shows up here, whether it is equanimity or upset, none of it is personal – no one is doing it – it's all like the weather – all of it another scene in another movie.

There is a great deal of spiritual mythology about enlightened people who are imagined to be totally beyond ego. I am not saying that there are not some remarkably clear, very awake people, but they all have poop chutes, as a friend of mine once astutely pointed out, and all too often these gurus who are supposedly so fully enlightened are also molesting young girls or embezzling money or drinking themselves to death or even sending out hit men to kill or terrorize ex-devotees, and of course, the faithful devotees manage to convince themselves that all such behavior is either untrue or else it's some form of "crazy wisdom" that the guru is doing deliberately as some kind of teaching. But really, what difference does it make who has more egoic moments or fewer egoic moments – who cares about this? It's the phantom me again. All we can work with is what is actually arising right now. What good does it do to worry about how enlightened or deluded someone else is?

If what is showing up right now is some manifestation of what is called ego, such as getting upset over an insult to my self-image, well, then that's what's appearing here right now. To have the added thought that, "I don't think Ramana Maharshi would ever have experienced this, he was so beyond all of this, and I wish I could be like him," that is suffering. It only confirms and solidifies the imaginary problem and the phantom "me" who supposedly has an ego or doesn't have one anymore.

P: Why can't devotion to these people be the source of our highest aspiration? Maybe I can get there too. That's how I see it.

J: If for you these are deeply comforting thoughts, and if they continue to arise, then by all means enjoy them. I'm not trying to convert you here. But again, I would suggest to you that what Ramana was pointing to was not some special future personal attainment that you might one day achieve, but rather, this ownerless presence, this boundless openness, this aliveness, this wakefulness that is right here, right now. He is not pointing to something you lack and might attain. He's pointing to the all-inclusive presence Here/Now.

Liberation and freedom from suffering is only possible now, and it doesn't happen by imagining "something better" in the future – that postponement *is* the bondage and the suffering. The problem can only be resolved now. Don't make an idol out of Ramana as some dead guru, but rather, *be* Ramana, *be* Buddha, *be* who you truly are – not in the future, but right now. What I'm talking about is effortless. It is already the case. It is what you cannot *not* be. Ramana is not "out there" somewhere, Ramana is –

[sound of screeching brakes from the street and then loud crash]

I hear a lot of car crashes in this apartment. There could be a guided meditation on tape: "Listen to the bird cheeps, the car crashes, the sounds of the ambulances..."

[laughter, and several participants have rushed to the windows to look out – after awhile everyone sits down again]

P: It changed the energy.

J: Nothing like a good car crash. [laughter]

P: Before the crash, I had been thinking about the fear of losing the "I," but when I got up to look at the car crash, I was not in the "I" mode anymore. There was no me story and everything was just happening. But then after a moment at the window, I found myself thinking that maybe I shouldn't have jumped up to look, and the "I" came back.

J: That's a beautiful account of how the I-thought comes and goes and how action happens by itself spontaneously. None of us could prevent the hearing of the crash or the particular response to it that arose in each bodymind organism at that moment. It all appeared here in this ownerless awareness, all of it empty of self. The thought, "I shouldn't have jumped up," creates the mirage of a "me" who is somehow separate from the seamless flow. It's only a mirage. And that thought appears in the same way the crash appears. No one is doing any of it.

We only have a few minutes left. Notice that our entire meeting together is gone. All the words, the thoughts, the questions, the car crash, everything that happened or appeared Here/Now is gone.

What remains?

The Pathless Path Through Suffering

There's an old Zen story where somebody asks the Zen master, "What is your teaching?" The master writes the word "Attention" on a piece of paper and holds it up, and the questioner says: "Attention, yes, but what does that mean? What is your teaching?" Again the master writes the word "Attention" and holds it up. And the questioner says, "Could you please say a little bit more about that? What do you mean by that? I don't get it." The master writes the word "Attention" again and holds it up: "Attention, attention, attention." Maybe that is the purest and most radical kind of religion – simple attention. Present moment awareness. Instead of a belief system, awareness *sees through* all beliefs.

Another word for awareness or attention is unconditional love. Jesus was always talking about love and seeing God everywhere, and if you read the Gospel of Thomas, Jesus starts to sound more and more like an Advaita, Taoist, Zen master. I suspect that at their root, in their most radical forms, if you strip away all the trappings, most religions are offering a way of seeing or being that is essentially a path through suffering to liberation.

The original founder of any religion is often a radical, iconoclastic outlaw who defies the prevailing traditions and overturns everything. But it doesn't take long before the followers turn it into one more oppressive, authoritarian organization with opulent buildings, codified beliefs and dogmas, and a bunch of clowns in fancy robes and silly hats pretending to be holier and closer to God than everybody else. Instead of being all about waking up, religion quickly becomes what Karl Marx once called the opium of the people. It becomes a belief system. We may think we're beyond such foolishness, but even radical nonduality, if it's nothing more than a comforting philosophy, is not really all that different from believing that Jesus saves us and we're going to heaven. It's just a somewhat more sophisticated and nuanced version of that same kind of opium.

So instead of that belief-based version of religion and spirituality, what's being pointed to here is *seeing through* all the words and all the beliefs, however wonderful they may sound, however comforting they may be, and returning to the bare actuality of Here/Now *as it is* before we conceptualize it. Being present without knowing what anything is. Attention, attention, attention. Or, as I would prefer to say it, open, spacious awareness. Listening, seeing, feeling, sensing – without judging, without moving away, without seeking a result, without doing anything at all.

Don't get me wrong. I'm not speaking *against* book learning or conceptual thinking. I enjoy reading about scientific discoveries, psychological theories, religious and philosophical ideas. I'm not in *any* way suggesting we ignore all this or throw it all out. It all has its place. But to see that ideas *are* ideas, and that *all* ideas can be doubted. There is something right here now that is not conceptual, something that cannot be doubted, and *that's* what's at the very heart of these meetings. And you don't need to be a physicist or a Buddhist scholar to find it. In fact, you can't avoid it or escape from it because it is all there is. But *see* it for yourself, don't take it on faith as an ideology.

Don't look for it or try to figure it out because then you just get more and more confused. Instead, attention, attention, attention. Open, spacious awareness. Nothing more and nothing less. And whenever you see the mind trying to codify, conceptualize or make something out of this bare attention, something you can hold onto – a belief system or a practice – let that go and come back to the simplicity of this moment, just as it is. The sounds of the traffic, the sensations in the body – this vast, open listening presence.

This can be quite easy when we're sitting here in a pleasant environment amongst friends listening to beautiful bird songs. But it isn't quite so easy if we're at the office or with the screaming children, or if we're feeling depressed or anxious or caught up in some addiction. Our habit at such times is usually to do *something* – we might try to distract ourselves by turning on the television, we might try to soothe ourselves by eating chocolate or drinking alcohol, we might *think* compulsively in whatever ways we habitually do – going over and over the past, dreaming about the future, beating ourselves up, beating someone else up, analyzing our situation, trying to figure out the nature of the universe. But none of these habitual ways of trying to escape from suffering or trying to find happiness actually works. They may bring momentary relief or pleasure, but in the end, they make the situation worse. What actually transforms the situation is not doing anything at all. And that's what I want to talk about this morning.

It's not easy to talk about because the mind can misunderstand what not doing anything at all actually means. It *doesn't* mean being a doormat, or sitting on the couch forever "doing nothing," or being totally passive. It doesn't mean you shouldn't go to a therapist, find an addiction recovery program, take an anti-depressant, get a job, or work out at the gym. It doesn't mean *wallowing* in thought-stories or in addictive behavior. It means, *at this very moment,* not moving away from exactly what is happening Here/Now. Going to a therapist or getting into a recovery program may be intelligent action, but *thinking about doing that in the future* is a form of moving away *in this moment.*

I'm going to give you an example from my own life. I've had this fingerbiting compulsion since I was a child. I don't bite the nails, I bite the skin. I pick at my cuticles or other rough places, and then I rip off little pieces of skin with my teeth. Sometimes I draw blood. I've spent a fortune on band aids over the years. And because I only have one hand, when I'm chewing on it, I can't do much of anything else, so it can be quite disabling. And although there's something compelling about doing this, it's actually a very tense and unpleasant experience when it's happening. Unlike being addicted to alcohol or cigarettes, a compulsion such as fingerbiting is not something you fantasize about doing or have trouble imagining living without. On the contrary, you dread this compulsion and long for it to be gone forever.

I've noticed that when this compulsion is occurring, it's hard to pay attention to it. There's a certain kind of attention because I know it's happening. I can start biting and do it for a few seconds without consciously knowing that it's happening. But within a few seconds, I know it's happening. So, there's some awareness of it. But it doesn't have my full attention.

I may be *thinking about it* as I'm doing it – wanting it to stop, judging it, analyzing what it means about me, going through the inner rolodex of possible cures – but my attention is not on the actual bare *sensations* of biting. The focus of attention is somewhere else – maybe thinking, maybe watching television, maybe reading. The sensations of biting are there, in the background somewhere, but they're out of focus, blurry. I'm hardly aware of them. The attention is somewhere else.

It feels as if I'm caught up in a kind of sticky hypnotic haze. There is a feeling of being torn apart, pulled in opposite directions, because it seems as though part of me wants to stop biting while another part of me wants to keep doing it. And although putting my fingers in my mouth is usually thought of as a voluntary action, when this compulsion is happening, it feels completely uncontrollable. There's a sense that I *have* to keep going with it because I'd feel something unbearable if I stopped.

This sense of avoiding something unbearable is very common with addictive behaviors, even very commonplace ones, like why we sometimes keep the television on longer than we really want to, flipping through the channels, as if we're afraid of the emptiness we'd feel if we turned it off. For many years, I viewed this as a psychological fear, or maybe a spiritual fear, but in recent years, I've wondered if it may not often have much more to do with things that are happening in the brain or the neurochemistry, things that may have nothing whatsoever to do with one's psychological or spiritual state. But it doesn't really matter what the cause or causes are. Whatever they are, there is this fear of stopping and this overpowering urge to keeping doing the addictive or compulsive behavior. And there is this conflict between two opposing desires, the desire to stop and the desire to keep going. And there is often a great deal of self-hatred and shame involved in such behaviors—stories about "me" being a failure or a loser.

Sometimes, seemingly out of the blue, in the middle of this tortured hypnotic haze, the thought-impulse will arise to pay complete attention to what's actually happening. And sometimes that thought-impulse is followed by a shift into this completely open, spacious, nonjudgmental, thought-free awareness. The biting is still going on, but now the thoughts *about it* fall away, and the lens of attention is on the pure sensory experiencing itself—the actual sensations in the body. It is a very open, spacious kind of attention, not seeking a result of any kind, but totally *open* and *interested* in what is happening—completely *accepting* what is, just as it is. There is no attempt to stop the biting, no wanting it to go away, no more tug of war between "wanting to bite" and "wanting to stop," no more attempt to control what is happening, no judgment of it, no story anymore of "me with a shameful habit I can't control"—*all* of that is gone completely. *There is no sense of "me" at all.* There is simply pure sensory experiencing and clear, open awareness. And *instantly*, the biting stops.

It may not stop for very long. It may start up again in the next moment, but with that open attention and complete acceptance, it always stops. Of course, if I try to *do* that open attention *in order to make the biting stop*, that doesn't work. The open attention I'm talking about is the absence of any such agenda or desire for change. And paradoxically, it is that total acceptance that seems to bring about the greatest change. But it has no *intention* to do that. It doesn't *need* any change. It isn't *seeking* change. It is completely open. Open to what is, as it is.

I've noticed that at those times in my life when there is a great deal of clear awareness and presence, as there is for example in these meetings, there's no desire at all to bite my fingers. It is only when that aware presence gets clouded over by some kind of neurochemical smog or agitation that this desire arises and takes over the organism. There are many different theories about what causes addictions and compulsions, and I don't think we really know. I suspect there are many variables, many variations and no single cause, but whatever brings these painful and destructive behaviors about, it is fascinating to see that in any moment of complete attention and open awareness, these powerful compulsions and addictions end completely. They may not end forever, but in that moment, they end.

It's very similar with feelings of depression, anxiety, loneliness, physical pain, or any other form of suffering. When we stop running away, when attention goes to the bare actuality, the problem vanishes. Not forever, but in that moment of complete acceptance and total attention, the problem ends completely.

In my own experience with depression, for example, I've noticed that the attention is usually lost in that hypnotic haze of thoughts and stories just like with fingerbiting. All these murky, half-seen thoughts and stories are spinning around, and there is a strong sense of "me" in the middle of it all. There are unpleasant sensations in the body – queasy, empty feelings. The mind tells us that these feelings are dangerous, they might kill us, so the impulse is to run away from them. Instead of truly *feeling* the sensations, we *think*. That seems safer. We think and we think and we think. We think *about* being depressed: "I have a serious problem. I need to do something. Maybe I need therapy or medication. I can't function. My life is going to be ruined. I'm drowning. What should I do?"

In all this thinking *about* depression, we are avoiding the thing itself. If we actually turn to face it, we may find that no monster is really there. We *think* we're already facing the depression and experiencing it fully because we're thinking about it all the time, we feel terrible, our life is a wreck, so obviously we must be facing it and experiencing it. But we're actually doing everything possible *not* to face it or feel it. We're looking *away* from the *actuality* of this thing called "depression" by thinking *about* it. We're avoiding the bare sensations by getting lost in that hazy world of thoughts and stories. Instead of completely *opening* to all of this with total presence and really *seeing* the whole thing clearly, our habit is to run and hide. And yet the faster we run, the more we seem to sink into the quicksand of depression.

What if we stop running away? What if we simply allow ourselves to *be* depressed, without seeking a cure? What if we let ourselves *be* unproductive, or *be* in bed in the middle of the day, or whatever is happening? Not forever and ever, but *right now*. What if we turn *toward* this so-called depressed feeling with curiosity and interest and explore the bare *actuality* of it rather than endlessly telling and re-telling the *story* of it and thinking *about* it? And by bare actuality, I mean the sensations – the queasy feeling in the gut, the hollow ache in the chest, the tightness in the throat. Totally allowing these sensations to be here, feeling them fully, without any resistance, exploring them carefully and lovingly with awareness – and also *listening* to the stories that are running through the mind and hearing them *as* stories, without believing them and getting entangled in them.

At first, we resist this possibility. It's scary. We think that if we allow ourselves to be depressed, it will never end. We think these feelings will be unbearable. Can we risk finding out if these sensations will truly kill us? Can we dare to explore this thing that feels so scary, so terrible, so deadly, so shameful? What *is* this? Not to come up with an answer – some word-label or verbal explanation or story about our childhood – but to actually *listen* and *look* and *feel* and *touch* and *see* and *hear* what's actually going on.

That looking and listening is love itself, isn't it? Giving attention to depression in the way a lover might explore the beloved, or as a child might explore the world with a sense of wonder. The *seeing* is what matters, not *what* is seen. The healing is in the awareness, the presence. *That's* the shift, from the *story* of separation to that open listening presence. It's a shift from resistance to acceptance, from entrancement to wakefulness, from thinking to being aware, from the *story* of separation to the *immediacy* of nondual experiencing.

And in my experience, once the attention shifts in that way, depression is completely gone. Yes, it may come back in the next moment, or a month later, or a year later, whenever the attention gets absorbed in the story again, or whenever the neurochemistry triggers it, but in the moment of complete attention to actuality, depression is not there any more, even if the neurochemistry is producing unpleasant sensations.

Please don't think this means you "should" be able to snap out of depression by applying this "attention to actuality" like a technique or a method in order to get the desired result. It doesn't work that way. What I'm talking about is the *absence* of any such result-oriented technique and effort.

We want a method or a magic bullet. We want to be in control of our life. We want to be able to engineer this shift on command. But the shift I'm pointing to is the disappearance of this very impulse to change and control and engineer and improve and fix. It is the disappearance of the one who would do that. There is no more conflict, no more resistance, no more judgment, no more strategizing, no more storyline, no more seeking a result. There is simply open awareness and total presence with what is. And in that open space, those old habits of thought and behavior that Eckhart Tolle calls "the pain-body" lose their power. They lose their grip. They disappear. Not forever and ever, but now and now.

Also, please understand that I am *not* saying you should be able to vanquish depression without medication, and if you can't, then you're a spiritual failure. *That's all another story,* and unfortunately, it's a rather popular story in the spiritual world. *There's nothing wrong with medication.* It is *not* a sign of spiritual weakness or failure. In many cases, medication may be entirely appropriate, and in some cases, absolutely essential. It's wonderful that science has discovered biological, neurological, chemical and genetic causes and solutions for many of what have previously been erroneously thought of as purely psychological, spiritual or moral problems. Some bodyminds have more stormy weather, bigger pain-bodies, more neurochemical smog than other bodyminds, and that's not personal. This is definitely *not* about what we "should" be able to do, and then beating ourselves up when we can't. Working intelligently with our complex human problems may involve a variety of approaches. There's nothing wrong with therapy or medication or recovery programs, and those people who think everyone should be able to resolve everything in *any* one particular way are not seeing very clearly. Just because something worked for one person doesn't mean it will work for everyone else.

But there *is* a great power in awareness. And there *is* tremendous freedom when attention shifts from the smog of storylines the clarity of direct perceiving and sensing. But there is no one who can *do* this shifting on command. That's where "being here now" teachings, *if they are misunderstood,* can turn into a giant club that can be used to beat oneself up for "not being here now." That's the tricky part.

Because as soon as you discover that shift, then the mind immediately wants to *get* that, wants to *do* that, wants to *have* that all the time. So there's a thought, "Oh, I see what has to happen. I simply have to pay attention all the time, and then everything will be okay." And the problem with that is that *it's only another thought*. There's nobody at the controls who can really *do* that. There is no executive in the brain who can carry that out or make that happen or even initiate the desire for that. *It all happens by itself.* Don't take that on belief, but look closely and carefully, and see for yourself.

There may be the thought, "I am never going to bite my fingers again. Whenever that urge to bite comes up, I'm going to pay complete attention to it." Sounds good, and in the moment when this thought-plan is arising, there is real energy behind it. But at another moment, the urge to bite comes up, and now there's a different thought: "I just want to get this one loose end." And now *this* thought and *this* desire has a lot of energy behind it.

This brain can provide incredibly elaborate justifications and rationalizations for anything it wants to do. If we're into radical non-dualism, thought may cleverly argue that, "There's no me to choose whether to bite or not bite. There's no free will. I'm totally helpless. It's all just happening. And there's no problem with it anyway. Everything is perfect. It's all unicity. It's all a dream. So I'm just going to get this one loose end. I'll stop after I do that." And the finger goes into the mouth.

Then a new train of thought arises: "No, no, no, no. You said you were going to pay attention, you were going to stop doing this, you were going to be aware of the urge and not give in to it." But at that moment, *this is just a thought* — and it's a kind of superego-thought that seems to come from our Inner Parent telling us how to be a good girl or a good boy. Naturally, we rebel. Right now, the desire to bite has much more energy than the desire to be a good girl, and so, the whole *idea* of "paying attention" (as an *idea*) seems kind of dead. (Of course, the *idea* of "paying attention" is not where the juice is – the juice is in the presence, the awareness, the aliveness of Here/Now). So in this moment, biting sounds like what I really want. So I bite. Or, more accurately, the bodymind organism bites. There really is no one at the controls producing the desires, authoring the thoughts, selecting which way to go, or performing the actions.

I suspect we've all experienced this back and forth process I just described, not necessarily with fingerbiting, but with various things in our lives. We take vows and break them. We have intentions and plans, and then we go and do something else. We discover the way through depression, and then we forget again, and depression comes back. This is very common in some form to all human beings.

So there *is* a way through suffering, and the way is attention, attention, attention (being here now), but the catch is there is nobody to do that. Nevertheless, it happens! Waking up happens. It happens when it happens, not on command. And when it happens, it's always now. *Asking how to do it is a form of postponement, a form of distraction. It's much closer than that.*

This isn't about some final cure, finally fixing all our problems and being perfect at last. It's about living with a spirit of wonder and wondering, looking and listening. Wondering, how does addiction or compulsion happen? How does suffering happening? How do decisions actually unfold? How does anger happen? What keeps it going? Not looking for a conceptual explanation, but *watching* and *being aware* of what is *actually* going on. No one is *doing* this looking and listening, and yet, *you* are doing it – not the phantom self, but the True Self – awareness.

The power is in the listening, the awaring, the attending. But not as a strategy with a goal in mind. The tricky thing about the path through suffering is that it is not a way out. It's a way in. It's a willingness to be with whatever is showing up, a willingness to be with fingerbiting for all of eternity if need be, and "all of eternity" is only now. The path through suffering is not about going anywhere else. That's the secret, the gateless gate, and the path is pathless. As soon as the thought of seeking something better pops up – getting rid of suffering, curing it – that very thought *is* suffering. The path through suffering is *seeing* that movement of the mind for what it is, and that seeing gets subtler and subtler and subtler.

I don't think there is any end to this seeing, this waking up. There are people running around saying that they never experience desire or fear or anger or anything else anymore except happiness and bliss. But my experience is that this waking up is a lifelong, moment to moment, exploration. Or we could say, a present moment awakening, now and now and now. Continuous change is the nature of life. As long as you have a garden, there are going to be weeds. As long as you are alive, there is going to be garbage to take out, and meals to prepare, and you are going to have to do another load of laundry and vacuum the living room again. Seeing the false as false is not something that you finish doing. And sometimes it's very discouraging. How can these things still be happening, we think, in spite of everything I've done – all the therapy and the bodywork, all the meditation and the satsangs and everything I've done – how can I still be biting my fingers or smoking cigarettes or getting angry or falling into depression or seeking salvation, or whatever it is? How can this still be happening to me?

We only need to look at the world, the Middle East for example, to see that this difficulty is not personal – it's part of our human condition. That doesn't mean it's inevitable or it's permanent. We don't know, but it's certainly very tenacious. It's both utterly nonexistent and amazingly tenacious. What I mean by that is, it's amazing how when there's that clear awareness, those powerful forces like anger and depression and addiction just don't exist. They're gone. *Pfff! Gone!* There *is* no depression. There *is* no anger. There *is* no addiction. It's *gone*! So it's amazing how utterly insubstantial and nonexistent these things are. And at the same time, it's amazing how tenacious they can be in coming back again and again and flaring up and reasserting themselves, and it's amazing how very real they can seem even after years and years of "seeing through the story." *Getting discouraged is part of the conditioned thinking pattern*. It rests on taking it personally – thinking that "I" should be getting somewhere, "I" should be doing better. And then we feel shame, discouragement and disappointment when "my life" doesn't seem to be working out the way "I" *think* it should. So, this is not about getting to a place where there is no more pain, no more suffering, no more imperfection. This is simply about being awake.

And being awake always naturally alternates with being asleep, so to be awake 24/7/365 is an absurdity, a nightmare. Actually, this is used as a form of torture! So to imagine a state of constant alert mindfulness is an absurdity. That is *not* what I'm pointing to. Sometimes the organism needs to retreat and shut down. But if the shutting down gets painful or compulsive, then there may be a natural interest in discovering the path through suffering.

And the path is not moving away from this moment. Picking up a belief system is moving away. Getting hooked on spiritual experiences is moving away. Chasing enlightenment is moving away. *Analyzing* your problem is moving away. Trying to "be in the now" in the next moment is moving away. Thinking about not moving away is moving away. Thinking you "should" never move away is moving away.

The only place that is truly alive and real is this moment, regardless of whatever shows up in it, whether it's grief, happiness, sadness, anger, addiction, depression, elation, bliss, fingerbiting, bird tweets – whatever it is – the aliveness is in the presence. Presence-awareness *is* the aliveness, the vibrancy, the freedom, the joy, the love that we long to realize. And more and more, a trust seems to develop in this simple presence. More and more, there is a willingness to let go of all the things we're holding onto – all the ideas and beliefs and methods and techniques – a willingness to stop running away – a willingness to simply be present and trust in the groundlessness of being from which we are never separate. *That* is the jewel beyond all price. But we all have to discover this for ourselves.

P: I once heard a teacher say, "You can't get it wrong." That idea freed me from judgments and desires.

J: Yes, beautiful – eventually we see that this wholeness of being includes *everything*, even fingerbiting and getting angry and feeling depressed and being lost in thought. It includes all the so-called setbacks, mistakes and failures. Unicity is all there is *in spite* of any shift that happens and not *because* of any shift. When we see fingerbiting or depression as another impersonal happening, like a cloud formation in the sky, then the whole self-centered concern with fixing it in order to fix "me" falls away. There's no evaluation, no judgment, no need to get rid of anything. Fingerbiting or depression is not personal. It simply *is*. The sensations of fingerbiting are as worthy of attention as the most beautiful work of art. There's no essential difference.

When we really *see* that "it's all perfect" or "you can't get it wrong," the belief that something *is* wrong drops away. That was my experience both in the kind of open, nonjudgmental attention that I've been describing this morning and also when I truly *heard* the message of radical nonduality. Something dropped. I was no longer opposing whatever was happening. I could see fingerbiting in the same way I might see a cloud or a tree. Biting my fingers was as worthwhile an activity as composing a symphony. It was another impersonal movement of the universe. It wasn't a *problem* anymore. Even any *idea* that being totally present with fingerbiting in the way I've been describing this morning was better than resisting it or being totally caught up in it, even that idea fell away. There was no need left to *do* anything.

But simply *believing* that "you can't get it wrong" as a philosophical idea doesn't help all that much when the shit really hits the fan. Yes, we can *say* it doesn't matter, and in the absolute sense, that's perfectly true, but when you are suffering or causing suffering, there may be a natural interest in what I've been talking about this morning – giving attention to the actuality of that suffering, discovering how it happens, waking up from the hypnotic entrancement of habit, seeing through the stories and beliefs. It's no longer the ego doing this in order to be spiritually correct or to get somewhere; it's the intelligence of the whole universe acting through you. Unicity is inquiring, unicity is meditating, unicity is waking up. Saying that you can't get it wrong or talking about life as a dream is one way of pointing to fluidity and impermanence. Buddha spoke of life as a dream, but he also offered a path through suffering, the path of awareness, the path of present moment attention, the pathless path of being awake.

P: What does attention mean?

J: As the Zen master said, attention means attention! Paying attention. Being aware.

P: Isn't that always happening?

J: Well, in a sense, yes. Awareness is always present. Awareness is what Here/Now *is*. We could say that attention is like the lens that focuses on different things, zooming in and zooming out and looking this way and that. When you're watching a movie, either in the theater or in your head, in one sense, there is total attention. The attention is completely focused on the movie. And, of course, there is awareness or the movie wouldn't appear at all. So in talking about attention today, I'm really pointing to a shift in the focus of attention. I'm talking about *seeing through* thoughts and stories and being awake to bare sensation or perception—a shift away from the encapsulated world of thoughts to the spacious open listening of thoughtless awareness. Sometimes the difference between conceptual thought and awareness is very obvious, but often it is really quite subtle.

P: In the last few days I've had a depression-panic thing, the worst I've had in a long time. I keep trying to do things with it. I tell myself that thoughts and feelings are just what's on the screen, but it doesn't seem to help.

J: Telling yourself that "thoughts and feelings are just what's on the screen" *in hopes of making the problem go away* is a strategy for *getting rid* of what's showing up. It's a way of avoiding it. As you've noticed, it doesn't work.

P: So it's an attempt at a comforting thought or a technique?

J: Isn't it? Nothing wrong with that—it happens—but maybe it's possible to drop all these nondual ideas that we've heard and read, and simply *see* what this "depression-panic thing" actually *is*. To notice that by labeling it, we are already making it into *something*. To notice that there's a whole feeling tone and judgment implicit in that label, because "depression" or "panic" is something we don't really want. We have the idea that it's not psychologically healthy or spiritually advanced, it's not desirable, it's a negative thing, maybe even shameful. It has all these associations. And then we're telling a whole story about it—"It's the worst I've had in a long time. It could destroy me." So to *see* that story *as* a story. And to wonder, what *is* this thing before the label, before the stories?

Of course that labeling process is quite automatic and conditioned, so it's probably going to continue to happen. It's not like we can make that not happen any more. It's part of what the brain naturally does—it labels things. So I'm not talking about abolishing labels. But to *see* that those labels are just words, and to let them go. To *see through* them. To see that the judgments and injunctions and past history and *all* of that is a bunch of conditioned ideas, beliefs and stories. And then to look more deeply and explore the bare actuality of this thing we've been calling depression or panic. Without the labels and the stories, what *is* it?

Not to *think* about it or analyze it and come up with a mental answer or an explanation—but to actually explore the thing itself with open awareness. So we might notice there's a feeling in the stomach or in the solar plexus or in the throat, and instead of passing over these sensations and trying to avoid them by telling ourselves some Advaita story about the screen and the movie, to instead explore these sensations with awareness. And to also hear the thoughts that go with the sensations, the stories. To listen to these thoughts without becoming entranced in the story, to be aware that it *is* a story. And to do all this with no idea or expectation of a result, but simply in a spirit of curiosity. To simply *be* aware.

P: Sometimes I do all that, but then it doesn't go anywhere.

J: What do you mean, "It doesn't go anywhere"?

P: It doesn't change.

J: Well, if you're really seeing and sensing and exploring in the way I'm talking about, you would never say it doesn't change, because if you focus on any sensation in the body – whether it's the sensations associated with an emotion or the sensations of physical pain – if you give it careful, sustained attention, one of the first things you discover is how it changes constantly – how insubstantial and ephemeral and protean it is. It's changing and moving, appearing and disappearing. But if you're giving it attention with the motivation that doing this will change things and bring results, then this isn't the kind of attention I'm talking about. What I'm pointing to is attention without an agenda, totally open, not seeking a result.

P: That's helpful.

J: Yes, so when somebody says, "There's this horrible depression and I've really been very attentive to it, but it's gone on and on," it tells me that this kind of bare attention I am pointing to has not really happened yet. Because when there's really this full attention, depression (or panic, or compulsion) doesn't go on and on. It ends. It may come back in the next second because the attention shifts again to the story. Or physical pain may persist as long as the cause is there (a wound, an injury, an illness, whatever it is), but if you examine the sensations that are being called "pain" very closely, you'll see that they're coming and going second by second – pain is like a vibration or a pulsation – it's not a steady, continuous, solid thing. It keeps changing. And there are moments when it disappears completely. But we put a word-label on it – "pain" – and then it *seems* solid, substantial, and persisting in a way it never really is.

P: It's like the reality is more mutable than the label we give it, which fixes it in some kind of steady state.

J: Yes.

P: Fritz Perls stated that depression was created by the avoidance of feelings.

J: Well, it certainly seems that there are many feelings under the surface of what we call depression – sadness, fear, grief, anger, whatever – and the outward manifestations are things such as fatigue, restlessness, obsessive thinking, feeling overwhelmed, lacking appetite, and so on. And it's not like, "Oh, now I get it. I just have to completely pay attention and feel all these feelings and that's going to get rid of my depression." Setting it up that way is the same old pattern again! It doesn't work! That's very different from the kind of open attention I'm pointing to.

P: That's the dilemma.

J: It's only a dilemma in the mind. It's always about what's right here, right now. So if result-oriented efforting is happening here and now, then simply to be completely aware of *that*. Not resisting that, not judging it, not trying to get of it, but simply *seeing* that result-oriented efforting clearly. Allowing it to be as it is. You simply start wherever you are, with whatever is here now. Right now, *whatever* is happening, is there the possibility of simply giving it open attention, without trying to change it or fix it or make it go away?

P: If there's no choice, then –

J: That question isn't asking for a conclusion or an answer. It is an open invitation from unicity to unicity to explore *what is* without knowing what you will find – without holding on to any beliefs about how everything works – simply wondering and not knowing –

P: But if there is no free will —

J: There goes the mental spin again.

P: You're not saying to make attention happen.

J: No, you can't. You can appear to "make it happen," but what really happens is the attention shifts by itself — or a thought that suggests paying attention may arise, but that, too, comes up by itself, and if it is followed by a shift in attention, then it seems like "I" did that. And in a sense, you did do it, but not the you that has a name and form. The real you, which is unicity, does everything. You *are* everything. So this gets very subtle. It's easy to disempower oneself with a *belief* that there is no free will. And yes, that belief also happens by itself. But so does questioning that belief. So to let *all* the beliefs go and remain open to surprises and to seeing something new.

That's the spirit of scientific investigation. Unfortunately, religion and spirituality often prefer to come up with conclusions and stick to them rather dogmatically. And it's not just the Catholic Church that does this. Radical nonduality can get quite dogmatic sometimes. I've had some incredibly sad exchanges with rabid nondualists who were as closed and as locked into their ideology as any fundamentalist Christian.

P: Is there a sudden, final enlightenment like some teachers seem to describe, or is it just this constant process of paying attention?

J: What is behind this question? Can we notice how the thinking mind creates the illusion of time — either a final event or a constant process? It imagines some kind of "permanent" enlightenment that goes on continuously for all time, or else it imagines this "constant process of paying attention" that sounds rather dreary and exhausting and that seems to drag on for a long, long time. But this is all thought! Imagination! What's alive and real and true is right here.

We can have all kinds of theories about whether there is or isn't some sort of big final enlightenment, but who cares about this? That's a serious question. Who is it that cares about this? Isn't it the imaginary character in the story? Is awareness or unicity concerned about such questions? Do such questions arise when there is simply open awareness and presence?

P: Free will or not free will is like that, too. Something to think about and get tangled up about.

J: Yes, exactly. It's a battle between different ways of conceptualizing what is actually inconceivable. It's something to think and argue and have discussions about. But what's alive is beyond words, beyond belief. It's amazing how many ways the mind comes up with to avoid the inconceivable aliveness of here and now. This moment is utterly new. It has never been here before. It will never be here again. It's already gone. Let go of every thought and every belief and see what remains.

Conversation with a Friend

Friend (F): What is enlightenment?

Joan (J): Enlightenment is when the bubble of encapsulation pops and there is simply everything, as it is.

F: Is it a permanent, final event? For many people, it sounds like a sudden, permanent shift.

J: Enlightenment is the popping of the illusory bubble that we call "a person," so it doesn't really happen *to* a person. It is a popping of the illusion of time, so it is timeless, only Now. Permanence, in the sense of infinite duration in time, is an idea, never a reality. The only real permanence is the ever-present Here/Now.

Unicity includes both enlightenment and delusion, both the recognition of boundlessness and the mirage-like experience of being apparently encapsulated in a particular bodymind. Some degree of being identified as a particular bodymind organism is functionally necessary and unavoidable and will be here, as needed, for the duration of the organism, unless you have a serious head injury or brain problem. So we're not talking about all sense of the person completely disappearing. But the story of being limited and encapsulated is what disappears or becomes transparent.

In enlightenment, there is no separation between "me" and "you." So in enlightenment, there is no impulse to say that "I" no longer identify as "me," but "you" still do identify as "you," or that all desire and fear have completely vanished "for me," but "you" are still stuck with them, or that "I" am like Ramana Maharshi and "you" are just another bozo on the bus. In enlightenment, it all happens Here/Now and none of it is personal.

Enlightenment sees from the perspective of unicity, and as unicity, it has no problem with playing the part of Joe Blow and having all the experiences of being a human being, but it doesn't feel limited to, psychologically identified with, or encapsulated inside, that character. Unicity sees only itself everywhere. It sees no other. Enlightenment sees from the absolute perspective, but it doesn't ignore or deny relative reality. Enlightenment is free. It has no need to maintain anything. It accepts everything and fears nothing. It even accepts resistance and is unafraid of being afraid! It recognizes everything as unicity, but at the same time, it can discern the relative difference between enlightenment and delusion, or between heads and tails. It recognizes that none of this is personal, and that all of it appears Here/Now to no one.

Delusion identifies exclusively as the character, and experiences itself as encapsulated inside that character and separate from everything else. It mistakes the appearance of duality for reality. It tries desperately to grasp or possess the absolute, which it mistakenly regards as another relative object. Delusion thinks of enlightenment as a personal achievement, a personal possession – a particular experience or state of consciousness that arrives on one day and then extends on through infinite duration in time. Delusion works constantly to maintain that special state of consciousness, to identify "me" as awareness or to "be here now" *all the time*. Delusion is imaginary bondage mixed occasionally with a faux freedom that must always be carefully maintained, remembered, practiced, reinforced and defended. Delusion fears delusion. It takes everything personally.

Enlightenment is nothing more than seeing the false as false. It is the popping of this bubble of delusion and encapsulation. It isn't an event in time, but rather, the recognition of timeless presence, the ever-present unicity that is all there is.

F: Do you think "be here now" teachings, like those of Eckhart Tolle or Toni Packer, are fundamentally different from what you call radical nonduality – the teachings of folks like Tony Parsons, Nathan Gill, Leo Hartong, Wayne Liquorman and Sailor Bob? And which group are you in?

J: I'm not exclusively in either group. As with any two things, we can find differences and we can find similarities. I resonate with both radical nonduality and "be here now" teachings, and I see no *essential* difference between them. They both aim at the same fundamental realization, and they both expose or see though the same basic delusion. But there are certainly differences in emphasis and tone, and they each have different strengths and weaknesses.

We might say that radical nonduality takes a step beyond a final veil that "be here now" teachings often do not. That step is the dissolution of any lingering belief that there is something to do that brings you closer to unicity and the recognition that all of waking life is a dream-like appearance. Some radical nondualists suggest that "be here now" teachings presume and reinforce the illusion of a separate self with free will, but many "be here now" teachers see through the separate self and the illusion of free will. Toni Packer certainly does. But with "be here now" teachings, there is always a sense – however subtle in some cases – of something to do that improves life for both the person and the world. These teachings emphasize a shift from being caught up in thoughts and stories to "being fully present Here/Now," *seeing* thoughts and stories for what they are, *seeing through* the illusion of the separate self, being awake as boundless awareness. Forms of suffering such as anger, jealousy or addiction are worked with by giving them careful attention. This shift from entrancement in thought to clear awareness is often regarded as something personal – something that happens *to a person* and that a person can learn or practice doing. It is often said that the person becomes clearer and more stabilized over time in presence and thought-free awareness. Whereas radical nonduality sees both the person *and* any kind of shift as dream-like appearances in the play of unicity.

In "be here now" teachings, there is often a sense of being engaged in this important work of moving from what Tolle calls the old state of consciousness to a new and more evolved state of consciousness. Tolle's books often have titles that appeal to our desire for improvement and empowerment, things like "The New Earth" and "Finding Your Life's Purpose." But then *in* the book, Tolle reveals that the New Earth is not some future utopia, it's Now. And your life's purpose is nothing more or less than being awake now. So he always brings you back to Here/Now. And Toni Packer *never* talks about utopian futures or methodical practices. On the contrary, I would say that she is inviting us to not do anything at all other than seeing through all our beliefs and all the ways we try to do something and get somewhere and make something out of nothing.

So how does that differ from radical nonduality? In *essence*, not really at all. In many ways, Toni Packer is probably the most radical teacher I've ever encountered. She won't pick up any kind of feel-good conceptual formulation such as "unicity is all there is." She strips away *everything* and leaves you with *nothing*—only the bare actuality of Here/Now. That's very much like original (as opposed to some popular) Buddhism—it is the deconstruction of every construct. Buddhism is very careful not to turn impermanence into something permanent. Buddhism might regard a notion such as "unicity" or "the One Self" as making something out of nothing. And that's where radical nondualists can sometimes get caught up in a subtle new belief system without realizing it. Toni Packer would spot that happening right away.

Because radical nonduality eschews any kind of practice, it tends to be communicated almost entirely through words, and it *can* be heard (or misheard) on a purely conceptual level. Of course, radical nonduality is pointing to something that isn't conceptual at all, but the mind tends to be easily seduced and mesmerized by the conceptual. So-called "seekers" in this radical nondual subculture are often trying to *think* their way to enlightenment, which never quite works. That kind of thinking is very frustrating—it feels like a dog chasing its tail and never catching it. The mind can hear these radical formulations, such as "it's all a dream" or "there's no free will," and it can turn them into beliefs. These beliefs can then become a tremendous source of confusion. "Everything is perfect" and "unicity is all there is" can be misunderstood to mean that running a concentration camp is every bit as enlightened as running a retreat center or a homeless shelter. Enlightenment is erroneously conflated with unicity, and all distinction between enlightenment and delusion is blurred or erased. In fact, although *everything* is a manifestation of unicity, *not* everything is a manifestation of enlightenment.

There is a real subtlety in all of this, and it's very easy to fall into a misunderstanding in one direction or another. That's one advantage to having an on-going relationship with a living teacher, *if* the teacher is truly clear. She can see where you get fixated and keep pulling the rug out from under you. But if the teacher isn't all that clear, she may just keep handing you more and more rugs to stand on! Of course, radical nondualism would say it's all unicity, and there is no one to fall into error and nowhere to fall, but again, to really *see* that is different from having it as a belief. Meditative approaches are more embodied, more experiential, less in the head, and therefore less likely to fall into that kind of confusion. Meditative approaches tend to become confused in a different way, and radical nonduality is very good at exposing that kind of confusion.

"Be here now" teachings often seem to reinforce the very illusion they are trying to expose. People get stuck trying very hard to "be here now" all the time. They get stuck on the notion of having a *practice* that they are *doing*. These teachings seem to take this process of waking up, and the whole movie of waking life, very seriously, while radical nonduality feels more playful and light and humorous. Radical nonduality dissolves that last veil of dualism between nirvana and samsara, between awareness and content, between "being here now" and "being caught up in thoughts." In radical nonduality, there is nothing to maintain or attain. Unicity is all there is, and even thoughts and stories are recognized as nothing other than unicity. Radical nonduality emphasizes what is always already the case *regardless* of what is appearing, rather than emphasizing some state of mindful presence that comes and goes. But of course, you can find plenty of places in the teachings of Krishnamurti, Eckhart Tolle and Toni Packer where they express this same ultimate understanding, so again, these differences are shades of grey, not black and white.

And in one way or another, radical nondualists also speak about some kind of shift, because even to recognize that no shift is needed is itself a kind of shift, and radical nondualists almost always make *some* distinction between being awake and not being awake. In a way, they also offer a (non-methodical, non-essential) "something to do" in the form of meetings, gatherings, books, and so on, and in these groups, people (labeled seekers) are often quite obsessed with the idea of having some kind of final breakthrough. Some radical nondualists criticize meditation for having methods and goals without seeming to notice that these same things can inadvertently show up in radical nonduality as well.

Both radical nonduality and "be here now" teachings would say the path is pathless, the gate is gateless, and the practice (or non-practice) is not about going anywhere else or getting something that isn't already here. Both would say it is about recognizing the ever-present Here/Now that is boundless and seamless, and seeing through the false sense of separation and encapsulation. Unlike "be here now" teachings, radical nonduality sees the person as nothing but an appearance in consciousness, but at the same time, there is often a strong idea floating around in radical nondual groups that some "people" have this realization and other "people" are still seeking it. *This is how the mind thinks!* And so *however* we talk about this, the mind will always tend to hear and interpret it in dualistic ways, until it doesn't.

Of course, in speaking of "be here now" teachings, I'm thinking of people like Krishnamurti, Toni Packer or Eckhart Tolle, whereas other forms of awareness or insight meditation may involve tradition, hierarchy, dogma and all kinds of elaborate rituals and practices. Radical nonduality obviously dispenses with all of that, although new forms of dogmatism, hierarchy and ranking can creep in very quickly and often do.

F: Many people, yourself included, seem to have gone from formal

Buddhist meditation, to more open and non-traditional teachers like Toni Packer or Eckhart Tolle, and then on to satsang teachers like Gangaji, Francis Lucille or Adyashanti, and then finally to radical nondualists like Tony Parsons, Sailor Bob, Wayne Liquorman, Nathan Gill or Karl Renz. I've rarely heard of anyone going in the opposite direction, but perhaps it happens. Any comments?

J: In my own journey, it's been more of a spiral than a straight line – I've doubled back many times and circled around. After years of radical nonduality, I recently re-visited Zen – it wasn't the formal tradition that drew me back, but the teachings on emptiness – I saw them in a whole new light and found them eye-opening. I did several Zen sesshins with Steve Hagen, a wonderful teacher, in Minneapolis. I've been back to Springwater many times in recent years. That's the retreat center founded by Toni Packer where I was once on staff. I love that place with all my heart, and I never stop learning from Toni. I almost became one of the teachers there, but in the end, I had to go my own way. On the recommended book list on my website, I include many different perspectives and approaches – they have all been helpful to me at different moments. Each one offers a slightly different piece of the puzzle. Each has different strengths and weaknesses, different pitfalls, different ways in which they cut through delusion, different ways in which they can inadvertently become obstacles.

And although I did go through what might sound like a progression exactly like the one you described, I feel it is important to see that any time we picture a linear progression or create a hierarchy, it is a conceptual map. I don't see radical nonduality as better or more advanced than "be here now" teachings or vice versa. I encourage people to follow their hearts, to go where the real resonance is, and that changes as it needs to change. Sometimes meditation is liberating, and at other times, a teaching that throws meditation out the window is liberating. There's a place for both.

We all find exactly the teachers and the teachings we need. Everyone's path is different. No two are alike. The teaching that wakes you up one day may lull you to sleep the next and vice versa. Everything changes. There are no mistakes, not really. Even a so-called "false teaching" or "false teacher" can be just what you need in order to see something. The flaws in a teacher may be as important in waking you up as the teacher's clarity and insight. The perfect teaching for you is exactly where you are right now. Tomorrow it might all be different. This Self-realization has no beginning and no end. It is a present moment journey that is always Here/Now, always going nowhere.

We can emphasize what different approaches have in common, or we can emphasize how they differ. Ultimately, all these teachings are about waking up, however you want to describe that. It's easy to get caught up in ranking and criticizing, but Buddhism, Advaita, radical nonduality, and folks like Toni Packer and Eckhart Tolle all point to that which has no rank, that which includes everything and sticks to nothing. Whether we call it emptiness or unicity or the Self or the Now or bloopity-bloop is not really what matters most.

F: I find myself always trying to see what it is that you and other teachers have seen that I haven't seen.

J: Yes, I remember that in the past, when I would go to see people who were supposedly enlightened or awake, or when I would read their books, I would always be wondering, is this person experiencing something I'm not experiencing? How is their experience different from mine? What do they have that I don't have? Or what has disappeared for them that is still active in me? What exactly *is* this shift they are talking about? What's different in their life and my life?

Early on in my spiritual search, I had seen through the mirage of the separate self and the illusion of free will. There was a clear recognition of boundlessness and an ability to relax into non-conceptual presence, and at some point, there was the realization that Here/Now is ever-present. Unicity was very clear to me. But there was also a lot of obsessive thinking and mental confusion at times, and for a long time, I was seeking some final event. There were many neurotic patterns in the bodymind — anger, fear, self-doubt, hesitation, addictions and compulsions. I had (and sometimes still do have) what Eckhart Tolle would call a heavy pain-body. In other words, there was a lot of clarity but also a lot of confusion.

So I would listen to these enlightened teachers and everything they were saying would make total sense to me and would sound completely congruent with my own realization and experience, and then suddenly I'd hit a bump, and something they would say would sound different. Some would say they no longer experienced fear or desire or guilt – or they'd say all seeking had completely fallen away, that they never had the urge anymore to see another teacher or read a book about this stuff – or they never felt confused or doubtful anymore about any of this – or they never identified as the character anymore – or they never got defensive or envious or anything like that – and I'd think, well, obviously that's not the case for me. For me, all these things can still arise. So then I'd think, I don't have what they do yet. Or, I haven't lost what they've lost yet. Or, I've lost it some of the time, but not all of the time. Basically, I'm not there yet where these enlightened folks are. There is some final finish-line I haven't crossed yet.

More and more, I began to notice that such thoughts were all about "me," and that they were thoughts. This problem of not being fully enlightened only existed in reference to the phantom self, and only when there was thinking. In any moment of thoughtless awareness, the whole problem was gone. The problem was *in* the movie of waking life, *in* the story.

But still, it often *seemed* very real. Many of these other teachers would describe a final line-in-the-sand kind of event that had happened on a certain day when the illusion of authorship or separation had permanently fallen away, never to come back ever again. And I had never had that kind of final event that I could pin down to a specific date and time. My own experience had been much more gradual and imperceptible – the same falling away they described seemed to have happened, but not with that kind of absolute finality. In my experience, sometimes the sense of being encapsulated and identified as "me" was present and believable and sometimes it wasn't. And of course, some teachers said that this back and forth business meant you were still a seeker and that the final understanding hadn't happened yet.

Enlightenment, they said, was the end of going back and forth.

The whole dilemma seems quite laughable to me now. Enlightenment isn't the end of ever-changing experiences, such as expansion and contraction. It's the end of *caring about* those differences and *taking them personally*. It's the end of believing in the mirage-like "me" who seems to be going back and forth between me-ing and being. People try to imagine not having a me, as if that would be some special experience "they" would be having, when "no self" is actually quite ordinary and within everyone's everyday experience. It simply goes unnoticed, those moments of thoughtless awareness when there is no thought-image-story of me. And, of course, there is *never really* a me. It's *only* a mirage.

It's worth noting that all these different teachers I listened to had slightly different explanations of what enlightenment was and what exactly had changed. Sometimes their descriptions were not even reconcilable. Gradually, it began to dawn on me more and more that these were all maps, and that everyone's experience was different. Some people had sudden changes, and for others it was more gradual. Some people had stormier psychological weather than others, different brain chemistry, different genetics, different hormones, different life experiences, and all of this effected how the person experienced and described enlightenment. Ramana was calm and gentle and beatific; Nisargadatta was fiery and sometimes angry. He even smoked cigarettes during his satsangs and died of throat cancer. Some teachers who claim to be enlightened are drunks, some are womanizers, some are quite abusive, some are even child molesters.

Anyway, for a long time, I felt that I was still in some way a seeker, but I also felt quite clear and awake much of the time. At a certain point after my first book came out, with the encouragement of all my teachers at the time, I was holding meetings. Sometimes, when I'd *think* about holding these meetings, I'd feel like a total fraud. There was this persistent habit of comparing my experience to the descriptions that other teachers gave of their experience, and a nagging sense that I wasn't completely "there" yet, that some final event had not yet happened "for me." This all seems quite funny now, but at the time, it seemed quite serious.

And then at some point, I noticed that this wasn't happening any-more – this comparing of my experience to other people's experience or this search for a final transformation or a final pop of some kind. I was no longer seeking enlightenment. It was clear beyond any doubt that Here/Now is ever-present and that there is no "me" to be enlightened or unenlightened. My problems hadn't magically disappeared, but they didn't seem to be problematic in the way that they had before. Every-thing was seen to be empty of substance, all of it a manifestation of unicity, even the stuff I didn't like such as fingerbiting, depression and anger. The *need* to get rid of that stuff or *do* something with it in order to fix "me" was gone. More and more, this whole movie of waking life lost its solidity and its heaviness. Something had shifted, but there was no moment in time that I could pinpoint when this had happened, and really, *nothing* had happened!

I would not say that I am enlightened (or not enlightened). I would say that Here/Now is always here, that unicity is all there is, and that sometimes enlightenment is here and sometimes delusion is here. Desire and fear still arise – sadness, anger, regret, sorrow – it all happens. My buttons can still get pushed. I still sometimes read nondual books and occasionally feel drawn to go hear someone else talk about this stuff, but the motivation is no longer about "me" getting somewhere and becom-ing somebody. It is simply that there is no end to seeing and learning and discovering. There are still moments when there is a strong sense of being a separate person, moments when I feel defensive, anxious, hurt, outraged, or whatever form it might take. What *has* changed is that these arisings are no longer taken personally in the way they were before as signs of "my" unenlightenment. When there is clarity, all of this is seen to be a dream-like appearance that isn't personal in any way. There is an understanding that even in moments of *feeling* separate and encapsulated, nothing is *really* separate or encapsulated, and that none of this is happening "to me" even if it sometimes *seems* that it is. I'm not at war with life anymore in the way I once was. But that doesn't mean I don't sometimes get upset. I do! It is seen that there is no "me" in control of this upset, that it is simply what the universe is doing at that moment. I am no longer *trying* to "be here now." I'm not *trying* to sustain any kind of mindful presence or any special state of consciousness. There is simply what is, as it is. Watching television seems no less spiritual than sitting in silence.

For me, a lot of the confusion around enlightenment and awakening had to do with reconciling the understanding and insight I had from working with teachers who stressed "being here now" with the somewhat different understanding and realization that I was coming to through Advaita and radical nonduality. For a long time, it seemed as if I had to choose between these seemingly irreconcilable approaches. And this was not an abstract struggle. It was intimately bound up with my relationships to people and places I loved. It was also very tied in, as I discovered, with my desire for approval and wanting to be on the winning team. The whole thing was so gut-wrenching that I actually developed a large lump the size of a tennis ball in my abdomen.

In the end, I didn't choose either side of this imaginary divide. I went my own way. In the process, my need for approval fell away. And the imaginary conflict that had been tearing me apart also disappeared completely, not because I found the right answer, but because the whole conflict was seen to be about conceptual maps and identities. Reality is so much simpler and more immediate. Waking up is not about joining the winning team, or crossing the finish line and being done forever, or being certified or approved by someone we look up to as an authority figure, or having all the answers. Waking up is simply seeing through the imaginary problem – not once and for all, but now. What remains is the groundlessness that needs no answer.

Although I don't belong to any team, I do feel profound gratitude and respect for *all* the teachers who have been important to me along the way, and especially for Toni Packer. I can't bullshit Toni. She has such clarity in seeing through subtle kinds of mental deception, and every time I visit Toni and Springwater, it wakes me up in some new way and reminds me of what is most simple and most true. I have never found anyplace as open and as unpretentious and unbound by dogma and ideology as Springwater. Toni is one of the finest teachers I've ever encountered, certainly my most important teacher. I have great respect for her and for the others who are also teaching at Springwater now as well.

I often realize that something I discovered through radical nonduality was exactly what my first Zen teachers were trying to get me to see years ago! I just didn't hear it then. There's a place for everything, and wherever you are is the perfect place to be right now. My advice to everyone is to follow your own heart and trust that wherever you are is exactly where you need to be, maybe not forever, but right now.

And if you find yourself thinking you haven't awakened or you're not enlightened yet, ask yourself, who is not awake? Who is not enlightened? See if you can find this phantom. Remember that all the descriptions of enlightenment are just maps, and all the personal stories are only stories, and everyone's experience is unique. There is no way it has to be. Ultimately, enlightenment is just a word. What matters is not the word, but the reality to which it points. There is nothing essentially different in what I am experiencing, what you are experiencing, and what Ramana was experiencing – different content, but the same Here/Now. The present moment is simple, obvious, unavoidable, and impossible to doubt. *That* is the jewel.

F: What would you say to someone who feels they only understand this intellectually, but they don't actually see it or realize it or embody it fully.

J: Here/Now is not intellectual. Hearing the traffic is not intellectual. Breathing is not intellectual. Being here now, which is undeniable, is not intellectual. Colors, shapes, sounds, scents, textures, sensations, seeing, hearing, awaring – this is not intellectual. And this bare being is not confusing in any way until we begin to think about it. All the confusion is in the conceptual overlay, the interpretations, the thoughts *about* this. The confusion is what is intellectual. This whole dilemma is *in* the conceptual overlay. It is an imaginary problem. The "me" who might not yet have the full realization or who might not yet be fully embodying it is only a thought-image that appears in awareness like the clouds and the traffic sounds.

Unicity is all there is, regardless of what appears to be happening. There is no way *not* to embody it fully because it is all there is. Of course, as a belief, that is unsatisfying and doubtful. So drop every belief and see what remains. This that remains is beyond doubt and it is not intellectual.

It is definitely very helpful to be able to discern the difference between a concept and a perception or a sensation, between the simple and undeniable fact of being here and all the conceptual interpretations of that undeniable presence, between the word-labels and the experiencing itself. It is helpful because all the problems are *in* the conceptual overlay, not in reality itself.

So there *is* a difference between intellectually understanding a philosophy and the direct experiencing of this moment Here/Now. One is complicated and the other is very simple. One takes effort and the other is effortless and unavoidable. One can be doubted and the other is impossible to doubt. One requires study and takes time and the other is effortlessly and timelessly present.

But there is no "me" who is closer to unicity in one than in the other, and there is no "me" who can embody realization. *Everything* is the embodiment of unicity, including Adolph Hitler and Jack the Ripper. But obviously, Adolph and Jack are not the embodiment of enlightenment. Any embodiment of enlightenment is momentary and ownerless. No one can permanently embody enlightenment for that would be a ridiculous contradiction in terms. Enlightenment is the recognition that there is no "me" behind the mask of any persona, and that no person exists as a solid, continuous, separate, independent entity. Enlightenment is seeing that I am everyone and no one. I include everything and I am no-thing in particular. Enlightenment sees from the perspective of unicity.

There is no way not to be here now, and there is no way out of unicity. This is the message of radical nonduality. And it is not an intellectual message. It is the sound of the traffic and the sensations of breathing. It is the colors in this room and the taste of tea. It is the energy in this conversation, the presence that is Here/Now.

F: Do you ever meditate anymore?

J: I often sit in silence doing nothing, in my armchair or on a bench in the park, but not with the idea that I am meditating. I'm not *trying* to be attentive or mindful or anything like that. I simply enjoy being in silence, being still, doing nothing, listening, being present. I don't really find a boundary line anymore between this kind of silence and every moment of ordinary life.

F: You talk a lot about how there is no choice and no free will and no need for moral codes and precepts. But is there no difference between an action that is intentional and one that is accidental? For example, stepping on someone's foot accidentally vs. stepping on their foot on purpose with the intent to hurt them. It seems very different to me. One seems like a choiceless mistake and the other seems like a deliberate choice that is morally wrong.

J: There is a misunderstanding here about what "no choice" means. Of course, there is an undeniable difference between accidentally stepping on someone's foot and deliberately doing so. Both of these different ways of doing what is apparently the same action may very well come from different places in the brain and the nervous system, and each of them certainly *feels* palpably different to both parties – to both the stepper and the one being stepped on. In the same way, there is a palpable, discernable difference between so-called voluntary actions (such as opening and closing my hand), so-called involuntary actions (such as the functioning of my kidneys), actions that are a mix of both (such as breathing), and actions that are compulsive or addictive (such as biting my fingers uncontrollably). There is an experiential difference between an instantaneous reflex action (such as pulling my hand away from a hot stove) and actions that are preceded by laborious rumination and indecision. No one is denying *any* of these relative differences and variations. They are all quite real and within everyone's experience.

But if you look closely, even the most intentional and seemingly voluntary action, such as a deliberate, carefully planned, premeditated act of stepping on someone else's foot with the intent to hurt that person, even that comes out of infinite causes and conditions, out of the whole universe actually – and in each moment of that action as it unfolded – from the first impulse, to the careful planning, to the execution of the action – it could not in any moment have been different from how it was. The whole universe came together as that urge, that plan, that action. In the next moment, the person who did this deliberate foot-stepping might be motivated to change their behavior and might be capable of doing that. But that, too, would be the only possible effect in that moment of infinite causes and conditions. It would *appear* to be a choice, but as far as I know, no independent executive has ever been found. I certainly haven't found it.

However, this realization of "no self" doesn't mean we deny the obvious fact that the body and the mind both have the potential to be trained so that the individual seemingly has more control and more possibilities – this happens all the time in athletic training, in the kind of brain gym exercises that have recently become popular, in somatic awareness work such as Feldenkrais, in meditation and yoga, in studying a foreign language, and so on. By training the bodymind or by shining the light of awareness on certain activities, the bodymind then has more choices, or better choices, or more possibilities, or more ability to control its actions, or less hesitation and second-guessing, or more ability to surrender to the flow, or however you want to express it. We've all experienced this, I'm sure, in some form or other. To take a very simple example, we all learned to write. In the beginning, back in first grade, we could barely draw the letters, much less spell the words. Over many years of practice and schooling, our vocabulary expanded and our penmanship, grammar and spelling improved so that we had more control, more ability, more versatility and agility, more choices and more possibilities for how to express ourselves in writing. But *all* of this happened choicelessly, out of infinite causes and conditions. Such improvement and refinement of our abilities is possible only when the right conditions come together. When conditions don't come together, it doesn't happen. No one "chooses" to be an illiterate crack addict, a serial killer or a child molester.

So when we speak of there being no choice or no self, we're not saying that if you're addicted to alcohol, then you might as well just keep on drinking because there is nothing you can do about it, or that if you step on someone's foot, you don't need to apologize because you had no choice. We're not saying that there is no distinction between voluntary and involuntary actions, or between spontaneity and rumination, or between clarity and entrancement in old habits. We're not saying people shouldn't be held accountable for what they do. We're only pointing out that everything is one seamless whole, that everything is the way it is in this moment because the whole universe is the way it is, that no individual agent is in control. But that doesn't in any way deny the *experience* of *apparently* making choices and taking responsibility for what we do. That's all part of the show, part of how the universe functions.

Every society has a moral code that is reflected in its laws. These moral codes vary from one society to another. Unless we are a sociopath, we all have a sense of right and wrong that develops out of some mix of genetics, cultural conditioning and life experience. But can we choose what feels right or wrong to us? Do we choose what society we are born into? Does believing that murder is wrong stop people from committing murder? Does vowing to never get angry again result in not getting angry again? Maybe it helps to have moral codes and vows, or maybe it just makes us feel bad when we fail, I don't know. What I can say is that nonduality is not *against* morality, but it understands that any moral code is relative and not absolute. But that understanding doesn't mean that *within the movie of waking life*, I have to buy into the version of cultural relativism that says it's okay for people to mutilate the genitals of young girls if that's their cultural belief, and those of us from other cultures shouldn't interfere because it's all relative. No, *within the movie of waking life,* as far as Joan is concerned, holding down young girls and mutilating their genitals with a knife is totally wrong and utterly abhorrent. There is no possible acceptable justification for it. I want to howl and weep every time I think of it, and I support every possible effort to stop this cruel practice. But ultimately, in the absolute sense, I can see that the whole thing is a dream-like event, that unicity is unharmed, that cutting off a young girl's clitoris and sewing her labia together is no more "wrong" than the female Praying Mantis biting off the male's head after they have sex. The key is not to mix up the relative and the absolute.

I think it's great for human beings to work against injustice and to explore and cultivate various disciplines that improve the ability of this bodymind organism to make wise choices and to function optimally to whatever degree we can. I'm very grateful for the Women's Movement and the LGBT Movement and the disability rights movement, all of which have made my life much easier and much less painful. I'm grateful that I'm not still drinking myself to death and smoking several packs of cigarettes a day and flying into uncontrollable rages as I was forty years ago. Certainly psychotherapy, meditation and martial arts training had something to do with facilitating that transformation. But the trick is to be able to engage in these various disciplines and political struggles without falling into the erroneous presumption that there is an executive at the helm who is in command or that there is any single recipe for transformation that always works, because when we believe those ideas, it's a setup for guilt, shame, blame, frustration, despair, self-hatred, and hatred of others.

Enlightened action comes from clear awareness – the unconditioned Here/Now of infinite possibility. Deluded action is reactive, compulsive and confused – it comes (at least in part) from a kind of hypnotic entrancement in erroneous ideas and beliefs. If we're lucky, we can learn to recognize delusion as delusion. We can learn to stop avoiding our pain and chasing after false promises. We can learn to unclench the heart and open the mind, to come back to the simplicity of what is. We can learn to shift from mental distress and confusion to the open space of "being here now." I know you've experienced this shift, so you know what I mean. But you've probably also noticed that you don't always *want* to shift away from habits and compulsions or wake up from being angry and defensive – and I'm sure you've noticed that even when you seemingly *do* want to wake up, that it doesn't always happen, that the very act of wanting it seems to get in the way because waking up is the falling away of intentionality and effort. This falling away is not something "you" can bring about through some exertion of force or will. This shift seems to happen by grace and surrender, in the same way falling asleep at night happens, not by our deliberate doing. Can we control what we want? Can we command grace? Even if it's true that the ability to "let go" and "come back to the now" can be developed and cultivated through meditation, why do some of us stumble upon meditation and have an interest in all this while others are never exposed to such possibilities or have no interest if they are exposed? Why does meditation seem to work for some people and not for others? And why do some people seem to wake up out of the blue without ever even *hearing* of meditation or nonduality?

There is no recipe for waking up in the same way that there is for baking a cake. Yes, potentially the bodymind can learn new skills, but this learning only happens when all the conditions in the universe come together in a certain way. It happens when it happens. No "me" can bring it about, and yet, there is a power *right here* that can act.

No way of expressing this matter of choice and choicelessness is ever quite right, and new discoveries are being made every day in neuroscience and consciousness studies, so I always recommend not coming to any fixed or final conclusions about these questions, but remaining open to new possibilities. And above all, I encourage people to look and listen directly – exploring for oneself – not just by thinking about it logically or philosophically, but more importantly, by paying attention to one's own life. Watch as thoughts arise, as powerful emotions like anger and jealousy come up, as urges and desires appear and "choices" happen, as conflicts play out and get resolved, as depression or addiction "overwhelms us" – watch and see how all these things actually unfold.

True enlightenment is not about being in control nor is it about being disempowered and passive. It is a fine line between erring in one direction or the other.

F: Adyashanti says we can become stuck in emptiness, and that it is important to return to the world and embody the awakened understanding in life itself. Do you agree?

J: Well, I can't speak for Adya, but I do have a sense of what he means.

Mixing up the relative and the absolute, or being stuck on the idea of "no choice" might be one example of being stuck in emptiness – or as I would say it, being stuck in the absolute. What people seemingly get stuck in is actually a misunderstanding of the absolute. I would say that the ultimate understanding is that there is no contradiction whatsoever between relative and absolute. Enlightenment includes both views and doesn't stick to either one. Enlightenment could be described as freedom from fixation.

Most people, who haven't heard of Advaita or Zen, are (we could say) stuck in the relative. They totally believe that they are a separate individual with free will in a "real world" of other individuals, a world which is "out there," made of matter, which we perceive, accurately or inaccurately, through our senses. This is the conceptual model that most human beings assume to be true, and it is so ubiquitous and deeply embedded, that most people don't even realize it is a conceptual model. They ignore their actual direct experience – pure perception – and "see" what they *think* is here.

Then some people take up spirituality, and a few of those find their way to Advaita, Zen or other radical, nondual teachings. They begin to wake up from this imaginary conceptual dream world. Many artists have the same experience. They begin to notice actual direct experiencing, as it is. They notice that the dividing lines we *think* are here are not really here. They begin to understand that everything is one undivided whole, that separation is purely notional.

At this point, many people begin to get the idea that relative reality is totally false and should therefore be shunned or denied. They refuse to use personal pronouns and always talk about themselves in the third person. They speak only in the passive voice. They change their name from Fred or Sue to Krishna or Joy Bliss. They deny history and give up making plans for the future. They say Africa does not exist and the genocide over there is not really happening. They drop out of school, quit their job, abandon their family, close their bank account, disconnect their telephone, and move to an ashram in India to spend their days in deep meditation. Occasionally they are forced to leave the ashram for the big city to renew their visa, and this seems like a terrible distraction, an assault on their nerves. They rush quickly back to the safety of the ashram to continue meditating. They prefer emptiness over form, and they assume that these are two different things. They try very hard to stay focused on emptiness (or what they imagine emptiness to be), and to stay identified as awareness and not identified as a person.

There's an old Zen story that says, before I encountered Zen, there were mountains and valleys. After I began to practice Zen, there were no mountains and no valleys. Finally, with enlightenment, there were mountains and valleys again.

At first there is relative reality, the world as we *think* it is. Then there is the discovery of the absolute perspective, but at this stage, there's still a big duality that is going unseen, namely this clinging to the absolute and denying the relative. In this mistaken view, the absolute is turned into an ordinary (relative) thing (emptiness but not form). The absolute is viewed as spiritual and the relative is viewed as unspiritual. One is seen as nirvana and the other as samsara, and there is a clinging to one and a pushing away of the other.

True enlightenment embraces and includes both views, the relative and the absolute. It moves freely between them. It realizes that nirvana *is* samsara and emptiness *is* form and vice versa. It sees no separation, no contradiction, no conflict – and yet, it is fully capable of discernment. It doesn't mix things up. It is truly nondual, which means there are mountains and valleys, but they are no longer mistaken for separate things that exist independently of each other. In fact, they can only appear together. They are not one, not two. The enlightened can function freely in the relative world without being tripped up by imaginary obstacles and limitations.

In the famous Zen Ox-herding pictures, in which chasing and taming an ox becomes a metaphor for the spiritual journey from delusion to enlightenment, the last pictures involve the dissolving of ox and person, and then the dissolving of enlightenment itself, and after all that dissolving, the final picture is called "Entering the Marketplace." An apparently ordinary jolly fellow is pictured coming into town. I suspect that is what Adya means by not being stuck in emptiness, and by embodiment as the final understanding. You leave the ashram and come back to earth. (Of course, some may stay in the ashram as their vocation, which is also perfectly okay, but they no longer see it in the same separate and rarified way, and the occasional trips to the big city are no longer perceived as a terrible distraction).

There is a wonderful line by Zen Master Sekito Kisen in the *Sandokai* or *Identity of Relative and Absolute,* a famous Zen text:

> *To be attached to things is primordial illusion;*
> *To encounter the absolute is not yet enlightenment....*
> *Light and darkness are not one, not two.*

Zen Master Dogen writes of *"leaping clear of the many and the one."* Zen teacher Thich Nhat Hanh notes that, *"a wave does not have to stop being a wave in order to be water."*

Nisargadatta Maharaj says:

> *You are taking duality so much for granted, that you do not even notice it, while to me variety and diversity do not create separation. You imagine reality to stand apart from names and forms, while to me names and forms are the ever-changing expressions of reality and not apart from it. You ask for the proof of truth while to me all existence is proof. You separate existence from being and being from reality, while to me it is all one.*

And Zen teacher Bernie Glassman:

> *A big mistake commonly made in studying Zen is to think there's something inherently wrong with the world of duality and that it's to be transcended or somehow discarded once and for all. The point is not to negate or transcend duality, but to totally immerse oneself in it. Totally becoming duality means totally becoming not only the relative but the absolute as well, because the distinction between the two is nothing but a notion.*

Or as Ramana Maharshi so beautifully put it: *"The world is illusory; God alone is real; God is the world."*

True enlightenment is not one-sided. It clings to no position. It isn't about being stuck in the absolute. It isn't about never saying "I" again. It isn't about quitting your job and moving to India (although that's certainly one possibility, but in no way is it spiritually better than staying in New York City and working at the stock exchange). It isn't about getting fixated on either side of a conceptual divide such as choice or no choice. Enlightenment is not dogmatic or fundamentalist – it is open and inclusive. Enlightenment isn't about holding on to some rarified experience or some *idea* that "I am Pure Awareness," and insisting that "I am not a person." Relatively speaking, of course you're a person! This isn't about constantly telling yourself over and over, "I am Awareness," like a mantra, and working very hard to maintain that view – and then feeling that the telephone ringing or having to go to work and deal with other people is all a terrible and threatening interruption. Enlightenment isn't about maintaining some kind of meditative state 24/7, or watching the evening news and not caring about what is happening, or not feeling sad if someone you love dies, or being perfectly calm all the time and never getting upset. It isn't about being detached – like a neutral witness viewing everything from far, far away. Enlightenment is totally intimate, awake and whole-hearted. It doesn't need to defend its purity because it recognizes that all impurity is relative and dream-like. Enlightenment is not about finally having the right answers, it is the absence (or the transparency) of all the answers and all the questions.

The absolute *includes* the relative, it doesn't deny it. It sees the relative for what it is – *relative* truth. It understands the difference between relative and absolute, between map and territory. But it doesn't deny or discard the map. It simply doesn't mistake one for the other – it doesn't mistake the relative world for the absolute, and it doesn't cling to the absolute as if it were some kind of relative thing that must be attained, protected and maintained.

There is no way *not* to fully embody the One Reality, since the One Reality is all there is, and *everything* is that. On the other hand, clarity is a different expression from confusion and not everything is an embodiment of clarity or enlightenment. To deny either side of the gestalt is to miss the whole truth.

So yes, I agree with Adya. It's possible (relatively speaking) to get stuck in emptiness. Perhaps it is a necessary stage (in a non-liner circular journey going nowhere). From the absolute understanding, there is no one to get stuck anywhere. It's all one undivided whole. But that one undivided whole includes the ability to make distinctions, to discern differences, to distinguish mountains from valleys, to make plans, to have intentions, to point out errors, to remember the past and anticipate the future. Unicity includes *everything*. It is not one, not two.

Sometimes it is important to hear an uncompromisingly absolute teaching, and sometimes it is important to hear a more relative teaching. Take what resonates in this moment. In fact, you cannot do otherwise. In another moment, something else will resonate. It isn't that one is "right" and the other is "wrong."

F: Is there a process involved in waking up?

J: Only in the imagination, after the fact, is there apparently a process. But relatively speaking, we can maybe identify certain changes that seem to occur. They are not necessarily linear, and how they occur in different individuals can vary greatly. There is no one right way. I can only speak from my own experience and observation.

F: What are these changes?

J: One is an increasing ability to discern the difference between perception and conceptualization – between awareness and thinking. An increasing sensitivity to thoughts, stories and beliefs – an ability to *recognize* that thoughts, stories and beliefs *are* thoughts, stories and beliefs – and to *see* that no concept is the truth (no map is ever the territory). Our suffering always has to do with false beliefs. Pain may come from physical circumstances, but suffering always entails some kind of thought, story and belief. Some of the most ubiquitous thoughts, beliefs and conceptualizations are so pervasive, so deeply conditioned, so widely accepted, and so constantly reinforced, that it takes a very subtle discernment to actually *see* that they are ideas and not reality itself. This ability to discern what is conceptual and what is actual is refined and cultivated over a lifetime. There is no end to seeing the false as false. It is always a present moment seeing. Perhaps most importantly, the "me" is seen to be a story made up of thoughts, memories and mental images, and as this is realized, there is a waking up from the imaginary story of my life. Waking up to pure perception, enjoying the simplicity of bare being more and more. Of course, this doesn't mean you stop thinking and conceptualizing and telling stories. It just means not being taken in by conceptual thought or confused by it in the same way.

Another important shift is the realization that Here/Now is always here, that this boundless field of awareness is ever-present, that *everything* (including this character called "me") appears within this boundless awareness, and that this aware presence is what I actually am. There are no boundaries anywhere to be found. I am not limited to or encapsulated inside this character I've been thinking of as "me," but rather, this character appears *in* me, *in* awareness, along with the whole movie of waking life.

Typically, even after this realization that I am awareness has occurred, there is still a persistent belief that "I" (as the character) go back and forth between the expanded sense of myself as awareness and the contracted sense of myself as the character. Eventually, it is noticed that this story of "me" going back and forth is nothing but a conceptualization that comes and goes in awareness. In reality, although there are ever-changing appearances and experiences, there is no one going back and forth between them. Here/Now is always here regardless of what shows up. The apparent owner of these ever-changing experiences is only a mirage. Contracted experiences or moments of identification as "me" are no longer seen as a problem "for me," but simply as another impersonal scene in the movie of waking life happening to no one.

This seeing is rarely a one-time occurrence that erases the believability of the mirage forever after. Within the movie, the illusion is quite deeply embedded and constantly reinforced by the world, so it tends to persist and pop back up. It's as if our true nature is remembered and then forgotten, remembered and then forgotten. But more and more, it is seen and realized that there is no "me" remembering and forgetting, that *all* of this is impersonal – like ever-changing weather – that it is only the mirage-character who demands a permanent state of expansion or a permanent state of remembering. Awareness has no problem with *any* appearance including contraction, distraction or forgetting. Awareness accepts everything, just as it is. No experience is permanent. And no experience is personal. The search for a permanent expanded experience "for me" falls away in the realization that unicity includes *both* expansion *and* contraction.

There may still be a subtle sense of duality or separation between awareness and the content of awareness, a lingering idea of "me" trying to stay on one side of that imaginary divide between form and emptiness, some effort to be detached and uninvolved, some attempt to keep remembering that I am awareness and not Joan. This is what we talked about before as being stuck in emptiness or stuck in the absolute. I am nothing, I am nobody, I am emptiness, and I reject the world of form. I stand apart from the whole messy affair of ordinary life. The relative world is seen as a distraction and a falsehood to be carefully avoided.

And then at some point, this last bubble pops and there is no separation at all anywhere. There is only unicity – everything just as it is – the honking horn, the screeching brakes, the breath going in and out, the breeze from the window, the shapes and colors of this moment, the arm reaching for the glass of water, obsessive thoughts about "me" popping up, clouds blowing across the sky, stories unfolding in the mind, fingerbiting, bombs dropping on children, an ant scurrying across the kitchen counter – *all* of it, one undivided whole – no separation. No subject, no object, no beginning, no end. Everything that appears is realized to be the One Reality, whether it is pleasant or unpleasant, square or round, blue or red, soft or hard. It is all emptiness showing up as infinite variation and then vanishing completely into the nothingness of deep sleep and death, like the tide coming in and going out. Nothing stands apart from this emptiness – there is *only* this. The present moment is utterly immediate, seamless, boundless and impossible to doubt. Nothing else is real.

And when I speak of this last bubble popping, please understand that this may not be a permanent line-in-the-sand event. It may not happen once and for all, but rather, it may happen again and again until finally, imperceptibly, either the bubble never reappears or else all concern with the bubble disappears and no one is left to care about the bubble. Of course, it takes thought and memory to construct the image of the bubble and the story of "once and for all" or "again and again." The only actual reality is Here/Now. The bubble is *always* only a mirage-like appearance appearing to no one. The separation is *never* real.

True enlightenment sees only unicity. And yet, that doesn't mean we lose the ability to differentiate between truth and illusion, or between Ramana and Hitler, or that we step in front of a bus because "everything is unicity and there's no one here to get hurt." We can discern relative differences and function appropriately in the play of life. I am everything and nothing. Everywhere I look, I see only mySelf. This feels not like detachment, but rather, like total intimacy. And this is not a great achievement or an acquisition, but more like a falling away of any misunderstanding until all that remains is the natural state that was here all along. It is utterly simple and ordinary, nothing special.

So is all of this a process? It looks that way if we think and talk about it. But everything I've just said is only another map. Another description. Another abstraction. Another conceptualization. Throw it away!

I've said all this in response to your question, but I don't really like the concept of stages of awakening. Any such mapping reifies and divides what is seamless and ever-changing, and it plays right into the habitual stories of personal lack and personal achievement. So I want to emphasize that everything I've said is only a kind of tentative approximation. Life itself is very fluid. Things can happen in a different way, and nothing *really* happens. Some teachers lay out all these different stages – kensho, awakening, enlightenment, liberation, seventh-stage sahaj samadhi, embodiment, full realization, blah blah blah – and they delineate all these different stages one after another in a very linear way, and it's easy to forget that these are all conceptual maps. Tibetan Buddhism has one map and Theravadan Buddhism has a different map and Adyashanti has his map and Adi Da has his map and Zen has its map. These maps of the journey may be useful to some people, but to me, that kind of linear mapping seems to get the thinking mind caught up in trying to locate "me" on the map and then advance "me" from the "lower" to the "higher" stages. It's like rising up the corporate ladder all over again. And in my experience, waking up is not a linear process. It isn't really "a process" at all until you reflect back on it, and then what you see is usually more of a spiral than a straight line. But the truth is, waking up is only Here/Now. There is no beginning and no end to it. That's the most important key: *Here/Now*. Not "once upon a time" or "once and for all" or "back then" or "someday," but *Now*.

F: I don't really know if I've had an awakening yet or not. Sometimes I think I have, but then I'm not so sure. I guess if I'm not sure, it must mean I'm not awake.

J: Awakening is simply waking up from, or seeing through, thoughts such as these and the imaginary situations they create in the mind like mirages. Above all, awakening is seeing through the "me" at the center of this whole train of thought, the "me" who wonders if "I" have had an awakening or not. This waking up is very simple. It is not some fantastic, spectacular, one-time event with trumpets blaring and fireworks exploding. Nor is it a personal achievement. We miss it because we're looking for something extraordinary, something that will enhance "me."

I run into so many people in my meetings who are seeking a big awakening experience – some huge, final breakthrough – just as I was doing for so long. And this is of course perpetuated by centuries of talk about enlightenment and nowadays people at satsangs gushingly recounting their awakening experiences and teachers telling their stories of final awakening. Naturally, it sets everyone up to want what is being described, to seek it, and to endlessly compare their experiences to those that are being described.

Even to speak of "awakening" or "waking up" or "enlightenment" instantly creates illusion. Once we have a word like "awakening" or "enlightenment," then the word immediately suggests a definitive personal event in time with a before and after. Words create all the confusion. The present moment itself is always very simple.

Everyone has a totally unique path. And everyone conceptualizes what happens to them and describes it in their own words, in their own way. Some people understate, some people embellish. But the stories are always stories, however relatively true they may be. They are fictionalized abstractions of something that really never happened at all – like memories and re-tellings of a dream.

· We often seek the experiences we have been led to expect, and then we often frame our experiences according to what we have learned. Christians see Jesus and get born again. Buddhists discover emptiness and the present moment. Satsang people have awakenings. Nondualists imagine a moment when "the self" drops away forever. People who expect dramatic enlightenments often have them! When I hear some of the big bang enlightenment stories on offer, I sometimes wonder if the teachers in question haven't constructed the whole experience out of thin air, convinced themselves of its validity, and now they're using it to sell themselves or make themselves special. Teachers dangle this notion of a final shift like a carrot in front of others. They may say that it isn't the person who gets enlightened, but then they keep on telling their personal enlightenment story. Whether the story is relatively true or untrue, it seems to me that this kind of final event story functions mostly as a way of focusing other people on what they apparently lack and what they might hopefully gain in the future.

This whole notion of a final breakthrough, in which all sense of being an encapsulated individual permanently vanishes forever and ever, never to return, is a total myth. That encapsulated "me" is *never* really here, *ever*, and the *idea* or *sense* of encapsulation vanishes in any moment that it's seen clearly for what it is. But that *sense* of encapsulation and identity with the bodymind "self" comes back any time there are thoughts and stories about "me" that are believed, including any notion of "me" identifying (or not identifying) as "me." To some degree, the sense of identity with a particular bodymind is a survival function, having a sense of location and boundaries, working to keep this organism alive. And in many ways, that's not a problem. It's functional. It becomes an apparent problem – it creates suffering – when it goes beyond what is actually needed in order to function and survive – when it takes the shape of total identification with this imaginary egoic center that seemingly needs to be protected, defended, and made special. This phantom "me" always involves a story of being incomplete and lacking, and a belief that "I" am in control, authoring and directing "my" thoughts and actions. It would appear that this illusion of an executive self is hardwired into the human mind as a way of functioning and surviving, and to some degree, it will continue to show up as needed in the waking state.

As far as I'm concerned, what is liberating is to see through the dysfunctional, illusory and unnecessary aspects of that egoic mirage *as it happens,* not to claim or believe that "I" have reached some mythological state where this "me" illusion doesn't ever happen any more "to me." Because that very claim *is* the reincarnation of the false self. And how does one ever know that something is gone forever? And to whom is it a problem if it happens again? It's only the "me" that wants desperately to be free of the "me" forever after. The "me" wants to be an Enlightened One, a perfect me. Special. Better than everyone else. At the top of the pecking order. Many teachers seem to be operating out of this need to be special, while insisting that they are totally beyond such things.

Enlightenment is Now. It's not a possession or an achievement. There is no final enlightenment. And an enlightened person is a total oxymoron. Enlightenment is the popping of the bubble of separation. It leaves no person to be enlightened or unenlightened.

As I've said, I think there is often a tendency to confuse unicity, which is all there is, with enlightenment, which is the absence of delusion. Unicity includes both enlightenment and delusion, both Ramana and Hitler. But Hitler was not enlightened. Enlightenment *sees* unicity. Delusion imagines separation. The very idea of permanently enlightened people is delusion.

There are characters running around in the movie of waking life claiming that they no longer experience fear or desire. Whenever I hear this now, it immediately activates my bullshit alarms. Maybe it's true, I don't know. But it seems to me that instead of *seeing* what is going on, many people who have swallowed the "I Am Enlightened" story may now be busy *denying* delusion, even to themselves. This is like putting on blinders. It's all about a new and improved identity – Me the Enlightened One – an identity that needs to be defended. Dogen expressed the truth beautifully when he said, "Those who have great realization of delusion are buddhas; those who are greatly deluded about realization are sentient beings." Those who see delusion clearly are, *in that moment,* enlightened, and those who believe deluded ideas about enlightenment are, *in that moment,* deluded. Awakening is not a flashy experience. It's very ordinary. It's simply seeing through false ideas. What remains is the ever-present, ever-changing aliveness of Here/Now. And *that* is actually never not here.

F: You've talked a lot about distinguishing between concepts and perceptions. Can you say a little bit more about why is that so important? Some teachers say enlightenment is all about some kind of energetic shift, that it has nothing to do with thinking or not thinking. And some teachers say it's not about any shift at all. In fact, you say that sometimes.

J: No verbalization can capture reality. If we don't *really* understand that, then we argue over different ways of verbalizing the same nothingness. It's easy to *think* we understand that "the word water is not water," but to really *see* that, moment to moment, is not always as obvious as we might think. If radical nondual teachings are heard merely as verbal formulations or intellectual ideas, they are meaningless and untrue. Only when the words actually hit the target, pop the bubble of the imaginary problem, and trigger direct insight are they true. And the truth is in the groundlessness that is revealed, not in the verbal formulation.

When we are caught up in obsessive, me-centered thinking, there is a very different energy in the bodymind than when we are fully present as unobstructed awareness. Once you've experienced this difference, as I know you have, it is undeniable. There are many ways to open the heart-mind and shift attention from the mental spin to bare presence – singing bhajans, chanting, dancing, insight meditation, sports, drinking a glass of wine, making love, walking in nature, blowing bubbles, attending a meeting with someone who says over and over that "no shift is needed" and that "unicity is all there is" – any of these things can bring about an energetic shift from contraction to expansion.

Is this shift important? Yes and no. *Something* is exactly the same in both expansion and contraction; unicity is all there is *regardless* of what shifts occur; no experience is any closer to unicity than any other. In the absolute sense, this shift from contraction to expansion, or from confusion to clarity, makes no difference at all. In fact, nothing really changes. Here/Now is equally present in every experience. But relatively speaking, *realizing that* is heaven and not realizing it is hell. So in terms of everyday reality, yes it does matter. It is the difference between heaven and hell.

One way of cutting through confusion and popping the imaginary bubble is to point uncompromisingly to the absolute truth that it makes no difference. Another way is to sing bhajans and do ecstatic dances. Another way is to point out the difference between concepts and perceptions, or between thought and awareness.

But whatever else we do, whether it is bhajans or radical nonduality, I would say that being able to discern the difference between concepts and perceptions is very important for being truly awake because all our suffering is in mistaking concepts for reality. The most basic concept that gets mistaken for reality is the separate, independent self. In pure perception, no such entity is ever found. In pure perception, there is no body, no mind, no me, no you, no inside, no outside. Those are all ideas, concepts, abstractions, mental images.

The tendency to form concepts and mistake them for reality is very pervasive, and to really discern the difference between a concept and what is real is not always easy. It can be very, very subtle. Many of the most pervasive concepts, like "the self" and "the body" and "the world," are so ubiquitous and so deeply conditioned that it is not all that easy to see that these are ideas and not our actual experience.

And in spirituality, we get new concepts. I've been noticing how easily the mind creates a subtle mental image of "emptiness" or "unicity" or "Oneness" or "Consciousness." And then immediately, it's another object, another mirage, and we're worrying about whether we "get it" or not.

What is *this*, right here, right now? The thinking mind always wants to supply a word, "It's blahbhahdybhah." And then we think we've got it. But no word is it. And on close inspection, there's no "it." There's no separate, independent, persisting *thing* of any kind. Waking up is not about coming up with the right answer, but rather, it's about throwing every possible answer away.

That's the key. Throw the answers away. See what remains.

And as soon as I say that, presto, *that* becomes the new strategy! And then, it's another answer, another formula, so throw that away, too!

Once we have some idea that "I'm an awakened person" and "I've arrived," then it's so easy to deceive oneself and put a lid on open inquiry and exploration. Instead of throwing everything away, we're holding onto something. Instead of deconstructing, we're constructing. Instead of groundlessness, we've found a place to stand. Instead of the freedom of being nobody, we're caught up in being somebody special.

I'm interested in what's here in the absence of any system, any idea, any conceptual overlay – seeing through all of the overlays that show up, all the answers, all the frames that the thinking mind comes up with.

This is one quality that I really appreciate in Toni Packer. You can ask her about something and she won't just regurgitate the answer that she had yesterday. She'll spend the next few days intensely looking into that question freshly, as if it were totally new to her. And to me, that's the essence of the old saying, "If you meet the Buddha on the road, kill him." If you find the answer, let it go. Yesterday's answer is today's dead meat. Any answer you find in one moment, as soon as it's formulated, let it go. Return to the aliveness of Here/Now, and *that* is not a word or something you can grasp and possess.

Waking up is nothing more or less than *seeing* how all the problems, all of the dilemmas, all of the conundrums are imaginary – they're all conceptual, they are all created by thought. In simple presence, there is no suffering. There might be physical pain or grief or fingerbiting or sad queasy feelings, but they aren't a problem. There is no need to *do* anything about them or with them. There is simply what is, as it is. No corrections needed. Very liberating!

F: There could be a genuine experience, or whatever you want to call it, and then right afterwards there could be a referencing of that experience in thought – thought is coming up more quickly than can be seen sometimes.

J: Yes, very often thoughts are not seen at all, they go by too quickly. And if they *are* seen, they are not seen *as* thoughts. Instead, they simply seem to be undeniable statements of *fact*. Our thoughts seem completely believable, like an objective report on reality. Thinking can be in images too, it isn't always in words, and it definitely isn't spelled out in complete sentences. It can be very quick little energetic mental telegrams. This is why meditation is often so helpful. When we sit down in silence with nothing to do, we begin to actually *see* our thoughts, where before they went by so fast they were often not even noticed. And we begin to see that they *are* thoughts, where before they were simply *believed*. Seeing through the conceptual dream-world can be very subtle, and there is no end to this seeing.

What we're always pointing to – the simplicity of awareness and bare being – this is no big deal. It's very simple and ordinary and always Here/Now. It's not some spectacular fireworks experience, though fireworks may happen for some people, but they're not important. In fact, fireworks can be a big distraction if they are thought to mean something. They're actually nothing but an entertaining display! What we're really talking about is that which is equally present as both fireworks and as the dullest, most boring experience. And *that* is utterly simple and ordinary. It's here right now. It's never absent. It is this aliveness that is showing up as everything – the rug, the water glass, the lamp, the trees, the birds, the way you just moved your arm, the whole show.

We have to use words to communicate, to talk – but any word is only a pointer or a description. There is no such *thing* as "unicity" or "beingness" or "awareness." What those words point to is absolutely ungraspable and inconceivable. It's not *something*! Once we start thinking of unicity as a particular something, we become very confused. Round and round goes the thinking mind on its little treadmill chasing its own tail faster and faster. We can get truly worked up over nothing at all! So this is about using words and simultaneously seeing through them.

Nisargadatta said, "Without words, what is there to understand? The need for understanding arises from mis-understanding." If there were no words, what problem would there be? The confusion is always conceptual. It's always in the way we're thinking and talking to ourselves and each other. Reality itself is not confusing or mysterious. It's absolutely obvious, undeniable, inescapable and never absent. And there is *nothing* that is not it.

F: You mentioned images. I might have a sense of present awareness, and then I might have an image of that which I am trying to carry over into the next moment. Already, before even a word, there is a kind of grasping to hold onto that sense I have, especially if it was a good feeling.

J: Yes, so simply *seeing* all of that – thought and imagination referencing "awareness" as a particular sensation, a particular experience, a particular state of mind, and then trying to hold onto that or get it back again. *Seeing* all of that for the wild goose chase that it is. We're not pointing to something that happened to you yesterday or that's going to happen in the next moment if you're lucky or if you do the right thing. We're pointing to what *is* – not *because* of anything you do, but *in spite* of whatever you appear to do or not do. Awareness *is* regardless of thinking or not thinking.

F: "Awareness *is*" directs me to *this*, right now.

J: Yes, and *this* is where Truth is. Here/Now. It's very narrow (the eye of the needle, the razor's edge) and yet at the same time, absolutely boundless (all inclusive and without limit). That's the paradoxical nature of Here/Now. You can't escape it, and yet, it can seemingly be overlooked.

When we reflect on this, in the imaginary story created by memory, waking up to this seems like an unfolding process. I often feel like I'm having the same realization or making the same discovery again and again, and yet, each time, it's absolutely new. The *aliveness* of this present moment is always new, always fresh. It's as if we keep realizing or discovering this same essential secret over and over. And in some way, over what appears to be time, it seemingly gets ever more clear, ever more subtle, ever more simple. And each seeing is seeing for the first time, because this moment *is* the first and only moment, the *now* moment. The past can only be there in thinking; awareness has no past.

And, of course, the whole story of changes occurring over time is a story. It takes thought and memory and abstraction and imagination to conjure it up. Reality is timeless. Here/Now, there is no continuity or evolutionary development. That's all *in* the story.

And yet, paradoxically, the story is also what is. The map is also the territory. Story-telling and mapping are part of how totality is functioning. The map (*as a map*) is as real as the landscape it describes. I think it was Dogen who said, "The moon and the pointing finger are a single reality." That is one step beyond "the map is not the territory" or "the finger pointing to the moon is not the moon." First, we see through the error of mistaking the concept for the actuality, and then we see through the error of imagining a dualistic divide where thoughts, concepts, stories and maps are "unreal," while trees, rocks, buildings and people are "real." Nothing is excluded from unicity, and while we can draw relative distinctions between different things, in the absolute sense, all appearances are equally real and equally unreal. They are real in the sense that the appearance itself is undeniable and that whatever appears is nothing but unicity. They are unreal in the sense that they are all momentary appearances with no inherent, independent existence. But if all that sounds confusing, just let it go. Come back to the sound of the wind in the leaves and the warm sunlight on the carpet. Come back to bare being.

Really, it's all very simple. Incredibly simple. As soon as there is confusion or complication, it's a clue there's thinking. Thought is busy chasing its tail again. The truth is always obvious. It takes no effort. It's fully here right now. This is it. Very immediate and unavoidable. This moment, *exactly as it is,* even if it feels uncomfortable.

Miss Scarlet in the Billiard Room with the Wrench

Nisargadatta famously said that "I am nothing" is wisdom, and "I am everything" is love, and between those two, life flows. The illusion that creates all our suffering is the false notion that I am *something*. But no "thing" actually exists apart from everything else, and no "thing" persists over time. What looks like solid form is nothing but seamless flux and change. We have a deeply engrained *idea* that there are separate, persisting *things* (including me and you). And then, seeing how vulnerable and impermanent every apparent form appears to be, we fear loss and death. That is our human suffering in a nutshell. But the joke is, *there is nothing to die*. The "me" or the "bodymind" that we think will die never existed in the first place!

We've *learned* to see chairs and tables and dogs and cats, to draw boundary lines conceptually. Babies are not born seeing chairs. They see colors, shapes and movements, and they learn over time where and how to draw the conceptual boundary lines. And pretty soon we lose sight of the fact that this *is* conceptual. Conceptual conditioning begins to shape perception, and by the time we reach adulthood, this is how we *think* we actually see everything, as a bunch of separate objects. And, of course, thought has created out of thin air the most seemingly important object of all – "me" – the star of the show, the center of the universe. And in a certain way, this has some truth to it. The true "I," which is common to everyone, is like that sphere whose center is everywhere and whose circumference is nowhere – boundless, seamless unicity, always completely present Here/Now. But we mistakenly think that the "I" is encapsulated inside an object, and that this bodymind is a separate "something" that is rushing along *in* the flow of life like a raft going down the rapids. This is a scary picture. But that isn't ever our actual direct *experience*.

In art class, I remember they told us, if we could truly *see* something, we could draw it. But the temptation is to draw what you *think* is there instead of what you actually *see*. That's why when most people try to draw a face, it doesn't look anything like a face. They draw what they *think* a face is like rather than what they actually see. That's why painters long ago couldn't create the illusion of depth because they were painting what they *thought* was there. When they finally began to paint what they were actually *seeing*, which was counter-intuitive, then *voila!* – we had paintings that captured the sense of depth and looked far more real.

If we pay attention right now to our actual direct experience, what do we find? There are sensations that are constantly changing, fleeting thoughts that appear and then vanish, bits of storyline and narrative, flashes of memory, mental images, the sense of being present. That's all we find in direct experience right now. We don't really *experience* ourselves as solid and independent. We *think* about ourselves that way. We have a mental image of everything that's like a map of the world, but the earth itself isn't anything like the neat and tidy picture on the map. The living earth is borderless – pulsing and flowing, erupting and quaking. As Zen Master Dogen realized long before the advent of modern physics, even the mountains are moving.

Every night in deep sleep, the most basic sense of "I am" is gone – even the first light of awareness disappears. This particular movie of waking life is turned off and there is no one leftover to miss it. The phantom viewer disappears along with the show because the phantom viewer is part of the show. Our life story is like a favorite television series. We get daily installments. When death comes, it is like the end of *The Sopranos*. This particular series finishes forever and the screen goes blank (except in real death, as in deep sleep, no one is left seeing a blank screen). This ending only sounds scary from the perspective of the phantom viewer who was actually an integral part of the show. We picture death as a scary scenario where the phantom viewer is buried alive in eternal darkness with the television turned off, unable to turn it back on and find out what's happening in our favorite series, "The Story of My Life." It sounds dreadful to the mind. Except that this isn't our actual experience. Every night in deep sleep, no one is left to miss the show, and we find it enormously rejuvenating.

Unicity doesn't end. Unicity never began. The terror we have about death is rooted in the mistaken idea of separation. It is rooted in imagining that we are the character in the story or the phantom viewer. Just like living in fear of stepping off the edge of the flat earth, death is an imaginary problem. There is no one here to die.

Did any of you play that board game *Clue* as children? It was all about solving a murder. You chose a character to move around the board, and this character was represented by a small wooden token. There was Colonel Mustard and Miss Scarlet and Professor Plum and various others, and you moved that "person" around the board by throwing the dice, and you visited different rooms trying to find out who had committed the murder, with what weapon, in which room.

As you played the game, Colonel Mustard or Miss Scarlet or whichever little piece you had chosen became your identity. And that's very much how we think of ourselves, as a piece on the board game of life. And we take this game very seriously. We lose sight of the fact that it is a game. It seems very important that Miss Scarlet needs to win and be the first to solve the mystery. We are trying very hard to get Miss Scarlet around the board, trying to keep her in the game, trying to pass go and win a million dollars and buy Park Place and get enlightened and all the things that Miss Scarlet wants to do. I'm mixing board games, but life is like that – the rules keep changing and there seem to be multiple games going on at once.

When we think about awakening, we think that it's something that happens to Miss Scarlet or Colonel Mustard. We think of it as an event or an acquisition, like passing Go, or buying Park Place, or solving the murder. Miss Scarlet is going to awaken, and everybody is going to notice she's awake. She's not going to have any problems any more. She'll feel only peace and bliss from now on. She'll be loved and revered. Devotees will rush to meet her every need. Miss Scarlet will have really done well. Her internalized parents will be pleased. But when the game gets folded up and put away, what remains? And when the movie of waking life turns off, in deep sleep or in death, what remains?

Nothing! All your progress is finished in an instant! Wiped out! Nisargadatta had a wonderful line, "When the dung dries, the worms are finished, however much progress they may have made!" [Joan laughs] It's very liberating – there's nothing to accomplish! It is already accomplishing itself perfectly, and nothing is even happening.

Where is this whole board game of life actually happening? We might say it's happening in the world, but then where is the world happening, or the universe? Where did the Big Bang happen? We might say the whole show is happening in the brain, but if you cut open the brain, you won't find this living room. Where is all this happening? How real is anything that appears? Do we actually need to "be somebody" and win the game of life?

Momentary identification as Miss Scarlet happens. But it doesn't happen *to* Miss Scarlet or *to* some imaginary phantom viewer – that's the illusion. And really, it doesn't even happen. All apparent happenings require time (which is a thought-form), and memory and imagination. Right here in this timeless instant, nothing is happening.

So the problem is always imaginary. The fall from grace is imaginary. The bondage is imaginary. Salvation is imaginary. Enlightenment is imaginary.

P: When Miss Scarlet dies as a separate identifiable thing, Here/Now still exists, right?

J: Can you hear the contradiction in the question? Miss Scarlet is presumed to be a separate, enduring entity that dies, and then we wonder, is Here/Now still going to be here, in the future, after that happens. What exactly are we talking about?

P: But after Miss Scarlet dies, is everything still here as it was before when Miss Scarlet was alive?

J: Was it any particular way?

P: Is there another show after death? Different levels? Different consciousnesses?

J: What is it that cares about this, what is behind this concern? It's that thought again of me buried alive, horrified, thinking, "My God, are they ever going to turn the television back on, or am I going to be buried alive in darkness forever?" But, in death, as in deep sleep, that phantom viewer who is concerned with this has totally disappeared along with the apparent problem. And possibly, that mirage-like phantom can disappear right now, or more accurately, it can be seen to be entirely non-existent and imaginary.

P: There is no difference before birth and after death? There really is no —

J: Birth and death are conceptual ideas. Where does anything begin or end? If you trace anything back, you find it to be utterly inseparable from everything else. You can't actually find any independent continuous *thing* that gets born and then persists and then finally dies except as an idea. What is it that dies? What is it that was born? What is it that persists? Can you actually find anything? I'm not saying there is nothing here in some nihilistic sense, because there is *this*, obviously and undeniably, but can you find any "one" who was born? Who you were ten years ago is already dead. The "you" who was here back when we began this conversation is gone forever. Everything has changed since then. *Everything!* The whole universe has changed. There isn't really a solid *entity* here to begin with — that's a mirage, a conceptual abstraction. The actual *reality* of you is a movement utterly inseparable from the rest of the universe. When Joan dies, the Joan Show is finished for good, and the phantom viewer of the Joan show is also gone for good — that phantom viewer was part of the show — but unicity is never destroyed. Unicity is the unborn, undying, ever-present wholeness that is all there is.

P: What's the difference between death and dreamless sleep?

J: Whatever difference there is between one apparent thing and another apparent thing is relative. It's an appearance. And in both death and deep sleep, all appearances end. So what would we be comparing? What is very clear here is that death is only disturbing when there is the idea of me as a separate somebody who is going to end and yet somehow still be here to be upset that "I" have ended. Otherwise there's nothing at all disturbing about knowing that this body will continue to disintegrate as it is already doing every instant, or that this entire movie of waking life might totally wink out in the next second as it does every night. Who would be left to care? Actually, that winking out happens every instant – you could describe the movie of waking life as a series of still pictures appearing in rapid succession, creating the illusion of continuity, like a motion picture or a flip book. The ever-present reality is the immovable Here/Now, the still point whose center is everywhere and whose circumference is nowhere.

P: What about physical pain?

J: Well, yes, there's physical pain. It's a fact of life. But a lot of the suffering that goes on around physical pain has to do with how we think about the pain. Even just labeling it "pain," can make it hurt more, and then anxious thoughts about it: "Oh my God, I can't stand this. What if it gets worse? What if it doesn't go away? This is killing me. I have to get rid of this. I hate this. This is unbearable. This is a nightmare." We tense up, we resist the pain, and then it hurts even more. This is observable, and it's fascinating to watch this when there is some kind of pain happening.

P: That's all mental, those thoughts.

J: Yes.

P: I'm talking about actual physical pain. How is it possible to get through the actual pain itself?

J: Well, if you're lucky maybe there will be a painkiller or surgery that works for you, but there are many people who live with severe, chronic pain. And many, many people live with mild chronic pain. Some people are being hideously tortured right now. Some people die painlessly and some people die slowly and painfully. That's life.

P: And there's nothing we can do about it?

J: Well, you can take an aspirin, or have a morphine drip, or do mindfulness meditation, or distract yourself by watching television, or kill yourself, or try to ward it off by eating goods foods and exercising, but whether any of that works or not is anybody's guess. And if you're in prison being tortured, or in a war zone, there may not be any morphine or good food available to you. There's no way to really avoid the vulnerabilities of the physical organism stemming from the fact that it can feel both intense pleasure and intense pain.

But when pain is actually happening presently, it is a different event than when you're sitting around worrying that this *might* happen to you in the future. When pain really *is* happening, my experience is that it gets much worse when the mind starts resisting it and having anxious thoughts about, "Oh my God, what if it doesn't go away? This is horrible. I can't stand this. This will kill me." With that kind of thinking, the body tightens up, and the pain gets worse. And the bottom-line is, we are resisting death. Pain seems most bearable when there's an ability to let go, to open, to die (metaphorically, and at some point, literally), to relax fully into this pain as pure sensation without a storyline, to be totally open and present to it (the mindfulness meditation approach, as it were, but without any *idea* of *trying* to do that). But sometimes that ability to relax into it just isn't there. It doesn't arise. Sometimes we resist and tighten up. Sometimes those anxious thoughts that make the pain worse just keep popping up. And I don't find anyone who can control that. At least, not always. (And in reality, never). Our effort works when it works, so to speak, and doesn't when it doesn't.

Our efforts at control are the result of ten million uncontrollable factors, and these efforts *appear* to work when they are followed by the desired result, and when these efforts are not followed by the desired result, then we say we failed, or we think we didn't try hard enough. But why didn't we try harder? Upon careful observation, it can be seen that there is no one in control. Thoughts arise. Actions arise. Apparent choices arise. "You" can do only what life moves you to do, and the results of "your" actions will depend on the whole universe. So you may, sometimes, be able to get away from pain one way or another, but in the end, there is no escape. Even if you kill yourself, no-thing really ends. Deep sleep, anesthesia, and death are temporary. So-called matter or energy continues endlessly. Consciousness always wakes up again. I'm not saying *Joan* wakes up again after her death because "Joan" doesn't really exist in the first place. And I'm not saying the phantom viewer of "The Joan Movie" wakes up again, because that phantom is part of the movie. I'm saying unicity always wakes up again. The pain and pleasure of life, the pain and pleasure of consciousness continues endlessly, and by "endlessly," I mean right now. The only real eternity is now. Pain relief has been the object of much spiritual effort – which is probably part of why Karl Marx called religion the opium of the people. Nothing wrong with pain relief – I'm all for it. By all means, take an aspirin, get palliative care, do mindfulness meditation, *if you can*. But ultimately, there is no escape.

P: Is it important to be aware of your physical body?

J: Important in what way?

P: Eckhart Tolle suggests feeling your body –

J: It's a way of tuning into sensory experiencing, waking up from the conceptual thought-mirage and bringing attention to the aliveness of Now. But thinking that this shift is "important" and making it into a heavy-handed practice only gets in the way of this simple, open, listening presence.

P: You talked about deep sleep being refreshing, but I feel that I'm just wasting time sleeping.

J: Sounds like there's an underlying thought or belief in there about how you're supposed to *use* time well. You're supposed to get somewhere and achieve something and make the best use of your talents. Heaven forbid that you are just sitting around doing nothing, daydreaming or doodling or masturbating or surfing the net or listening to the rain or watching television or dissolving completely in deep sleep or something utterly useless like that. You should be productive! And in the spiritual world, that translates to being constantly mindful, attentive, "aware of the energy field of your body," or "aware of awareness," or whatever it is. "Don't get distracted. Pay attention. Be Here Now. Don't lapse. Don't get caught up in the movie." That's the message. It sounds like elementary school all over again, doesn't it?

Yes, there is something wonderful and wonderfully liberating and alive about present moment awareness, sensing the energy field of the body, being awake now – absolutely – that's the heart of life. That's freedom. Love. Joy. Happiness. But as soon as the mind conceptualizes this and turns it into a method or a goal or a project or a desired result, it becomes drudgery. Then we're back in the dream world of thoughts and ideas, trying to succeed and always falling short.

P: How was the understanding for you? Did it come suddenly or gradually?

J: Suddenly. I was a real mess, and then one day I had this enormous experience that totally changed my life forever – waves of energy shot out the top of my head, I saw an intense blue light, I went tumbling down a dark tunnel, it seemed like I was dying, and suddenly there was an explosion of ecstasy beyond anything I could ever have imagined. I felt the self drop away forever as I merged with the whole cosmos. Ever since then, there has been nothing but radiant brightness and profound bliss. [laughter from group]. I don't know why they're laughing.

P: Are you kidding or serious?

J: I'm kidding! Some people actually do take themselves seriously when they tell that kind of story. But nothing like that ever happened here. Certainly there are moments when things change, sometimes dramatically – a thunderstorm ends, the sky clears, the sun comes out. But I don't find an owner of these experiences. And no sunny day proves to be a lasting state of affairs.

Joan doesn't experience perpetual sunshine. As unicity, I can say that all problems are imaginary. But, speaking as Joan, I can acknowledge that it doesn't always *feel* that way. Maybe the storyline behind the darker moments is never entirely believable anymore. Maybe the darkness doesn't last as long. Maybe there is a recognition that darkness is also unicity, that it's all part of the show. But sometimes consciousness gets absorbed in a story, hypnotized and mesmerized by the plotline and the drama. Momentarily, the rope looks like snake, and the snake seems very real. The bodymind tenses up and mobilizes to fight, take flight, or freeze. Joan says something nasty, trembles in fear, or feels depressed. It happens. That's all part of the organism and its conditioning. It's all an appearance in the movie of waking life.

A word such as "enlightenment" points not to a momentary insight, nor to a fleeting experience, nor to a sustained experience, nor to an enduring state that one enters and then never leaves. Rather, it points to recognizing the unicity (by whatever name) that is being and beholding it all. In fact, there is no one coming and going, entering or leaving, being momentary or sustained. That's all *in* the dream, *in* the story.

So, a lot of people *in* the movie of waking life do tell that story of a big bang awakening that "they" apparently had on such and such a day, and maybe for some characters in the movie, that may indeed be an accurate reflection of their actual experience. For some, I suspect it's more of a construction that they've convinced themselves is true because that's what they thought they were supposed to experience. The mind is very good at producing what it expects. Maybe for some, it's simply a way of expressing the understanding that unicity is all there is, that there's no possibility of being anything else in reality. And if that's what is being pointed to, the undivided wholeness of being, that's fine, as long as people don't confuse that with some false idea that "I" (as a character) am having a permanent *experience* of clear skies and sunshine, or that the me-story no longer arises at all "for me."

There are certainly some very clear people in this movie, I'm not denying that, but it's easy to idealize dead gurus, or living teachers if you only see them during satsang or on a retreat. But if you get close enough to them or live with them, you often discover they're not quite as perfect as you had imagined – they are human and flawed. I've lived in close proximity to several of my teachers. And that's a very important part of the teaching actually – to discover that the messenger is imperfect and flawed – otherwise you tend to idolize and idealize the messenger – you put them up on a pedestal – you focus on the finger instead of on the moon to which it is pointing.

Frankly, I'd be very dubious of anybody who claims that hypnotic entrancement or absorption in mental movies *never* happens anymore *ever*, unless they're pointing to the fact that there is *never* "somebody" that is getting absorbed. And that's *always* the case – not just for "some people," but for everybody, or more accurately, for nobody – because *really*, there are no separate, continuous individuals. The "me" is *always* an illusion. It has *never* been here. Usually, when people talk about "their" permanent awakening, they make it sound like they personally never get caught up anymore in the illusion of encapsulation or the illusion of authorship, whereas other people still do. And that picture always sounds very suspicious to me – more like delusion than true awakening – it always sets off my bullshit alarm.

I'm not saying there are no enlightened people – there *are*, in a sense, but they are only enlightened here and now. There are no enduring persons to be permanently in some ongoing state of enlightenment.

That is delusion. Enlightenment is the seeing through of that illusion. It is not a personal achievement. The clearest and most enlightened people I have known are very ordinary and unassuming. They have a lot of genuine humility. They don't go around telling their enlightenment story ad nauseum or acting like they are on a whole different plane of existence from everyone else. Believe me, there is a lot of pretense, delusion and bullshit in the spiritual world, just like in any other world.

I've had people tell me that they never think anymore, or that they haven't had a thought in three hours or three weeks or three months, and I just smile, because "I haven't had a thought in three hours" is itself a thought. To even make such a claim requires thinking. What they really mean is that they're thinking less, or maybe in less obsessive ways, or else maybe they're simply not *aware* of thoughts, particularly subtle thoughts, and now they've overlaid a story (a bunch of thoughts) about being thought-free over their direct experience. And that story becomes an identity, and that identity *discourages* clear seeing rather than *encouraging* it.

But, regardless of how true the personal awakening story is or what people mean by it, what seems unfortunate about the popularity of this story is that it tends to get other people caught up in this search for some kind of a "big bang" event, some permanent shift in perception or experience. Luckily, this search is only a dream-like happening. And if you investigate that expectation of some big transformation, it's always all about Miss Scarlet. It's all about thinking that awakening is something that happens *to* the characters on the board game, and then mythologizing and idolizing those characters. Colonel Mustard said that he had a "final awakening" and ever since then he has been totally problem-free, and Professor Plum says he has no sense of personal authorship anymore, and Mrs. Peacock says her self dropped away one day as she was walking across her kitchen, so then naturally Miss Scarlet wants all those experiences too. Awakening is *seeing through* that whole movie story.

P: So you've been always like that?

J: Like what? There's simply *this*. It's not *like* anything. It *is*. You may *seemingly* be overlooking it right now, or *apparently* not noticing it, but –

P: When did you notice?

J: Now! Actually you can't *not* notice. You just *think* you can't see this. You *are* this. It's all there is. I'm pointing to this present experiencing that is impossible to avoid. Not some special "thing" that you lack and certain other special people possess, but the inescapable presence that is Here/Now, the utter simplicity of what is. When you wake up, you realize that Here/Now has never been absent. As Buddha famously said, ""I truly attained nothing from complete, unexcelled Enlightenment." The whole problem was a dream problem, it was imaginary. There are a lot of different personal stories, and in truth, they are all fiction.

If you get focused on the stories of the characters in the board game, which is what's happening here now, and it's a popular activity in Advaita circles, it just reinforces the story of somebody who needs to be different. It's a big sidetrack. I'm pointing to what is fully present Here/Now *in spite* of what happens in the board game and not *because* of what happens.

P: But something has to help you to understand it.

J: You don't need to understand anything to know that you are here or to hear the sounds of the traffic. You can't *become* what you already *are*. And whether there's clarity or confusion, unicity is all there is. There is no way out of unicity. Sunny days and cloudy days, unicity includes it all. Unicity is always already attained, impossible to ever lose. You are it, just exactly as you are, warts and all – or more accurately, it is you, and it is every wart and every breath and every thought and every action you appear to take. By seeking something else that you imagine others have achieved, you overlook what is right here, being and beholding this whole show.

I'm not suggesting we adopt an alternate storyline that "there is no enlightenment" and that "being a child molester is just as enlightened as being a Zen master," and "it doesn't matter what you do because it's all a dream." That's another story, another ideology, another spin job by the dreaming mind. Because relatively speaking, *of course* it matters what you do – whether you are hurtful or helpful – but there is no "you" to be permanently one way or the other. And you actually contain the whole world. You contain the Zen master *and* the child molester. So, it is not about landing in some one-sided view – relative or absolute. It is about the fluidity that includes both at once.

Even in moments of absorption in the story of Miss Scarlet, in some way, you *know* it's a story. This isn't some high-level Advaita secret that only the most enlightened sages in the board game realize. You have always known this: *Row, row, row your boat, gently down the stream, merrily, merrily, merrily, merrily, life is but a dream.*

It's like when you're at the movies. On the one hand, there's a real absorption in the movie to the point where you're actually crying or sitting on the edge of your seat with anxiety, but you also still know it's a movie. And there's some recognition that this waking dream is also a movie. Think of how it is when you're arguing with a loved one, feeling all self-righteous and defensive and offended and angry, and yet part of you knows the whole time that your position is thin air. It's make-believe. You're acting in a drama. Right? We all know this. At some moment, the pretense (the pretend) collapses, and you kiss and make up. Right?

P: But in real life you have to act, you have to do something. It's not like watching a movie.

J: You *are* the movie. You, the One Self, are seeing and being the whole show. In the movie, you *seem* to be Miss Scarlet, and you *seem* to be both acting in the movie and also watching it. But as the imaginary character, as Miss Scarlet, you don't control anything. You are moved around the board by an unseen hand (the infinite causes and conditions of nature and nurture). Action happens. The way we conceptualize it inserts a doer into the picture who isn't really there – a thinker of the thoughts, a doer of the actions, a maker of choices – someone at the helm steering the ship. And thought also conjures up the phantom viewer, the witness who is also "me," standing back and watching the show. We think that *this* "I" has to see through the I-illusion and not get identified as Miss Scarlet. But if you actually pay attention to direct experiencing moment to moment, it will be discovered that there is no separate entity doing *any* of it. *Everything happens by itself.* There's no me, no actor, no chooser, no phantom viewer. *All* of this vanishes every night in deep sleep and no one is left to care. That's a big clue.

P: No choice? There's no choice?

J: Is there? Did you choose to say what you just said?

P: Yes, I think so. I choose to ask questions or not.

J: If you examine very closely how those words that just emerged actually occurred, what do you find? Where did the question or the answer come from? Who was in charge of asking or answering?

P: I could choose to be silent.

J: Well, I would invite you to really carefully watch that. And in watching, it's important to discern the difference between how we *think* it is and what's *actually* happening if you pay attention to the *actual* experience. Really watch as you "decide" to speak in this meeting. Or, as you go through the day, watch and see how apparent choosing actually happens. Watch it in simple little choices like maybe you're sitting in a chair and then you "decide" to get up. Or you suddenly "decide" to watch television, or you "decide" to turn the television off. And before you "make a decision," maybe there is a so-called "decision-making process" that happens, but if you examine this process closely, all you find are thoughts and impulses going back and forth – first, the urge to turn the television off and the arguments for that, then the urge to leave it on longer and the arguments for that. Back and forth these thoughts and impulses go in succession, and in each moment, whichever impulse is stronger wins out. So you leave the television on until the impulse to turn it off is stronger than the impulse to leave it on, and then your finger pushes the "off" button. Watch and see how that happens. It may *seem* like "you" are authoring these thoughts, that "you" *chose* to push the off button and could have done otherwise. But is there anyone in control of thoughts and impulses? Can you control your next thought? Your next impulse? If it *seems* that you can, where does this ability come from? From where *exactly* does that action of pushing the off button actually emerge? Can you find the origin of the impulse and the thought and the movement? Don't *think* about these questions, but watch closely *as it is happening.*

You "choose" to ask a question or you "choose" to remain silent. Look carefully and *see* how this "choice" arises. Or watch it in big choices like whether to take a job or buy a house or get married. Really pay very close, very careful attention to how this all unfolds. How does choosing and deciding happen? How do actions actually get initiated? From where do they emerge? Again, I'm not suggesting you *think* about this. I'm suggesting you actually *watch*, with awareness, and really *see* how it is.

[Joan takes a sip of water] A conceptualization of what just occurred would be: "I took a drink of water." That thought makes it *seem* like there's an "I" doing the drinking. But what *actually* occurred right there? How exactly did it happen? In one sense, we could trace that action back to the big bang! How this arm and eye and brain evolved from simpler life forms, how tap water and water glasses were invented, how I was born, how my parents and their parents and their ancestors met, how I ended up in Chicago in this room, the ten trillion conditions that made all those events possible, how this feeling of thirst arose at that moment, what forces in my nature and nurture prompted the arm to reach out rather than wait awhile longer. If I really fully give attention a simple action like this one as it happens, what do I actually find? How did this reaching out and taking a sip of water actually occur and who did it?

P: You made a choice. When you felt thirsty, you decided to take a drink.

J: Well, that's how we conceptualize it, that's how we describe it, that's what we *think* happened, but if you actually *look*, what do you find? Simply the impulse to take a drink, the arm reaching out, the hand clasping the glass, the arm bringing it up to the mouth.

I have not found any executive in there making all that happen. But we *think* there is. We *talk* as if there is. We say, "*I* made a choice." And we think, "*I* could have done the opposite." But the thought that I could have done the opposite is only a mental idea. It's not what happened. What is actually happening is how the universe in this moment actually *is*. But there's a persistent illusion that it could be different. "I could be living in San Francisco right now." As if we could somehow separate time and space and me and the rest of the universe – as if we could pull these things apart and rearrange them. That's the way we *think* – the deep-seated idea that life is a collection of separate things, a bunch of Newtonian billiard balls crashing around. But look closely and see, where are the boundaries? Could I be somewhere else right now? Is that really true?

P: How about responsibility for your actions?

J: There really isn't any. We have the *idea* that Hitler shouldn't have done what he did, and could have done otherwise, and if *I* were in his shoes *I* certainly wouldn't have done that. But if you were in his shoes, meaning if you had the same conditioning, the same genetics, the same neurochemistry, the same nature and nurture, the same programming, the same childhood, the same everything, then you would be Hitler and you would have done exactly what he did. That's the illusion again – that there's a "me" here who could have been somebody else and then would have done *that* life a lot differently.

When we see that there is nobody at the helm and no choice, that doesn't mean we feel fine about what Hitler did, or that we wouldn't try to stop someone like Hitler. That, too, simply *happens* (or not).

But if you really look, you don't find anybody steering any of these apparent ships. And actually, if you *really* look, you won't find any "ships" either (any "people" in the way we *think* of them as solid, separate, independent, persisting objects). Ships and people and all other apparent things, including thoughts and feelings, all turn out to be nothing but flux and change, inseparable from everything else. The dividing lines are purely conceptual. It's all one undivided functioning happening by itself.

These words – they're coming out. I'm hearing them for the first time, too. Even if it were a speech that I had planned and written out last night, that planning and writing last night would have simply *emerged*. From where? We could trace it back to my educational background, my hormone balance, my neurochemistry, my genetics, and ultimately, to the entire universe, because it's all one inseparable dynamic whole. There are no separate pieces. "You" and "me" are conceptual illusions.

How can an illusion or a concept have responsibility for its actions? When you *see* this, when it's really seen, you may still put the child molester in jail to keep them out of circulation and away from children, but you no longer *blame* them and *hate* them for what they did. Or if you happen to *be* the unlucky child molester, you may feel deep regret, remorse and sorrow over your actions, but if you really *see* that you had no choice, that you could not have done otherwise in that moment, then you don't feel the guilt and self-blame that comes with thinking you "could" and "should" have behaved differently. With this understanding, guilt, blame, shame, vengeance and hatred dissolve. It doesn't mean you don't try to overcome or cure certain tendencies. You may try your very best to cure yourself of addictions and compulsions, to be a kinder, gentler, better person, but that trying for improvement also happens by itself and whether it fails or succeeds is never in your hands.

But again, the most interesting thing is not to consider this as a philosophical idea but to really watch as choices and decisions unfold, because that's when it becomes clear, if you pay attention to actual direct experience *as it happens*. It takes a careful, subtle kind of attention. You have to *see* the difference between *perceiving* and *conceptualizing* what is being perceived. And then it becomes very clear that "choice" is a conceptualization, a description. It's a way in which we *think about* and *describe* something, but you really can't put the actuality itself into words. The word "water" is not water!

So we can say "there is no choice," or "there is choice," and these are both abstract descriptions, and neither version is quite right. You can't really replicate the actuality of life in words. If you say there is no choice, that doesn't entirely capture the reality either, because *experientially*, I can *seemingly* raise my hand at will [Joan raises her hand]. We can't deny that experience. But how exactly does that happen? From where did the impulse and the ability to do that come? How exactly does this raising up of the arm occur? I really have no idea how "I" do this. Is this a choice? Is there a "me" lifting "my" arm?

The *idea* of not having free will is disturbing to the mind because, as you say, we *think* that would mean no one is responsible for anything, and if somebody decides to go out and murder people, they would have no choice. Well, actually they don't. Who would do that if they really had a choice?

P: It's a compulsion.

J: Yes. See, the illusion is that if we don't believe in free will, that means there will be no constraints and more people will be committing crimes. We *think* that without free will, life will be meaningless and everyone will become completely irresponsible. This misunderstanding is rooted in still believing that there is *someone* who lacks free will. But seeing through the illusion of an autonomous self with free will doesn't make life any less meaningful, nor does it make you any more likely to murder people. I doubt that there is any way that you could go out and murder ten people this morning. Your conditioning, your genetics, your nature and nurture would not allow you to do that. The very idea of it would be totally abhorrent to you.

P: But there are people who do that. They must be disturbed.

J: Yes, one doesn't tend to do something like that from a state of happiness, clarity, and peace.

P: Some sages distinguish between actions that cause karma and those that were just called up in the moment. Do you have any thoughts on that?

J: That word "karma" gets used in many different ways, but I'd say that everything causes and effects everything because it is all one seamless unicity. There is no such thing as an action that causes only good, or an action that causes only bad.

Cause and effect is only a conceptual description of life – it has a relative truth to it, but not an absolute truth. Cause and effect implies separation, and in the absolute sense, there is no separation. So relatively speaking, we can say that a gunshot to the brain causes death, and it is functionally useful to know that, but in the absolute sense, you can't divide it up that way.

We can make a relative distinction between action that comes out of confused thinking and action that comes out of clear seeing and open awareness. We could say that Ramana Maharshi's actions come out of, and in turn create, a very different space and energy from Adolf Hitler's actions.

But to be aware that these are all *relative* distinctions, because to imagine that Ramana and Hitler are two separate, discrete, independent beings, rather than indivisible aspects or activities of One Reality, is a false way of thinking. Hitler and Ramana are like two sides of a single coin. Where does the front turn into the back? You'll never locate the place because there isn't one. And yet, relatively speaking, we can discern the difference between heads and tails. Our mistake is that we think the head is actually *separate* from the tail, and then we imagine that we can have one without the other, or that the head caused the tail, or whatever other nonsense we posit. So did Hitler's confused thinking *cause* the holocaust, or did those two things (confused thinking and the holocaust) arise together?

Conceptual divisions are useful and necessary for how we

function. They may be relatively more or less accurate. But our delusion is to mistake these conceptual divisions for actual reality, for absolute truth, and then to identify ourselves with the little imaginary piece in the board game and think, "I'm Miss Scarlet and I have free choice to decide whether I'm going to behave like Ramana or like Hitler." Is it true?

P: It's all happening by itself.

J: Yes, and from the perspective of Miss Scarlet, everything we're talking about sounds very frightening. Death, no free will, no one at the helm! Oh my God! But as unicity, why would you worry about anything? It would be as ridiculous as worrying right now because I'm not in control of the functioning of my spleen, or being grief-stricken because one of my skin cells just died, or terrified because one of my eye lashes might fall out.

P: On the surface, this understanding looks like it's a lack of caring or a lack of responsibility.

J: Actually, I would say this understanding is total compassion, unconditional love, absolute acceptance of what is, as it is (including the desire to change it and the action of doing so). Imagine a world without blame and guilt and vengeance, where we realize that everyone is an aspect of ourselves, where we see that there is only unicity. Would we fight wars and put each other in concentration camps and torture and shame each other? "Responsibility" and "caring" are interesting words. "Responsibility" is the ability to respond. Do our responses and our abilities come from the phantom executive, the ghost in the machine – or do they come from the Totality? Do we as individuals choose what we care about? Or does what we care about and what we want come out of the whole universe? Could this moment be any different from exactly how it is?

Right now, as thoughts may be popping up – are you choosing or authoring those thoughts? Or do they show up unbidden? And whether your attention suddenly goes to a memory that pops up, or to a sound in the street, or to a thought about another participant here – are you in control of that movement of attention? It may *seem* like you are if a thought arises such as, "I must stop daydreaming and pay attention to the discussion again." That thought suggests there is a "you" who can direct your attention. But did you choose to think that thought at that moment? Hadn't the waking up from the daydream already happened spontaneously before that thought arose? And can you choose the action that will come next after that thought? If your attention really *does* return to the discussion, then it may *seem* as if "you" have successfully controlled your mind. But it's an illusion. Don't take my word for this. Check it out.

P: What about compassion?

Another P: Words like empathy and compassion all have a dualistic flavor to me, as if I am in some kind of superior position doing something for you.

J: That's what I associate with the word "pity" – that sort of oozing, paternalistic, pseudo-compassion that people sometimes cultivate in spiritual circles – the kind that feels solicitous and self-serving. True compassion sees wholeness, not lack. It sees perfection, not imperfection. It isn't about feeling superior. It isn't patronizing. It's the recognition of not being separate. True compassion takes care of another in the same way one would take care of oneself.

P: It seems like we were sold a bill of goods about compassion in Buddhism –

J: Yes, where we were trying to *cultivate* that, then it was just a big ego trip wearing spiritual clothing.

P: There could be so much hypocrisy about that, and internal conflict, and shame, as in, "I am not feeling compassionate now, so that says something bad about me..."

J: Whenever we get into believing that there's a spiritually correct way to be responding to any of life's events – that's absurd. The mind can get caught up in wondering, How would Ramana have responded? What would Jesus do? As if we could find the right response "out there" and then imitate it. But maybe just to see what response *is* occurring, right here, right now, and to explore, was there any choice? Could it have been otherwise?

In seeing that this phantom chooser cannot be found, what happens to all the anxiety we have about doing the right thing and making our lives work? What happens to our judgments of the world and how the others should be? What happens to our understanding of George Bush or Adolph Hitler or fundamentalist Christians or child molesters or serial killers? Maybe that clear seeing *is* true compassion.

Beyond the Conceptual Divide

I talk a lot about how there's no choice or no one to make a choice. And I encourage people to really investigate the making of choices and decisions to discover firsthand how it actually happens, to see if there's someone doing it and if the decisive moment can actually be found. But if we turn our findings into a conceptual *idea* or *belief* that there's no choice, that's not really quite true either. Because there certainly *seems* to be an undeniable ability *right here* to open and close my hand or to put my attention on my big toe. If we look closely, we see that the impulse and the "decision" to do this and the execution of it are all the result of infinite causes and conditions. But still, there is a felt-sense that there is an ability or a power *right here* to open and close my hand. In saying there is no free will or no self, we are trying to put into words something that is actually impossible to capture with any combination of words or any conceptual abstraction. If you merely adopt the *idea* that there's no choice or no self or nothing to do, that *belief* can mix you up and be a means whereby you foolishly disempower yourself. Of course, "you" are not doing any of that either — that, too, is all happening choicelessly, but so are these words.

There are two very different boat stories floating around as allegories of our human situation. One version compares life to an amusement park ride over which the rider has no control. Advaita teacher Wayne Liquorman has the most developed rendition of this one that I've come across. In his story, it's the motorboat ride at Disneyland. You get into a boat with four other people, each of you has a steering wheel, and you get to pretend that you are steering this boat through a watercourse. In his story, you actually *believe* you are steering the boat. Of course the boat doesn't always go the same way that you turn the wheel, so then you conclude that you must be a bad boat driver, and you take a boat driving seminar to improve your skills. You get back in the boat and are momentarily pleased by the results of the seminar, but before long you are again disappointed. You turn left and the boat goes right. So you take more seminars and more boat rides, and the story goes on and on at great length, until finally Wayne concludes by saying, "This whole time, it never once occurs to you that *your wheel is not connected!*" Free will is an illusion.

The other boat story is from Katagiri Roshi, a contemporary Zen teacher. He is responding to a hippy back in the Sixties whom he has met on a streetcar. Katagiri asks the hippy where he is going, and the hippy says, "I don't know. Ask the streetcar." Katagiri calls this a big misunderstanding. He goes on to say that if you're in a boat just drifting along, depending on the boat to do everything, not knowing where you're headed, then you're "completely confused." You've forgotten that *you* have to pick up the oars and row the boat. Of course, his boat isn't a ride at Disneyland.

Both stories aim to reveal a certain aspect of how reality is. Wayne's story points to the fact that there is no "me" at the helm – no boat driver, no ghost in the machine, no executive self. Katagiri's story points to the fact that totality functions through all of us and through our ability to act. This ability is never really "our" ability, since the separate owner / author is only a mirage, and yet in another sense, it *is* our ability, because "I" and "totality" are not two. The illusory self is not calling the shots because the illusory self does not exist, but what I truly am is not the illusory self. If we drop the oars because we've mistakenly adopted Wayne's story as a *belief* or a *prescription* for how to behave, rather than understanding it as one possible *description* of reality, then we've missed something very obvious. We've left ourselves out of totality. We've overlooked this ability right here to pick up the oars and start rowing. On the other hand, if we imagine that "I" exist as a separate entity driving "my" boat with free will through an "outside world" that is independent of me, then we will be endlessly subject to frustration, disappointment, guilt and blame as our lives keep turning out differently from what the thinking mind imagined, intended and planned.

Each of these boat stories is a useful and accurate map, but any map is always only an abstract representation. Both of these stories can open our eyes, each in a different way. But once the truth to which each is pointing has been seen, we must discard the pointer. Otherwise, if we cling to the map and try to set up camp in that symbolic world, we end up very confused, arguing over whose vision is correct – the left eye or the right eye.

Some teachings emphasize picking up the oars and rowing; other teachings emphasize the absence of the boat driver. Some teachings emphasize the absolute truth that there is *only* unicity; other teachings deal with the relative or practical problem that human beings often *feel* separate from unicity. Some teachings seem to take the world very seriously; other teachings compare the whole show to an amusement park ride, a movie, or a dream. But the truth isn't in any map. Truth is the territory itself.

Although unicity is all there is, as human beings, we often feel separate. We get tangled up in mental confusion. We stumble and fall in ways no other animal ever would. Many spiritual teachings are about untangling this confusion. I studied martial arts years ago, and when I was really "in the zone," there was a complete letting go, a kind of absolute abandon. There was no holding back, no hesitation, no thought. It was as if I had, by an act of grace, surrendered to a power far greater than the controlling mind and merged completely with the flow of energy that is the whole cosmos. I was willing to die. There was no fear of getting hurt. In one sense, it seemed as if I were completely out of control, and yet in another sense, I was perfectly in control. It was quite a powerful experience whenever it happened. It didn't seem to come about through gritting my teeth and *trying* really hard. It was almost the exact opposite of that. It was effortless.

When you watch great athletes performing incredible feats, they make it look easy. They often seem to be floating or gliding through the air. But of course, there is enormous concentration, training, disciple, effort and skill that goes into being able to let go that way in sports, martial arts, music, painting or any other discipline. Being in the zone requires both complete concentration and complete surrender. In Zen they call it No Mind. If you worry about falling or getting hit, you probably *will* fall or get hit. Because those thoughts create a sense of separation. They *seemingly* take you out of the seamless flow. There is a moment of hesitation, a split second of holding back and worrying about death or failure, a moment of doubt, of feeling separate and vulnerable, and in that split second, you seemingly lose the flow. You stumble and fall. Being in the zone is being completely one with the flow with no thought at all for success or failure or even survival.

That flow is what you actually *are*, of course, and even when you hesitate or fall, you are nothing *but* flow, inseparable from everything else – so in the absolute sense, there is no way to lose the flow or to fail. Seamless flow is the ever-present reality, what you can't *not* be. Even hesitating or falling is nothing but flowing. But at the same time, for a human being with self-reflexive thought, *realizing* or *actualizing* or *embodying* this ever-present reality and no longer *feeling* separate from it often takes years of training. No wild animal has this problem. It comes along with our complex brain.

Part of why this all gets so confusing is that we mix up the relative and the absolute. If everything is unicity and it's all perfect and there's no choice, then why do we bother with meditation or martial arts training or coming to meetings like this or reading books about nonduality? We could say that choice and choicelessness each refer to different levels of reality. In the absolute sense, there is no choice, no chooser, and no such thing as success or failure. But relatively speaking, within the movie of waking life, if you are teaching karate, for example, and you are training a student to punch through a board, you're not going to tell the student she has no choice. It would be absurd if you told her, "There's nothing you can do to learn karate, there's no you, there's no choice, and either the punch will go through the board or it won't, but there's nothing you or I can do about it because we do not exist." As a teacher, you're going to show the student, to the best of your ability, how to make a fist, how to move her arm and her whole body in the most effective way, how to visualize the punch going through the board. You are going to try your best to help the student refine her control and improve her ability to make the choices that add up to punching effectively, and you're going to encourage her and tell her she can do it.

Should the student then try to punch through the board and fail, if you truly understand the nature of reality, you are not going to shame or blame the student (or yourself) for her failure, because you understand that infinite causes and conditions create each moment just as it is. You won't imagine that "you" or "your student" can control the universe. You'll know that whatever happens in this moment is the only possible, and that ultimately, it's okay. But you won't *think* that this absolute understanding means that you can't or shouldn't offer advice. That is your function as a teacher, and that functioning emerges from the same unicity that is keeping the planets in their orbits and growing the trees. As a teacher, you are (hopefully) going to do your best to show the student how to correct her mistakes and improve her punch. We could say that you are functioning from both levels simultaneously — you're helping the student to develop her skills, to refine her power of choice, while at the same time being aware that both your teaching and the student's ability to learn come out of the whole universe and are actually choiceless and could not be otherwise.

The apparent problem (or conflict) between relative and absolute only arises when we try to conceptualize and map this all out after the fact. Then we seem to have two conflicting models and it feels like we must "choose" between them. But actuality itself is simple and obvious! Opening and closing your hand is not confusing.

We might say that one view (no self, no choice) is a *description* of how reality is, and the other view (free will, the power to make choices) is more like a *prescription* for functioning within the play. Everything *is*, in fact, choiceless and without self — one undivided whole that could not be other than it is. But at a relative level of reality, within the play of life, prescriptions and intentions arise (choicelessly) for how to improve and enhance functioning, and these prescriptions must by their very nature *act as if* there is choice: "Look both ways before you cross the street," or "Eat more green vegetables," or "Do your homework," or "Question your thoughts," or "Bring your attention to the present moment," or "Visualize your punch going through the board." Such prescriptions arise choicelessly and whether they work or not is equally choiceless.

But to think that "you" *should* (or could) avoid prescriptions or apparent choices because you *believe* that "there is no one to choose," is to confuse relative and absolute. It is to confuse description and prescription. It is to imagine yourself separate from the totality. It is to not notice that the mind is imagining a separate "you" *in* the picture trying to leave yourself out of the picture, trying to do the spiritually correct thing! Such confusion comes from making "no choice" into a belief. As Wayne Liquorman once put it, "There is a great difference in having the belief that you are not the author and not having the belief that you are the author." The latter is true freedom and the former is simply a belief. Belief is always shadowed by doubt.

To say that meditation is dualistic because there is no one to meditate is like saying that football training is dualistic because there is no one to play the game, or cooking lessons are dualistic because there is no one to cook. In fact, you *can* learn to be present with the bare sensory experiencing of here and now in much the same way that you can to learn to play football, or cook, or ride a bike, or speak a foreign language. And that's what intelligent meditation practice is all about – learning to "open the hand of thought" and reside in simple being, learning to bringing attention back to the bare actuality of the present moment, learning to see thoughts *as* thoughts and to discern the difference between thinking and perceiving, becoming aware of awareness, and ultimately, seeing that all division is imaginary, that there is only one seamless whole. This seeing is the end of suffering. It is liberation.

If you turn your attention around and look for the one who is supposedly *doing* this meditating (or bike riding, or learning, or speaking, or choosing, or deciding), you find nothing at all (apart from everything). The "me" that thought and language tell us is doing all this cannot to be found in actual direct experience. True meditation is about discovering this directly – investigating (with awareness) and seeing through the illusion of separation and encapsulation.

Is there free choice or not? Is spiritual practice necessary and essential or does it merely reinforce the central illusion? Does waking up take effort or is it effortless? Is nonduality about "being here now," or is it about "all there is, is being"? Which way of expressing things is truly nondual? These questions all seem to assume that the answer must be either/or, which is already a dualistic way of thinking. Life itself is simple.

The survival mind always wants to get control, locate itself, sort things out, develop a strategy. This is natural, and in practical situations, it makes perfect sense and is vital to our survival as an organism. But in many situations, this mind activity only serves to obfuscate matters. The mind tries desperately to figure out which map or model of reality is most real. We take a position, identify with it, and then defend it to the death. If we pick up a different map, we can be very quick to dismiss it without ever really seeing it. Can we listen without instantly making judgments or coming to preconceived conclusions? Can we remain open to the possibility of seeing things differently, of being surprised, of changing our mind even?

We could say there is choice, but not in the way we usually imagine it. Or we could say there is no choice, only the appearance of choice. But finally, we have to *see* that the reality of how life functions doesn't fit neatly into either concept ("there is free choice" or "there isn't free choice"). On the conceptual level, this seems paradoxical and confusing. But reality itself is obvious. Opening and closing your hand is obvious. There's nothing philosophically confusing about it. Only when you begin to *think* about these activities and whether or not "you" can freely choose to do them, does it all suddenly seem to get very confusing. We can describe these actions as choiceless or as a free choice, and neither description is quite right nor entirely wrong.

If you insist that you can freely choose to open and close your hand, then where does the impulse and the ability and the intention and the millions of nerves and muscles involved all come from? And what exactly are "you"? How exactly do "you" do these things or "decide" to do them? If you look deeply into these questions, you see that the whole universe is doing everything. There is no separate "you" calling the shots. But if you insist you *can't* freely choose to open and close your hand, and you wait around for "grace" to open or close it for you, then you will have a long wait. You will be foolishly disempowering yourself from doing something that you (as life itself) obviously *can* do (unless you can't!). The apparent conundrum is only in the words, the conceptualization, not in the actuality.

Now, of course, enlightenment is not exactly the same thing as learning how to punch through a board. Because in the case of enlightenment, the board we are trying to punch through is actually imaginary, as is the one who is punching. Enlightenment is the recognition that Here/Now is ever-present *in spite* of what happens in the appearance and not *because* of what happens. To offer a solution to an imaginary problem would only seem to confirm the imagined reality of the problem. So if someone asks me to help them get enlightened, I may point out that there is no one to get enlightened and that this problem is imaginary.

But at the same time, enlightenment doesn't mix up relative and absolute. If someone is thirsty and asks me for a glass of water, I'm not going to tell them there's no self, I'm going to get them a glass of water. And if someone comes to my meetings and hears over and over that there is no self and no problem but still looks totally bewildered and miserable, then I might very well suggest that they take time to sit quietly and explore the present moment, or that they investigate the unfolding of choices and decisions and see if any executive can be found. My suggesting such possibilities is the action of the whole universe, as is the person's response, whatever it may be. Some teachers would never make such suggestions. They'd keep hammering away uncompromisingly at the absolute truth that the whole problem is imaginary and that *whatever* the universe moves you to do or not do, *unicity is all there is.* And that uncompromising message is also the action of the whole universe. Apparently, there is room here in this movie of waking life for many different ways of skinning the imaginary cat.

I'm bringing all this up today because sometimes people hear these talks about "no choice" or "nothing to do" and think it means they must stop doing anything that might seem like an intentional activity, that they have to be totally passive. People get the idea that they "shouldn't" meditate or that anyone who suggests meditation is deluded. One fellow I talked to even thought these nondual teachings meant he didn't need to wear a condom anymore when he had sex even though he was HIV-positive because nothing is really happening and everything is unicity. That is a big misunderstanding of the message. And yes, that misunderstanding is also unicity, and in that moment, it could not have been otherwise – but that doesn't mean I can't now point out the error in it. My words are also nothing but unicity. Unicity is falling into confusion, and unicity is clearing up confusion.

No verbal or conceptual formulation can ever capture reality. Do we have free will? Can I stop smoking? Is there a difference between being awake and not being awake? Is there anything to do to wake up? Is there a choice? Does it take effort? No answer quite hits the mark.

When we take words too literally, or don't understand their limitations, there is a tendency to get stuck ideologically on one side or the other of an imaginary conceptual divide, defending either the "no choice" position or the "free will" position, the "train hard" position or the "nothing to do" position. But the truth is not in either position. It's in the actuality of life which cannot be boxed up in any position. And what is liberating is to *see through* any position where the mind gets stuck.

You know how I always say at the beginning of the meeting before the silence that "there's nothing to do," and to "just allow whatever is here to be as it is," and "we're not trying to get into any special state." Well, I remember once somebody said to me, "This is so wonderful to be somewhere where I can just totally daydream and fantasize." And I thought, hmmmm – it is so hard to communicate what I actually mean! Because of course, the person was right in one sense. I'm *not* urging people to do the kind of deliberate *practice* that we are often instructed to do in formal schools of meditation, where we are told to willfully stop any kind of thought activity as soon as we notice it and immediately bring our attention back to the breath and keep it there. I'm not saying, "Don't daydream," or, "It's bad to daydream," or, "We're trying really hard not to daydream," and in the absolute sense, daydreaming is nothing other than unicity appearing as a daydream. But in fact, I'm not actually encouraging mindless indulgence in daydreaming and fantasizing either. I'm really talking about a kind of alert but relaxed listening presence with sensitivity, openness and that same quality of letting go and abandon that athletes have when they are in the zone – an effortless energy, a relaxed precision, a total surrender that is at once concentrated and boundless.

Zen Master Dogen's burning question as a young monk was why we needed to practice – if everything already has, or *is*, Buddha Nature, then why do we need to practice? After many years, his discovery was that practice is not something we do in order to *attain* enlightenment, but rather, practice *is* enlightenment – practice is the *expression* of enlightenment. He has this great little story at the end of Genjo Koan, one of his most beautiful works. In the story, this Zen master is fanning himself, and a student walks up to the master and asks, "If the nature of wind is permanent and there is no place it does not reach, then why are you fanning yourself?" In other words, if "this is it," then why are you making some effort or doing some practice? And the master says to the student, "Although you understand that the nature of wind is permanent, you do not understand the meaning of its reaching everywhere." So the monk asks, "What is the meaning of its reaching everywhere?" And the master just keeps fanning himself. In other words, our activity, our apparent choosing and correcting and refining and practicing and doing, is all the expression of the One Reality. The student was leaving himself out of the picture.

By telling this story, I'm not trying to suggest that you should take up formal Zen meditation practice of the kind Dogen was engaged in. I'm simply pointing out a possible misunderstanding. I'm pointing out that however we try to put reality into language, no words can ever really capture the actuality. The actuality always slips through the net of words – reality itself is too delicate, too slippery, too ephemeral, too boundless, too empty, too immense, too non-existent for words.

So all of these ways of trying to put nondual reality into language are to some degree inaccurate and they can all be taken by the mind and misunderstood.

Brrrhuummmm [Joan imitates sound of car going by] – so simple. No subject, no object, no problem, no mystery to solve, no dilemma to untangle. Just the simplicity of what is, as it is. *Brrrhuummmm*. And then the mind pops up and begins trying to sort it all out and make sense of it, and next thing you know, the mind is racing frantically on its little treadmill, chasing after the imaginary carrot. The solution is to stop running. Stop running away from the messy stuff, stop running toward the carrot, stop trying to figure it all out – just *stop*.

And if the mind pops up and says, "how do I do that?" or "who can stop if there's no self?" – just stop. *See* that this is the mind leading you in circles. Of course, I'm not saying that thinking is some alien force and that our goal is to totally stop thinking and always be in some state of non-conceptual, thoughtless awareness. That would be impossible, and it's another false dualistic divide. Thinking is wonderful! But when thinking is misused, when concept or imagination is mistaken for actuality, then we suffer. And in this sense, we can say that thinking, or more accurately, the *misuse* of thinking, is the cause of all our suffering. Waking up is to see thinking *as* thinking, to *see* how conceptualizing confuses us, how it creates imaginary conflicts and false problems.

To *think* about all of this is maybe not so liberating. It may produce a big headache. But to *see* this conceptual dividing up of life and this mental spinning as it is happening, to discern the difference between functional thought and useless thought, and between thinking and being aware, this is liberating.

Nonduality doesn't mean you ignore or deny relative reality. But it is such a delicate balance to express this. Even clinging to oneness is dualistic! That's why Zen prefers to say, "Not one, not two."

So, when suffering or confusion arises, is there anything we can do? Stop, look, and listen. Let go of everything you are trying to remember and practice and maintain. Let go of trying to figure it all out. Completely give up. See what remains, and see if that is a problem.

The thinking mind makes this all seem very complex and difficult, but the actuality is extremely simple and obvious. The mind says,
"I don't get it," or, "This doesn't look like unicity to me," or "There's
got to be more to final enlightenment than hearing traffic sounds!"
These are all thoughts. Waking up isn't about vanquishing thoughts or
eliminating them, it's about *seeing* them as what they are and not being
taken in by them.

The more we try to fix the imaginary problem of being unenlightened, the worse it seems to get, and the more convinced we are that
there really *is* a problem. Waking up is about relaxing, opening, sur-
rendering, letting go – *realizing* that there is nothing here to fail or to
die. How do you *do* that? It's like falling asleep. You can't *do* it. You can
only allow it to happen. You can only *see* the ways you are holding on.
The seeing has its own action.

And even if there is holding on, tensing up or thinking obsessively,
there is no "you" doing any it, and all of it is nothing but sensations
appearing Here/Now, a scene in a dream, and there is truly no way out
of unicity. Whatever can shift is part of the dream, and what you truly
are is ever-present and needs no fixing. But just be aware of how the
mind spins that.

P: It's only when the story of me shows up that there are even questions
about things like choice and intention. Without the me or the I, there
isn't even a question.

J: Yes, exactly, these questions like choice and intention only come up
in relation to the bodymind or the person. Without that, these questions
don't make any sense. They don't exist. Without that identification as
"me," *most* of our questions cease to exist. The confusion is *always* in
the conceptual overlay, never in reality itself.

When I was studying Feldenkrais, this awareness through movement somatic bodywork, we would spend a lot of time down on the
floor doing these very subtle movements. Many of the movements were
designed to recreate some of the process we go through as an infant

learning to do very basic things such as rolling over and sitting up. And as I was doing it, it was really interesting to contemplate what it must be like, as a baby, to begin to discover that I can move my arm. Or that I can reach for something and bring it to my mouth. Or that I can turn myself over. Because of course a baby isn't conceptualizing these activities in that way – it has no language yet. The baby isn't saying to itself, "I can turn myself over now." The whole event is one whole happening.

P: It's like the baby is drawn to motion or sound somewhere else in the room maybe, and it turns to it, and it discovers almost accidentally in the process that it can turn over.

J: Yes. It's very much one flowing wholeness undivided by thoughts. So as a baby, there is this discovery that I can pick up an object and bring it to my mouth, but without conceptualizing it that way. It is simply pure movement. And then as thinking and languaging comes into the picture more and more, we begin hearing a description of that action: "You are picking up the glass and taking a drink." And on top of that, we begin getting this conditioning where the parents are saying, "Good girl. You picked up the glass. You did that." Or, "Bad girl! You spilled the water." And this conditioning gets expanded upon more and more. We are told, overtly or covertly: "You are Joan and you have to do something meaningful and important with your life." So the mind starts formulating this whole mental image and story of who "I" am, based on the assumption that I am this bodymind, this person, and that I have all these traits that others tell me I have or that I observe in myself on some occasion and then turn into what I think of as enduring characteristics: I'm smart, I'm stupid, I'm a girl, I'm a boy, and so on. That simple, direct, undivided experience of pure movement gets overlaid with this whole, very complex story: "If I don't win the gold medal or publish a book or get dharma transmission, that means I've failed in life and I'm a worthless human being," and all that kind of stuff. Next thing you know, we are smoking cigarettes and seeking enlightenment, all in an effort to regain what has never really been lost.

P: What's wrong with daydreaming?

J: Nothing is "wrong" with it. But my experience is that if I daydream a lot of the time, then I don't feel very well. I don't function as well. There's no rule for how much of anything is too much. A sensitivity can develop to how things make you feel, what they do to the bodymind, how they effect you. Everyone's threshold is different, and our own threshold one day may be different from our threshold on another day, so it requires a sensitivity to here and now, not some conclusive or formulaic idea.

You have to see for yourself how it is right now. How do I feel after this hour of daydreaming or after this beer? Or this dish of ice cream? What compels me to turn on the television or light a cigarette at this moment? Am I avoiding something? Seeking something? This isn't about right or wrong, good and bad, should or should not. It's not some moral injunction about good behavior. It's about developing a sensitivity to what brings happiness and what brings suffering. And one of the things that brings suffering is taking all of this too seriously, making it into a big project that "I" need to do correctly. So that's not the kind of sensitivity and curiosity I'm talking about at all. I'm talking about simple, relaxed, nonjudgmental awareness with a sense of humor.

I used to spend an enormous amount of time, maybe 90% of my time, thinking about the future. This was years ago. And I would literally, all the time, be thinking about what I was going to do with my life. Where I would move next, what my next career path would be, what I would do tomorrow, what I would do in the next moment, and so on. I'd be on retreat making plans in my head about coming to the next retreat! There was a certain pleasure in it, the kind of pleasure that we get from an addiction, but like any addiction, it wasn't really bringing me true happiness. It was a form of suffering. It was all about, "This is not okay right now, this is not enough, but some day I'm going to have a perfect life." Except of course, the future never arrives. It is like the mirage lake in the desert sands. The closer we come to it, the farther away it recedes. And so if our life is nothing but daydreaming, thinking about my past or my future or where I'd rather be, that is not a satisfying life. In fact, you actually miss your real life!

Of course, in the absolute sense, you can't miss it. There is no "you" apart from it, and it is as it is, and could not be otherwise. It is perfect and complete just as it is, however it is. But when you are lost in fuzzy thoughts about the past or the future, you don't see the beauty in front of your eyes. You dream of a future that never arrives, or you go over and over a past that is long gone, and you miss the actuality and the perfection of life, because you are overlooking or avoiding the only place where life really *is* – here and now. Here and now *seems* unsatisfying or boring or meaningless only because you are lost in *ideas* about how it is, and how it should or could be better, or how you screwed it up, or whatever your particular habit of thought happens to be. But you aren't awake to how it actually *is*.

Again, I'm not saying that one "shouldn't" think such thoughts, or that such thinking is "wrong" or "bad." It happens! And likewise, activities such as daydreaming and drinking beer and watching television happen, and all of those activities can be harmless and enjoyable if we do them in moderation. And even if we do them in excess every now and then, that's no big deal. But if they become addictive or compulsive in an on-going way and we find that our whole life is nothing but drinking beer and daydreaming and watching television all the time, in my experience, that's not going to be very satisfying. And neither is telling ourselves that "it's all unicity."

Finally, after many bottles of beer and many trips to India, we may discover that what makes for a truly satisfying life is being awake in this moment. Being fully alive here and now. From that, everything else follows naturally. The right diet, the right activity, the right companionship, the right location. And even if circumstances force you to eat the wrong diet and be in terrible surroundings, being awake is the best way not to suffer.

Sometimes pain killers and distraction can temporarily relieve pain – if you have a toothache, taking Tylenol and watching an entertaining television program might temporarily relieve the pain, although you might eventually need to visit the dentist and have a root canal. And if you are depressed, drinking a beer and watching television might bring temporary relief, but you may discover that this leaves you even more depressed the next day. Sometimes we *do* choose the escape or the distraction, and that's okay, but the more sensitive we become to how that actually affects us, the wiser our actions become and the less suffering we create for ourselves and others.

With drinking, for example, I've noticed that when I have more than one glass of wine, I usually don't really like how I feel after the second glass. It's not that having a second glass is "bad" or "wrong," it's simply *noticing* that, *for me,* it doesn't actually feel good. For someone else, it might be different. Sometimes I seem compelled to have a second glass, but if I pay attention, I notice that I don't actually like the effects.

And we're talking relative reality here. From the perspective of unicity, there are no mistakes. But realizing that doesn't mean we can't make relative observations and adjustments of this kind. Of course, "we" don't make them. They happen.

The way my obsession with thinking about the future fell away was through paying attention and becoming more and more aware of this habitual pattern and how it actually felt to be doing it. I'd probably been doing it for years without even being aware of it, until one day, on an all-day sitting at the Zen Center, I suddenly *saw* it happening. It was like a light had been turned on in a previously darkened room. And once that light had been turned on, this habit of thinking about the future started to be seen more and more. I was *seeing* what was alluring about this habit, and I was also noticing how unsatisfying it was. I began to *see* that it was a form of suffering very much like any other kind of addiction. It didn't fall away forever in one instant never to return ever again, but every time it happened, it was seen more and more clearly. And then at some point, about a decade later, I noticed that it wasn't happening any more. Not that I never think about the future at all, but I almost never sit around and dream and obsess about it in the way that I did back then. So that's an example from my own life of the kind of change that happens through simply paying atten-tion and being aware. And I wasn't *doing* this paying attention in some heavy-handed, goal-driven way. It was simply happening by itself very naturally.

If I had "decided" that day at the Zen Center that I was never going to think about the future ever again for the rest of my life, that would have been just another thought about the future! It wouldn't have worked. But what happened instead was simply a *noticing* of this habit. And gradually, that seeing, that simple awareness dissolved the habit – it fell away. It didn't fall away on demand, on my timetable, and it didn't end permanently in some dramatic fireworks moment, but rather, it was eroded gradually, slowly, over time. And I think that's how change usually happens. In one sense, it only happens now, and in another sense, it seems to unfold gradually over time.

I've noticed that other modifications happen in that same way, with diet or how much I'm drinking or any number of things. Just by being aware and paying attention and noticing, "Oh, this is not really very satisfying," something shifts. Because the body has its own intelligence. Life has an intelligence, and awareness *is* that intelligence.

Any *idea* we adopt about what is satisfying or healthy is only an idea, and if we cling to it, it becomes a hindrance because things are always changing. I went on the macrobiotic diet once, and I felt great for a long time. And then after several years, I began longing for things like meat and cheese and fruit that are not part of this diet, and I was literally gagging when I was trying to eat the macrobiotic food, but I kept eating it because I had a *belief* that, "This is the right diet. This is good for me." I couldn't *see* that things had changed. When I finally let that macrobiotic diet go and started eating meat again, I felt much better. But that doesn't mean meat is "the answer" any more than macrobiotics was the answer. The answer is only the answer in this moment. The next moment is new. Everything changes. The tendency of the mind is always to fixate. And that brings suffering because things are always changing.

When we are fully present here and now, all the other questions about secondary matters answer themselves. But the thinking mind doesn't trust that – it wants to think and figure it all out – but when you finally let that thinking go, then the answer comes. Great scientists like

Einstein have often described their breakthroughs in exactly that way. And I've had that experience countless times – I'm sure everyone has. The thinking mind is spinning around and around desperately trying to figure out what to do about something, and finally, in some moment of not thinking about it at all and simply being totally present, the answer comes with absolute clarity.

Confusion requires thinking. The present moment is not confusing. To become confused, you have to start trying to figure out how to solve some imaginary problem – then you get confused. For example, you've heard one teacher say that you should choose to be here now, and then another teacher says there is no free will and you can't not be here now, and you are trying to figure out which one is correct and you feel confused. You are trying to solve an imaginary problem. And the more you try to solve it, the more confusing it seems to become. But the actuality of doing whatever you are doing in this moment is not confusing in any way until you start to think about it. Picking up a glass of water is not confusing, but if I start *thinking* about who did it, and how it happened, and whether or not I have free will, and whether the glass is mind or matter, then suddenly it may seem very confusing.

A certain amount of thoughtful analysis may be functional in making a decision, but you can actually begin to feel when it ceases to be functional, when it becomes nothing more than obsessive loops repeating themselves again and again. And of course, if you try to *make* this stop, it doesn't work. Awareness is the opposite of trying to control something. Awareness allows it all to be as it is. Awareness sees and listens. Awareness sheds light. And that light, that clarity, that seeing has its own action. The attempt to assert control over the thoughts (to *make* them stop, for example) comes from the thinking mind, from conditioning. It only tightens the knot.

With my thoughts of the future and my obsession about where to live, I began to notice more and more clearly that wherever I went, Here I always am. And by Here, I don't mean Chicago or California or this living room. Chicago appears Here, California appears Here, this living room appears Here, the bodymind appears Here, all our emotions and thoughts and stories appear Here. But Here is always here. *This* is the real jewel, our true home – this Here that can never be lost. Only this placeless place, this timeless presence, can offer true happiness because it *is* happiness. There is no "me" in this placeless place of Here/Now. And whatever location appears Here – whether it is Chicago or California, India or Kalamazoo – the happiness is not in the location, it's in the presence.

That's not to say you shouldn't move. There are natural attractions that arise, and that's part of how life functions, people are attracted to different places, to different people, to different lines of work, to different interests. There's nothing wrong with being attracted to California and going there, or falling in love with a particular person and marrying them, or feeling drawn to a particular vocation and pursuing it. But if you imagine that California or your partner or your vocation will provide you with ultimate happiness, or that you have to be in California or with that person or in that vocation in order to be happy, then obviously you will suffer and that story will always end in disappointment. You'll discover that California isn't perfect. Your partner isn't perfect. Your vocation isn't perfect. Or life will take them away from you.

But in most cases, you won't figure out where to go or what to do by thinking. Clarity arises in the absence of thought. And however it happens, it's always life itself that is calling the shots. I'm speaking from a more relative perspective today – but that, too, is unicity!

P: If I choose to inquire into thoughts, I worry that I am empowering the me. I've heard Tony Parsons say that any kind of meditation or inquiry empowers the me. He says that his "me" has fallen away for good. But I still feel like an individual and I feel confused about this.

J: Notice that it's only confusing when you think about it. This is the kind of confusion I've been talking about today. I would say, *you* are not choosing to inquire, this interest is arising out of the whole universe. You did not create this interest and you cannot destroy it. And the "me" who "has a me" or "doesn't have a me" is another layer of the same mirage.

A certain functional identity as the bodymind is vital to survival. Those who lose this end up in books by Oliver Sacks and become unable to board the bus because they can literally no longer distinguish between themselves and the bus. It is a serious neurological malfunction. This functional identification with the bodymind appears when it is needed, and it isn't going to leave you permanently unless you get a brain injury or dementia or something like that. Tony Parsons turns around if you call his name. He knows whose mail to open. He can tell the difference between his wife and the sidewalk. That sense of identity is functional. But this is not the "me" that we speak of as an illusion. The "me" that causes us so much suffering is the thought-story of being "somebody" apart from everything else, somebody who is forever trying to "get somewhere" or "become somebody." That "me" is the phantom executive who seems to be thinking the thoughts and making the choices.

But there are many moments in any ordinary day when this mirage-like "me" is totally absent, when there is no sense at all of being a person – there is simply seeing, hearing, doing, with no thought of "me" in the picture. But these ordinary moments go unnoticed. And then we imagine that "no self" is some kind of exotic experience that we've never had. And the "me" wants this experience! The "me" wants to get rid of the "me" and be a successful no-self! Of course, this is just layers upon layers of the same mirage, the same thought-story – "me" trying to become a winner.

This phantom self is *never* really there. But even after that has been seen very clearly, the mirage may still appear from time to time, just as a mirage lake may still appear in the desert sands even after we know it is only a mirage. And for a moment (a second, an hour, a day, a week – it really doesn't matter – the only reality is Now), we may be fooled – the mirage may seem real. But there is no "me" being fooled – that is part of the mirage. Language keeps inserting a subject in the sentence, but it's only a figure of speech.

Believing these thoughts, believing in the mirage-self, we may experience guilt, blame, anger, and all kinds of unhappy emotions. And then at some point, the bubble of illusion pops and we wake up to the utter simplicity of seeing, hearing, doing, with no thought of "me" in the picture. This waking up is not necessarily a huge or dramatic event – it usually isn't – and it is rarely, if ever, a permanent, final, one-time happening after which the mirage never returns again. But the return of the mirage is only a problem *within* the mirage. Whether the mirage appears and fools us again only matters from the perspective of the false self who takes this happening personally and regards it as a sign of personal failure. *Awareness has no problem with anything.*

All teachers are dream teachers, including Tony (I'm sure he'd agree). Every experience is a dream experience including this meeting and this conversation. Every enlightenment is a dream enlightenment. Every delusion is a dream delusion. The whole movie of waking life is a dream-like appearance that vanishes as quickly as it appears.

Everything that appears to happen is happening spontaneously and naturally by itself. Everything is the cause and the effect of every-thing else, all of it one seamless whole. There is no "you" apart from this seamlessness who needs to acquire it. You *are* this seamlessness. This is all there is. Only when the mirage of separation and encapsula-tion is believed to be real do we *seem* to be vulnerable and endangered. But when seamlessness is realized, there is no fear and no desire, no birth and no death.

But don't imagine that there are people walking around with no fear and no desire. Within the movie of waking life, *of course* there is fear and desire! These are vital to our survival. We fear the predator and desire the next meal. It keeps us alive. *Psychological* fears and desires may fall away more and more – the desire for success, the fear of failure, the dread of death – that kind of thing. But *whatever* appears, it is only a momentary appearance. And even when we are finally devoured by death, nothing real is ever destroyed. Formlessness just continues form-ing and unforming and reforming, eating and being eaten. Predator and prey, parasite and host are one movement, one being, one dance – all of it a dream-like play. Whatever happens, nothing is really gained and nothing is really lost. But at the same time, if you're HIV-positive, put on the condom.

Words, words, words.

It's a delicate balance – trying to express the inexpressible. But *this* [Joan gestures to include everything] is not confusing or paradoxical or mysterious in any way whatsoever. Until we start thinking about it.

The Imaginary Vantage Point

In this listening presence here now, is there a me? Or is there simply the humming of the refrigerator, the whooshing of cars, sensations in the body, the breath rising and falling, coming and going – all of it one seamless whole appearance?

Where does "inside of me" turn into "outside of me"? Feel into this inquiry, actually *look* for this boundary, see if you can really *find* it. See if you can actually locate the boundary between awareness and the content of awareness. Is there really a seer and something seen, or is there simply *seeing*?

You can *think* of a boundary line – you can *imagine* one – you can *picture* the skin as the boundary between inside of you and outside of you. But where is this mental picture of the skin appearing? Inside you or outside you? With our eyes closed, we can't even find skin. We can find sensations maybe, but they don't hold still. They're not solid. You can't really find exactly where "the skin" ends and "the chair" begins. If we looked at skin through a powerful microscope, we'd see that it's porous and it's made up of cells that are dividing and dying. This so-called "skin" is a process of constant flux, exchanging things with the so-called "environment" that surrounds it. And at the subatomic level, it's mostly empty space. Not a very solid boundary!

Where does awareness begin and end? Does awareness have an age? A gender? A location? Or do all apparent locations appear *in* awareness? Does awareness have an owner? Or does any image or idea of a possible owner appear *in* awareness in the same way chairs and clouds and people appear?

What are you? Are you the image in the mirror? The character in the story? If you have a brain transplant, will you still be you? What were you five minutes *before* the moment of conception? What was your face before your parents were born? Every night in deep sleep, what happens to you? What happens to these questions and the one who cares about finding the answers? Who are you?

In deep sleep, there's no experience at all, there's no story, there isn't even that first *sense* of non-identified, impersonal awareness or presence. In deep sleep, *all* of this vanishes completely – there's *nothing* perceivable or conceivable. In death, what is it that dies? If everything totally stopped right now, totally winked out, who or what would be left to care?

We have this fear of death because we *think*, "What will happen to *me* afterwards? Where will *I* be? Will *I* be missing something? Will *I* go on to a better place?" But if everything stopped right now, who would be left to care? Who's left in deep sleep to miss the soap opera of dreaming or waking life? And in fact, who is here right now experiencing all this? Is there an experiencer?

There is an idea and maybe a mental picture that there's "me" encapsulated inside the bodymind looking out at everything else through the windows of my senses and manipulating this outside world as best I can. Relatively speaking, within the movie of waking life, this makes a certain amount of sense: "I" can apparently seek dinner outside myself and find it "over there" in the refrigerator. "I" can seemingly manipulate various ingredients and turn them into a cake. Relatively speaking, this makes sense. But can I find enlightenment or love or happiness "out there" somewhere? Can I manipulate my thoughts or my desires in the same way I can manipulate the ingredients of a cake? Or has this way of thinking that *seems* to make sense for survival tasks (like food-gathering and shelter-building) suddenly become totally incoherent when the thinking mind tries to apply it to finding happiness or freedom "out there" somewhere? And in fact, even with those survival tasks, is there actually a "me" who chooses to do them and who could have done something else instead? Or did everything in the whole universe come together at that moment as the baking of a cake or the building of a house?

Maybe if we get spiritually advanced and sophisticated enough, we think that the experiencer is "awareness" or "consciousness" or "the witness." But is there any such *thing* as "awareness" or "consciousness" or "the witness" that can be isolated out from everything else? Or is there only this indivisible seamlessness that includes sleeping and dreaming and waking up – this boundlessness being and beholding everything? Is this boundlessness actually divided up into subject and object, seer and seen? Is there any *thing* containing all the other apparent *things*? If there *were* a "thing" containing it all, that thing would have to be another relative object, like a giant container, and what would be seeing that? Does awareness have any boundaries, limits, or edges? In fact, does *any* apparent thing actually have boundaries, limits, or edges? It *seems* that way when we're talking about a pencil or a table, but if we look carefully, we discover the boundary-lines are very fuzzy and permeable, and the apparent object is actually nothing but flowing change, and it always arises together with the rest of the universe upon which it totally depends (there would be no pencil without trees and people, and no trees or people without sunshine, oxygen and water, and so on). Where are the separations? We can see, if we look, that they are only conceptual or relative, not real. There is no permanent, abiding, separately existing *thing* anywhere to be found, except conceptually, in thought. So how can "awareness" be a big container or a gigantic blank movie screen? These are analogies, and they may work well enough as helpful pointers, but ultimately, they fall short. Awareness is not an object. And actually, *nothing* is really an object in the way we imagine.

Is there *someone* who gets born, who lives for eighty years and then dies, *someone* who goes on to another incarnation or an afterlife in heaven, or who perhaps totally escapes from the wheel, whatever *that* might be like? Is there *someone* going through all this or is there only thoroughgoing flux?

When we really see that there is only flux and change, then we see that nothing separate and enduring is ever formed in the first place to *be* impermanent or to die. Death is an illusion, as is birth – a notional boundary conceptually dividing up what is actually boundless and seamless. What we speak of as "ever-changing," we could just as well speak of as "ever-present." We can call it flow or we can call it stillness. I sometimes call it unicity. Advaita calls it the Self. Buddhism calls it emptiness. These are different words for a single reality.

I used to think emptiness was the opposite of form. Emptiness was the space that contained the forms. But I came to see that when Buddhism talks about emptiness, they are pointing to something much more subtle and nondual. There's an old Zen story about a Zen master who asked his student, "How do you take hold of emptiness?" In response, the student makes this gesture of grabbing at empty space. And the master says, "Well that's very nice, but there's an even better way of grabbing hold of emptiness," and he takes hold of the student's nose and twists it.

Emptiness is not some mythic blankness – it's the sensation of nose twisting, it's the microphone, it's the rug. It's the neurochemistry, it's awareness, it's the thoughts, it's *everything* – or more precisely, it's the no-*thing*-ness of everything. Form is emptiness and emptiness is form. Because we have two different words, form and emptiness, everything and nothing, awareness and content, we *think* that there are different *things*. So we imagine that pencils and chairs and tables are "forms" and then there's something big and ephemeral called "emptiness" which is like a big empty space that contains all the pencils and chairs and tables. This view is delusion. It is a conceptual abstraction. It turns emptiness into *something*.

In reality, all form is notional. Reality doesn't hold still. It isn't divided up. Reality is empty of division, empty of solidity, empty of continuity. And there is no such *thing* as "emptiness" apart from form. Emptiness *is* form, and form *is* emptiness. They're not two. There's only this undivided, immediate, Here/Now – ever-changing and ever-present.

In order to talk, we use words. So we might say, "Everything is appearing in awareness." But as soon as we use words, they create this mirage of duality or separation. To say that "everything is appearing in awareness" is a description that invites a certain insight. It has a usefulness, but no description *is* what it tries to describe. And as soon as we have different *words*, it seems as if we have different *things*: "awareness" and "content." So in using words, notice how quickly they create the mirage of duality, the mirage of separation, the mirage of substance. In the immediacy of pure perception, there is no such separation. There is variety, but not separation.

We have to use words to communicate, so we use them. And that's fine. But there's no such *thing* as awareness. There's no such *thing* as consciousness. There's no such *thing* as you or me or Chicago or America. I don't mean there's *nothing* here, in the sense of a nihilistic blank void. But there's nothing solid, separate, fixed, persisting and substantial as we come to *think* there is.

There's no need to get rid of the words or the mental movies they generate. In fact, that would be impossible. But the more they are seen for what they are, the less we have to run after an imaginary mirage lake in the desert in search of water, or tremble in fear at the thought of stepping off the edge of the flat earth. But if running after an imaginary lake *does* happen, so what? This, too, is simply another dream-like appearance. It isn't personal. The "you" who seems to be having this experience is *always* a mirage. The movie and the empty screen are both equally empty.

We could say that reality is everything or nothing – however you want to describe it. The illusion is that there is *something*. Some separate, independent, autonomous, solid, persisting *thing*. In truth, there is only seamless unicity.

And if right now the mind is trying to work it all out mentally and take hold of "seamless unicity" – that is a very frustrating endeavor. But it's amazing how long hope can persist. Joko Beck once said that no rat would keep going down a tunnel that had no cheese at the end of it, but we humans will! The thinking mind keeps trying to work it all out. After awhile, the thinking mind even *knows* that thinking is the problem, so it begins *thinking* about how to stop thinking! And like any addict, it wants to quit, it really does, but first it wants just one more last hit – it has to work out this one last little problem, because this time it really *is* getting close to resolving things, or so it thinks.

Of course, there really is no "thinking mind" – it's a figure of speech. There aren't really even any such *things* as thoughts. Again, there is only seamlessness. Words divide it up and then thought tries desperately to put it all back together.

Seamlessness is not an experience or a state. It has no opposite. Nothing is outside of it. It is all there is, even in the midst of contraction and agitation. There's no leaving it and no finding it. Unicity appears as stories and traffic noises and thoughts and chairs and tables and the whole universe. And in deep sleep, the whole manifestation is erased and even to say that unicity remains is saying too much. There is no such word as "unicity" in deep sleep.

Drop all the words right now and see what remains.

P: I keep trying.

J: Trying happens. It's a habit of mind. And then there's an additional story: *"I* keep doing that." It's all nothing but unicity showing up as thoughts.

P: These discussions of oneness and emptiness and unicity do not seem to describe what happens here. There are two things here, not one thing. There is a perspective which is empty, and there is no person involved in that – it's like a standpoint. And then there's the illusion. There is a perspective that's like an empty point – no self – and then there's what is occurring within the perspective. So there's still duality, but the other half of the duality is not a me. It's the perspective in which the movie of waking life is seen. And the movie is separate from the perspective. Two things.

J: What is the perspective?

P: Well, it's not a thing. It's an empty point – a timeless, spaceless, dimensionless point.

J: Okay, we could call it awareness, right? [participant nods] Is there an actual boundary between awareness and the content of awareness? We draw dividing lines with words, but is the separation really there? In your own experience right now, can you actually find this boundary?

P: Yes, there are two things.

J: Conceptually, there are two things. But when you actually investigate your own direct experience in this present moment, can you find a dividing line between awareness and what is being seen and heard right now? Is "awareness" actually a separate *thing*? Is there really this "empty point" *apart* from what is appearing?

P: It's not a thing; it's a vantage point.

J: Is there actually a "vantage point" right now seeing everything else? Or is that "vantage point" a very subtle reification and conceptualization? Isn't any "vantage point" that you can conceptualize another object that is also part of the appearance? Does it really exist as a separate thing?

P: When I remember, yes. There's either total caughtupness in everything, or else, when I remember, then there's caughtupness plus a vantage point.

J: Let's stick to right now. Right now, is there a vantage point? There can be a *thought* that says, "There's a vantage point, and everything else is the content of that." But isn't your actual present moment experiencing really one immediate, seamless, undivided, whole? Yes, there is diversity – many different shapes, colors, textures and so on, but all of it is appearing altogether at once, right here at zero distance, isn't it? Where is the separation?

P: There is a vantage point, but it's not a me.

J: Right. I understand what you're pointing to. We might also call this vantage point "impersonal awareness" or "the witness," right? And I'm not denying the *reality* of awareness, but as soon as the mind turns it into some *thing* that is separate from everything else, *something* that must be remembered and maintained, then it has become a subtle mental object, a concept, an idea. Can you see that? As you say, you *remember* to think it. It's a thought.

What is aware of the vantage point?

There is an awareness of both the imaginary vantage point and the objects within it. So there is something prior to any vantage point that you can imagine or conceptualize or perceive or experience or think about or remember or describe. And actually, this awareness that is prior to everything is not separate from everything. It *is* everything. It is the common factor in every experience, the formlessness that is forming as every form. It is not *something* you can objectify and then have to keep remembering. Awareness cannot be separated out from everything else and made into a separate object. Any such object would just be another momentary appearance. Right now, right here, is there really any separation between seer, seeing and seen, or between awareness and content, or between subject and object? Aren't those simply ideological categories that thought has created? Isn't your actual experience undivided *seeing, awaring, being*? Is there actually *something* separate looking *at* everything else, or is there simply *this* [Joan gestures to include everything] – one seamless and boundless whole?

P: There's "this" when totally caught up.

J: Right now?

P: Yes.

J: What's totally caught up?

P: "This" is totally caught up, and then there's a vantage point that isn't caught up. "This" is a totally caught up sinking feeling. And then there's a vantage point that stops the sinking, that isn't caught up. If I let go of the vantage point, there is total caughtupness.

J: Right now there's total caughtupness? Or is that a story? What is it that is caught up? What is it that needs to be rescued by remembering this vantage point? Look at the rug here. Without thinking about it, where is the boundary between awareness – or the imaginary vantage point – and the rug? Can you actually *find* this boundary? Can you see that it takes conceptual thought to divide "the vantage point" from "the rug"?

P: The rug is occurring in a context. The rug is a form, and yes, there is something besides that.

J: Yes, there are different shapes and colors and sounds – visual, auditory, tactile, olfactory, somatic sensations. Yes, there is awareness in which it all appears. But without the words, awareness and content are one undivided whole, aren't they?

P: It's like those pictures which can be seen two different ways. You know, where it can be either a picture of a lady or a vase and you can flip back and forth. It's like a painting in a frame. So there's that form of the rug appearing in a frame.

J: What sees the frame? What is aware of awareness? What is witnessing the witness? What is conscious of consciousness? Can you see that any answer that might arise, anything perceivable or conceivable, would be another appearance, another object? Is the seeing really divided up into seer and seen, or is your actual experience simply *seeing*?

P: If the idea goes, if the perspective goes, then there's just total sinking into the form, totally caught up. Plodding along.

J: That's a story. Look at the rug there in the center of the room – what's caught up and plodding along? Doesn't there have to be a mental story of *somebody* "caught up and plodding along"?

P: But that's set in a frame. Everything is set in a frame.

J: I'm questioning whether that frame isn't a subtle idea. And I'm questioning whether there is anybody who is really in danger of sinking into form.

P: The frame is emptiness.

J: *This* is emptiness. The rug is emptiness. You are emptiness. Everything is emptiness. There is *only* emptiness. Form *is* emptiness.

P: I don't see that.

J: Actually you do, but you're overlooking it. Thought is overlaying it with a conceptual story, and the focus is on the story. You're trying to see something special. You imagine that emptiness should look different than this present appearance. You think that if you were seeing emptiness, it wouldn't look like this. It wouldn't look like people and chairs and rugs.

P: True. When I really see it, it doesn't look like this. It's vibrant and it's a different experience.

J: Well, every second is a different experience. And *every* experience is emptiness, whether it's a vibrant experience or a dull experience, an expanded experience or a contracted experience. It's *all* emptiness. You can't *not* see emptiness. Emptiness is all there is. The seeing *is* emptiness. And *everything* you see is empty. But if you imagine that some *particular* experience is emptiness and not every other experience, then you've got an *idea* of emptiness that's only an idea.

P: When I'm stuck in form, it's like being lost in form completely. The frame is not a me.

J: Right, it's a bigger idea, like "awareness" or "witnessing," but if it's something you are trying to remember, then it's only an idea.

P: It's a helpful idea.

J: Maybe at some point it was helpful as a way of realizing that you are not really an object *in* the story, but that you are *seeing* the story and the characters. You are not encapsulated inside the bodymind; you are the awareness that is beholding the bodymind and the whole universe. So maybe at some point this idea of the vantage point was helpful as a way of waking you up from the story of encapsulation.

But now "awareness" (as an *idea*, as a "thing" you need to remember and maintain and identify with) is becoming a burden. In Buddhism, they compare the teachings to a raft, and when you reach the shore, you leave the raft behind, you don't carry it with you, because if you do, it quickly becomes a burden. So this once helpful idea of the frame, or the witness, or the empty container, or the screen of awareness, or the dimensionless point, if clung to, it becomes a burden. Now you really believe there is a danger that you might lose sight of the frame and get totally caught up in the rug. Can you see the joke here?

P: No, I really might drown in the rug – in the world of form.

J: Who's going to drown?

P: Katagiri Roshi kept saying, "Don't fall into the scenery." I need to remember it's scenery and keep a perspective on it. Remembering that the rug is just part of the scenery helps.

J: I can't speak for Katagiri Roshi, but I'm guessing he meant don't fall into the story. I'm not talking about the story. I'm talking about the bare sensory experiencing of this present moment. In that bare experiencing, *who* is in danger of drowning? *Who* is falling into the scenery? *Who* has to keep remembering the frame? There has to be some underlying story there, and there has to be some idea of "me." You can only get lost in the scenery when you imagine there is someone to get lost, and this getting lost is always an imagination. It has no reality. If you allow your attention to fall deeply and completely into pure sensory experiencing right now, which is all that form really is, then you may discover that you don't exist as anything separate from the whole – that there is nothing here but boundless emptiness appearing as colors and shapes and sounds. You may discover there is no one to drown! Unicity is all there is. Unicity can't drown!

P: It makes me feel better to remember the perspective. It gets me out of prison. Oops, "me."

J: So, is there really a "me" and is there really a prison?

P: Without the frame I will drown in the character.

J: "*I* will drown in the character." Can you hear the joke?

P: I'll drown in the rug. I'll drown in the grey sky.

J: *This is all a story!* Can you hear this? Can you hear how ridiculous this is? Who is going to drown in the rug or in the character? Where is this grey sky? What are we talking about?

P: I and the grey sky become one and we just spiral down.

J: That's a story. In direct experiencing, right now, is there any spiraling down or any grey sky or anyone drowning? You've got your eyes closed and it looks like you're straining –

P: No, no, I'm thinking.

J: That's what I mean, you're thinking.

P: I close my eyes when I listen carefully. Otherwise I won't hear you, and I'll pay attention to the TV antenna or something.

J: The TV antenna is saying exactly the same thing I am.

P: I try harder and it only makes it worse.

J: That's right. Trying harder makes it worse. So you notice that. But even that trying and that so-called worsening is only a dream-like happening coming out of the whole universe, and it's no more personal than a traffic jam or a thunderstorm. It's a habitual story about how something seemingly needs to be acquired or attained or achieved or protected or eliminated or maintained. And there's this phantom "me" who somehow needs to make this happen. That's the story, the trying harder story. And closing your eyes makes no difference at all. There is no boundary between inside and outside. As long as we are looking inside, we're still looking outside – and no outside is anywhere but inside. It's one whole seamless Here/Now.

P: The perspective makes it all okay. Empty awareness. Remembering empty awareness.

J: What exactly is it that is "not okay"? There's a story about me sinking and drowning and being caught up in the evil world of form, and then a thought pops up and says, "Remember the vantage point. Remember the frame. *Be* the witness. Don't fall into the scenery. This is all appearing in empty awareness. You are the empty awareness. Remember that." And for a moment that feels better.

P: Yes.

J: Okay. So this contracted, caught up, straining, grasping experience (which is actually only a bunch of thoughts and bodily sensations) breaks open and there's a sense of spaciousness and freedom –

P: Yes, Yes.

J: And that's fine. But as you've noticed, it's only another fleeting experience. And it takes a lot of maintenance. As soon as you try to hold onto this spacious experience, it instantly turns into contraction and suffering. As soon as you *think*, "This is it! Now I must stay focused on awareness so I can avoid drowning in forms," as soon as you think that, there is instant suffering. Right? I'm pointing out the difference between awareness itself, which is ever-present and all-inclusive, and a *concept* of awareness as *something* that must be remembered and maintained (some *idea* of "formless emptiness," "a dimensionless point," "the witness," whatever it is). *Something* that is separate from the supposedly unspiritual and dangerous world of form. I'm pointing out the absurdity of working very hard at this spiritual task of remembering the vantage point and making sure that "me" is identified as emptiness and not as form.

Being aware is actually effortless. You can't *not* be aware, so it's always already the case. But instead, it gets turned into an imaginary project for the "me" to accomplish, an imaginary "thing" that must be remembered and maintained. This may all have been a helpful pointer at one time, to distinguish awareness from content, and to notice that there is something bigger than "you" the character, something that is seeing the character, and to realize that you *are* that awareness, that seeing. It may have been very liberating to hear that. But now it has become a burden. The invitation now is to put it down. To drown in what looks like form. And to see what dies and what remains.

Unicity is appearing as awareness and the content of awareness. Words divide it up, but it is all unicity, and unicity is all there is. To talk about it, we use words, and then it seems as of "awareness" and "content" are separate, and "you" have to align with one and not get sucked into the other. But do these "things" really exist? Is the separation real? Is this phantom self real? Are "you" actually in danger of sinking into form?

P: It seems like there are two things, awareness and content. I don't get unicity.

J: Okay, forget unicity. It's only a word. I'm talking about *this* [Joan gestures to include everything]. This present moment Here/Now, as it is – one whole picture appearing seamlessly all at once. Thought divides it up into little pieces and gives them labels. We *learn* to see separate things. Like there's Bob and Roger – two separate people. Or there's the rug and the chair – two separate things. And relatively speaking, yes, we can distinguish the rug from the chair, and we can distinguish Bob from Roger, and this is functionally useful. We can also distinguish a contracted experience from a spacious experience, and conceptually, we can distinguish awareness from the thoughts and sensations that appear *in* awareness. And at a certain moment on the pathless path, that is a functionally useful distinction. We're not denying the variations that appear or the mind's ability to draw dividing lines. Thought creates forms out of formlessness. And when I say formlessness or emptiness, I don't mean some indistinguishable, undifferentiated, mush-like blob or some empty void. I mean *this* [Joan gestures to include everything] – exactly as it is.

Our actual experience if we pay attention to pure perception or bare sensation is that it is all appearing here as one whole seamless picture. And when I say seamless, I don't mean that there is no *apparent* border between the color and texture of the rug and the color and texture of the microphone. I mean they show up together. To a baby who hasn't yet learned to pick out and identify rugs and microphones, it is one flowing whole. The differences and variations are there, yes, but not the particular dividing lines that must be learned and the separate objects those dividing lines define and create. And above all, "you" are not there as a separate, independent "thing" that could drown in form and die.

It is only when we imagine separation that we fear dying. The boundaries and divisions are only conceptual, created by words and thoughts. And that can be seen by looking at your actual direct experience and discerning the difference between perception and thought.

We also know this from science. The apparently solid "things" (like rugs, chairs, and people) are not really solid, not really independent, not really continuous. They only continue as an idea, a thought-form – an object in a story, and only apparently, only conceptually. In reality, your body is utterly inseparable from the environment and all of it is changing every second. Your actual experience of the body is ever-changing sensations and vibrations. If you look carefully at your actual experience, you can't actually find a real or substantial boundary between you and the room or between your body and awareness. There is no "body" except as a concept, an idea.

P: But when it all happens at once, it is a feeling of total contraction and caughtupness. There's no me, but it's total grasping. Unicity is chaos and horror – and then this perspective of remembering awareness frees it. Like totally rushing around in the grocery store, for instance – there's only one thing – but it's totally caught up – that's unicity, right? And when the perspective happens, that opens.

J: If you are trying to hold on to a sense of distance and detachment, then maybe it *seems* like rushing around in the grocery store is "chaos and horror." But that feeling you are calling "chaos and horror" is itself nothing but sensations and vibrations. Without a story, there is simply what is, even if it is neurologically unpleasant or jangling in some way. Freedom is the absence of anything to save or protect or defend.

Of course, we may be using words in different ways, or we may be seeing something differently here. You might be describing the effects of a particular neurological or brain condition, maybe something akin to what I've heard autistic people describe, where too much sensory information seems to be pouring in all at once and it feels overwhelming and chaotic and painful to the nervous system. Or maybe the nervous system is highly sensitive and easily over-stimulated for some other reason. There are all kinds of things like seizure disorders and brain tumors that effect how the brain and the nervous system process information, and some people are simply more sensitive than others and get more easily over-stimulated and overwhelmed. And for some people, the *thought* of having no boundaries, and maybe even the first hint of expanding into boundlessness, may trigger a deep psychological distress, perhaps a fear of losing the ability to say no, or the ability to set limits, maybe because there was something like sexual abuse in one's childhood where personal boundaries were repeatedly violated. Or maybe there was psychosis at some point in the past where the functional sense of identity was lost, and so any experience of boundlessness triggers a fear that I'll lose the ability to function, or I'll go mad and everything will be chaos and horror, as you say. But I'm not talking about going mad or losing the ability to function or not having personal boundaries in the sense of being able to say no and set limits. I'm not even talking about a particular experience, but rather, the emptiness at the heart of *every* experience.

I'm guessing that when rushing around in the grocery store feels like "chaos and horror," as you put it, that unless there is some neurological or psychological condition such as what I just described, then there *has* to be some kind of story running, maybe something like, "How am I going to get everything done today? Which cereal should I pick? What if I get the wrong brand and it triggers my allergies? There are too many people here, this is a nightmare. I've lost awareness. I'm sinking into the scenery. I'm drowning in form and chaos. I'm dying." This is all a story with the phantom "me" at the center of it. In reality, there are simply a bunch of thoughts and sensations creating an experience that feels overwhelming and scary, perhaps triggering a survival fear, a fear of dying. That releases chemicals in the body to flee, fight, or freeze, as if you were in actual physical danger, and those chemicals in turn generate more thoughts and more sensations. It *feels* like you are drowning.

If, on the other hand, there's no story and no idea of me, and there is simply moving around at a high speed through the aisles of the grocery store and the appearance of colored boxes and cans and other shoppers, and the arising and passing away of thoughts and sensations, including neurologically unpleasant sensations, I'm guessing that unless there's some kind of brain anomaly or serious psychological or neurological disturbance involved, that this would not be an overwhelming nightmarish experience of "chaos and horror." It might be unpleasant, there might be a sense of over-stimulation, but without any me-story in the middle of that, it would be simply sensation and movement.

But rather than go off to the grocery store in our minds, which right now requires memory, imagination and speculation, let's stick to this room, right here, right now. Is there any problem with the direct experiencing right now of presently arising sights, sounds and sensations?

P: I think it's an extremely unpleasant experience of total identification with the character in the play.

J: Identification with the character is not a sensation, it's a thought-story. And yes, thinking there is a "me" to identify or dis-identify with the character is painful. But I was talking about sensory experiencing without any storyline.

P: There's always a story. And then this other thing, remembering awareness, liberates it. And when I hold on to both, life is good, but it's duality.

J: It sounds like a lot of work to "hold onto both" and to always be in danger of forgetting and sinking. And always this imaginary "you" in the center of it all who has to manage and control it. But really, there's no you to hold on or to sink. Just different words, different ideas, different sensations. And there's no such thing as a continuous *experience* of expansion – that's never going to happen. There's always going to be pulsation and vibration – some degree of back and forth between contracting and expanding. That's part of the manifestation. Even if there is some brain condition like autism or psychosis or epilepsy and the experience of sensory input is sometimes overwhelming and chaotic for neurological or biochemical reasons, even then, that is simply happening, like a thunderstorm or a volcanic eruption, and without a story of "me" in the middle of it trying to resist or manage it, then I wonder if the same kind of nightmare you're describing would be occurring. Maybe it would be, I don't know. But I wonder. And actually, either way, nothing is occurring except as a dream-like appearance in the movie of waking life. The problem only *seems* to exist *in* the nightmare.

And *is* there always a story? Is that true? I would question that.

P: The duality frees it.

J: Becoming aware of the awareness that is beholding everything is freeing, yes, because awareness is free, and you see that you are not encapsulated inside the dream character. But now is it possible to notice that awareness isn't a separate *thing* that "you" have to keep remembering? Awareness is here effortlessly, inseparable from the forms that arise within it. It is, in fact, the very *substance* of every form.

Is it really necessary to hold the world of form at bay as if it were something very dangerous and alien? Is looking deeply at the forms in this room actually going to kill you? Does this one who appears to be in danger really even exist? Can you find any form apart from awareness or any awareness apart from form?

P: There's a sense of frustration. I just don't see unicity.

J: Instead of trying to see unicity or getting caught up in the story of being a failure, what if you explore that experience of frustration right now, not by thinking about it or analyzing it, but simply by being aware of the actual sensations and feelings in the body. Thought labels it "frustration" and attaches a story to it, but without the label and the stories, what is this so-called "frustration" actually like? What do you find?

P: It's still there.

J: We're not trying to get rid of it. We're exploring it with interest and curiosity.

P: It's associated with body tension.

J: Okay, but go into the actual sensations of what you're calling body tension. What do you find?

P: A sense of sinking and a kind of dark energy.

J: Okay, drop the words. Go into the actual, bare sensations themselves. What do you find?

P: Going into it just keeps going in and in and in. I haven't been coming out the other side.

J: That's because you are going into the story and not into the actual direct experience.

P: Well, all I can do is believe what you say.

J: No, no, don't believe what I say. Look and see. Can you see that "not coming out the other side" is a story, an imagination? Is it possible to give complete open attention to the actual sensations themselves?

P: Frustration and dark energy is pervasive.

J: That's another story. That's not actual sensations. Do you see the difference between direct experience and these thoughts, stories and labels? When you tune into the actual sensations, do you find anything solid there?

P: It doesn't seem that solid or not solid applies.

J: Right. If you go into any sensation, you'll find that there's nothing there that's solid or persisting – and you won't find any real boundary between "you" and "it," because "you" and "it" are only thoughts.

P: It persists.

J: What is "it"? Something persists only in the story, in thought – as an unexamined concept. Thought says this is the same sensation I had a minute ago, or the same frustration I had a minute ago. Is it?

If you are only paying attention to bare sensation for one microsecond and then immediately flipping back into thought and analysis, well, then you can *think* there is an "it" that persists. But if you're really paying careful attention to any object, you can *see* that it's not always the same. This is more obvious with auditory or somatic sensations than it is with visual sensations. If you are really paying attention to a somatic sensation or a sound, does it stay exactly the same?

P: No, but it stays.

J: What's the "it"? You say, "it" stays. Can you really find an "it" in there that stays? If "it" doesn't stay the same, then what do you mean by the "it" that stays? How can something change and still be the same? Isn't that "it" a concept?

P: I can always sort of feel the sensation of tension.

J: But this so-called "tension" is actually changing, pulsating, moving, maybe disappearing for a moment if your attention goes elsewhere. What is the "it" that is "always" there?

P: Yes, but the mind doesn't want to attend to sensations because it gets boring.

J: Okay, another thought. "It's boring." What is this thing called boredom? It might be a cover for fear because our whole solid picture of reality is collapsing and thought can't get a grip on what is being revealed, so it says, "This is dangerous," or maybe, "This is boring. Do something else." Is that possible?

Certainly, you don't need to keep attending to sensations as if this were your new task. That's not what I'm suggesting. But actually *exploring* the difference between perception and conceptualization, that might be interesting to play around with and look into – if it interests you. And when I say look into, I mean with awareness, not with thought and analysis. It's subtle, you know, the difference between the *conceptualization* of what's here and the actual direct *experiencing*.

The direct experience is never a problem. It might be painful at times, but it isn't a problem. Even if you're dying, it isn't a problem until you start thinking about it. Our suffering is always in the conceptualization, the thinking.

P: The sensations are not a problem?

J: Are they? They might be painful, but without the story, there is simply pain, and no overlay of suffering. There isn't even "pain" (as some solid and persisting *thing*) until we begin to think. The sensations themselves are always changing, coming and going, pulsating. There isn't really a solid "it" to be found anywhere in direct experience. We have a word, like "sensation," and immediately it seems to refer to a solid object – the word actually creates that object in the mind, like a mirage. Something is there, but it isn't ever a continuous *thing* as words would suggest.

We can't talk or think without creating the appearance of objects and dualities, and to some degree, this appearance is also created by conditioned perception which has learned to reify and organize what is showing up in a particular way, to see tables and chairs and so on. But perception itself isn't troubling or problematic. The troubling aspect is always in the thought-overlay. Seeing the *it-less-ness* of everything is what is meant by emptiness.

Another P: The naming of the name is equivalent to drawing a boundary.

J: Yes, an imaginary mirage boundary. And when you die, the whole show is going to go off, as it does every night in deep sleep. Gone. *Poof.*

P: How do you know it will all be gone?

J: Because it happens every instant. Everything is gone from moment to moment. And every night when you go to sleep, the whole world disappears. *You* disappear.

P: What if you just don't remember?

J: It amounts to the same. But let's be clear, I'm not saying there is *nothing* after death, or that deep sleep is nothing at all. Death itself is an idea, just as birth is an idea – they are conceptual lines in the sand. Reality itself is undivided. That which is present in deep sleep is unborn and undying. It is equally present in the waking state and the dream state. It is here before birth and after death and in every moment of life. It isn't anything perceivable or conceivable, nor is it limited to what we usually think of as consciousness – sensing, perceiving, thinking, feeling, imagining, remembering – the whole movie of waking life. That disappears every night in deep sleep.

P: So there's the screen on which the show is playing, and that doesn't end when the movie ends.

J: Any screen we can imagine disappears too. The analogy of the screen may be useful for making a certain point, like the raft in Buddhism is useful for crossing the river, but in deep sleep, it all disappears. What remains is the reality that is prior to every image and every pointer.

P: But there was a time when you didn't see that, wasn't there?

J: There was no time before now and there is no me who sees that. You cannot *not* see that because there is *only* that. Wherever you look, you are looking at that. You *are* that. Reality is timeless, always Now, and it isn't divided up and encapsulated inside separate organisms. It isn't personal. You can't pull it apart. You can't have the contraction without the expansion or the expansion without the contraction. The valley makes the mountain and vice versa, just as there cannot be up without down. It's all happening together at once. One seamless unicity.

The mind tries desperately to unite what has never "existed" (or been apart) in the first place (to exist comes from *ex-sistere*, to stand outside). *You can't stand outside,* except in imagination (by mentally dividing outside from inside, or you from it, and then you can *seem* to stand apart, but only *in* the movie image that thought has created).

Direct perception is always nondual, undivided, whole. Nondual unicity is perfectly obvious in everyone's ordinary experiencing right now — you don't need to see anything other than what you are seeing right now. I don't mean that it all appears as indistinguishable mush or white light, or that you can't distinguish the chair from the rug, or that you lose the ability to recognize Roger or Bob, or that the whole room vanishes into thin air. I am not saying this one present moment isn't magnificently diverse and full of wondrous variety. I'm saying that nothing is really separate or separable. The chair only appears along with everything that's apparently not-the-chair. It could not appear otherwise. If there were *only* chair, no chair would appear!

And every night in deep sleep, this dimensionless point of consciousness totally disappears and nothing perceivable or conceivable remains. You remain, but not as anything experiencable or describable. Not as a person or a dimensionless point or an empty screen, for all of that has disappeared.

P: Is there any free choice involved in any of this? Can we choose to drop these stories?

J: You tell me. Can you?

Participant: Not always.

J: That's been my experience as well. Stories can be seen, but there's no "me" who can do that seeing at will. It happens, or not.

Let's say I'm a smoker, and a thought arises that, "I'm going to quit smoking," and it's followed by the cessation of smoking. That sequence of events reinforces the belief in free will, and it seems as if *I* deliberately thought that thought and had that intention, and *I* quit smoking. *I* decided to do that and *I* did it.

But then there are all of the times when "you decided" to quit smoking and then kept right on smoking. Or all the other people who tried to stop and failed. If it's a simple decision, a matter of free will, then why is it apparently so difficult? Why doesn't it always work?

It's amazing how many times you can decide to quit smoking and then start again and still keep deciding to quit, each time with the belief that, "I should be able to do this." And if it doesn't work, we feel like a weak-willed, neurotic failure. "What's wrong with me?" we wonder. If it works, we feel proud: "I did it!"

If we look closely, the decision to stop arises out of nowhere. That thought or intention, "I'm going to quit smoking," pops up, and then smoking either ends or it doesn't. There is no "you" involved at all.

Now if we just understand this in a conceptual way, the thinking mind might cleverly say, "Okay, I get it. I can't decide to quit smoking. I'm powerless. I'll just keep lighting up. Hooray!" This thought, too, just pops up, unbidden, but it's a slippery thought. The mind is very clever.

We say, "I picked up the glass," as if there is an "I" who does that. [Joan picks up her water glass] But that's only a way of putting this happening into words. What actually happens is an impulse arises, the hand shoots out, the fingers curl around the glass, the arm moves, the glass rises, and this way of conceptualizing and languaging it emerges: "I decided to pick up the water glass and I did it." But how did that really happen? Is that phantom decider, that phantom doer really there? Or is it only a mental image, an idea, the subject of a sentence, a grammatical convention? Whether we are talking about the body or the mind or the ego, this so-called "self" is always more like a process than a thing. What we call "the self" is the functioning of countless interrelated systems, and ultimately, it is inseparable from the functioning of the whole universe.

P: So in a sense, much more is going on than we acknowledge.

J: Yes, the whole universe is involved in everything that happens. Everything is caused by, and everything effects, everything else. Everything is inseparable from everything else. In Buddhism they call it interdependent origination. That's what they mean by emptiness. Everything is impermanent, constantly changing, and interconnected with everything else. There is no inherent, independent, autonomous existence. No "thing" actually ever forms to even *be* impermanent. There is *only* seamless wholeness.

But there's a powerful illusion because of the way that we conceptualize all of this, that this glass is a separate object, and I'm a separate object, and "I" can get control of "the glass." And in a practical situation like that, with picking up a glass, it seems to work. It's coherent. Relatively speaking, it makes sense. But then we think that our mind is an object, and that "I" can get control of that object, too. And that doesn't work out as well because now we're trying to lift ourselves up by our own bootstraps. But we don't see the incoherence. We can't understand why we're having such a hard time controlling ourselves!

P: That's pretty scary for the brain that wants to be in control.

J: Yes, it's scary from the perspective of this illusory phantom, this "me" who doesn't really exist. It's very scary to *think*, "Oh my God! I have no control." It's a scary thought. *But it's only a thought.* There's nothing real or separate here to have control or to lose control. The "me" who wants desperately to survive is a mirage! It never has been in control, ever, because it is an illusion!

P: It sure seems like I have free will.

J: Yes, it does, until you look carefully and closely. And, relatively speaking, we go on functioning *as if* we were making choices. We have no choice! I mean, suppose somebody calls you up and says, "Which movie do you want to see?" You're not going to say, "There's no one here to make a decision. There's no you. There's no movie theater. We'll just see where we end up."

P: *You* might. [laughter]

J: Well, we're out of time, which we were never in, so before we end or begin again, let's have a few minutes of silence in which everyone can enjoy the sound of the cars, the cool breeze, the breathing, and the utter simplicity of being alive.

If you notice that the mind is grinding away, still trying to work out the things we've been talking about, maybe it is possible to let that life-preserver of thinking go, and to drown completely in the utter simplicity of sensation. And if there continues to be grasping at ideas in an attempt to stay afloat and survive, then maybe it will be noticed that this grasping is simply another appearance in awareness, no different from wind gusts churning up the ocean. It's a moment in a dream.

Seven Steps to Dissolving the Imaginary Problem

I guess for the squirrels and cats, the absolute simplicity of what is, is obvious. But for human beings, it's not so obvious because we have this capacity to remember the past, to project into the future, and to refect on this thought-image of "me."

We imagine "me" trying to *merge* with the flow, or be *in* the flow, or *understand* the flow. But actually, there is *only* flow. There's no way in or out and there's nothing separate to *be* in or out. But it doesn't *seem* that way because the very nature of thought is to divide up and freeze what is actually indivisible and fluid.

Memories seem to be a reliable recording of an actual past, even though we know intellectually that they are notoriously unreliable and can never possibly capture the totality of what actually happened. If everyone in this room were to report tomorrow on what happened here tonight we'd have many different versions of what happened and what was said. Of course, we might think that the "real version" would be on the tape.

I once had an interesting experience. I had been to an event with a popular satsang teacher, and in an exchange with a questioner, I heard this teacher say, "The thing standing between you and facing your fear is me." I found it a very curious and compelling statement. Some weeks later, I listened to the tape of this exchange and heard the teacher say that same thing again. Many months later, I listened to the tape a third time and realized that I had mis-heard the line. The teacher actually said, "The thing standing between you and facing your fear is fear." I had heard the word "me" instead of the word "fear," not just once, but twice! And the word "me" doesn't even *sound like* the word "fear." How could I have heard something so utterly false, not just once, but twice!? It was a shocking revelation of something I knew intellectually but had never knowingly experienced so vividly, that we can see or hear things that are not actually there. Maybe my brain had simply inserted the message I needed or wanted to hear and then heard that instead! Perhaps I thought that what was standing between me and facing *my* fear was my involvement with this teacher, so the brain just changed the message. And even when I finally heard it correctly, or so I assumed (and I did replay that exchange several more times to double-check), who knows what was *really* there? If fact, is anything "really" there? Or is *everything* a subjective present-moment creation?

Is there actually an objective reality "out there" as we think there is?

Another time, I heard a tape recording of a talk I had given, and I discovered that at one point in the talk, I had said something quite different from what I had intended to say. The interesting thing was that I didn't *hear* my own mis-speaking when it occured. I wasn't *aware* of my mistake at the time. As I spoke, I heard myself say what I *meant* to say, not what I *actually* said. If anyone had quoted me afterwards saying what I actually said, I would have adamently denied it. And I would have been *completely convinced* that I was right.

Both of these experiences showed me how unreliable perception and memory can be, and it helps to explain how human beings can misunderstand each other as much as we sometimes do. Not only do we see things differently and have different views, but on top of that, we're not always saying what we think we're saying or hearing what we think we're hearing.

What is real here and now? This is a wonderful question to consider.

Even though there might be a tape recording or a video of what happens here tonight, the tape can only capture some small part of what's actually going on, some abstraction of the flow, and then you can listen to the tape and not even hear what's really on it, if *anything* is "really" on it! And every time you listen to that tape, it will be a completely different experience because the bodymind that is listening and the circumstances of the listening will be totally different than they were before. As they say, you can't step into the same river twice. Upon close inspection, this seemingly solid world all begins to look very unsolid – an ever-changing appearance. And yet *something* is undeniably here.

If I actually pay attention now to what's happening, I can't find a source for these words that are pouring out. These words are emerging out of the same darkness from which my next inhalation or my next heartbeat is emerging. No one is in control of what is being said. Everything is arising out of the same energy or intelligence that is growing the trees and rotating the earth around the sun and causing the leaves to fall off the trees after they turn beautiful colors.

Nothing needs to be done other than exactly what is happening now. You can say, "Wait a minute, I have to pay the rent or the mortgage. I have to get the kids to school. *Of course* there's something that has to be done." And yes, there are all these things that apparently have to be done in the movie of waking life, and they all happen quite naturally in the same way that these words are happening, and the breathing and the beating of the heart and the dropping of the leaves from the trees.

Even when there is effort and confusion and resistance and rumination and indecision, that too is happening effortlessly. There is nothing other than than this seamless movement that is ever-changing and ever-present. The flow isn't just the stuff that looks or feels harmonious or flowing – it's *everything.* Even the blockages are nothing but flow.

If you don't have the mortgage, then maybe you lose the house, maybe you become homeless, maybe you go to jail, maybe you starve to death, but whatever is happening is happening effortlessly and could not be otherwise. It *is* the flow. And the bare *fact* of it – the *suchness* of it – is very simple.

Being here is very simple. Breathing, seeing whatever shapes and colors are appearing right now, hearing these sounds, thinking whatever thoughts are arising, doing whatever you are doing. *This* is utterly simple. Effortless. Unavoidable. Isn't it? Even getting the kids to school is very simple in the moment it is happening, even if they're late and they've just spilled juice on their new shirt, and the eggs are burning, and the television is blaring and the phone is ringing and you are feeling panic and yelling at the kids – *all* of that is happening effortlessly and simply. It *is* the flow. The *sense* of complication and struggle is in the accompanying story – the story about how we have to be on time, the juice should not have been spilled, I should not have yelled, this shouldn't be happening, life is too overwhelming, I've lost the flow, I'm a terrible mother – *that's* all a story. And that story is also the flow. That story arises unbidden, effortlessly, as does the *sense* of complication and struggle – the sensations of tightening muscles and jangling nerves and changing neurochemistry, and then maybe the irritated words pouring out and the children crying or screaming. The whole chaotic, frenzied mess is all happening with effortless simplicity. It *is* the flow, absolutely *all* of it. It *is* as it is. An hour later, the whole scene has totally vanished. Gone! Thirty years later, or a hundred years later, nobody even remembers it. It was like a dream. It had no substance, no actual existence. It was an appearance in consciousness, a painting in emptiness.

In fact, life is always simple, even when it *looks* very complicated and confusing and chaotic. It is one whole happening. There is no one at the helm – not "you," not "God," not "Zeus," not "Consciousness." There is, in fact, no helm and no ship. Those are mental ideas. Even "unicity" or "the flow" is only a word, a pointer – what it points to is nothing you can grasp. And no matter what appears to happen, even if you murder the children, or the whole planet explodes, nothing real has been destroyed. The energy, the beingness, the wholeness of life is still complete. Forms dissolve and new forms emerge, but formlessness is unchanged. The problem and the need to solve it are *in* the story.

So then the mind may say, "Okay. I want to get rid of those troublesome stories. I want to see that simplicity or that flowing wholeness that she's talking about." And we imagine that what I'm talking about is something that is missing right now, something we need to search for and find.

And here's where we have my special program, and I take credit cards. I call it "The Seven Steps to Dissolving the Imaginary Problem." [laughter] These are very difficult steps and there are multiple levels that you are going to progress through, up, up and away. And in the end, after all this hard work, you'll be right here where you are now. But to get here from here, which is very tricky and hard to do, you'll have to work extremely hard and pay lots of money and attend lots of events, and if you succeed at this difficult task, as I obviously have and as a few other special people have, then, with my blessing and transmission of the flame, you, too will be empowered to become a teacher of the Seven Step Program, and you can then help others to find perpetual peace and happiness. [laughter] If you're not lucky and you don't try earnestly enough, you will fail at this as so many do, and then you'll know that you just didn't have the right stuff. You didn't try hard enough. You didn't really want it. You were just slightly more interested in chocolate or sex or trivia. Your attention flagged a little bit. [laughter]

When we really see this movie for what it is, it's the Cosmic Soap Opera. But believed and taken seriously, these ideas about "me" progressing through the Seven Steps can appear very serious. Death is our greatest teacher in this regard, for it reminds us of how fleeting everything really is. Every night in deep sleep, or at the moment of death, this whole movie of waking life stops playing. *Everything* disappears including you and the seven steps. And this disappearance is the deepest peace.

Looking for happiness *in* the movie, as a particular outcome *in* the movie, is a losing endeavor. The movie is always moving – it is nothing *but* thoroughgoing, ceaseless change. Anything you appear to find will be lost, and whatever you find is always only another dream object. All the Seven-Step Programs are *in* the movie. All the enlightenment experiences are *in* the movie.

Is there something that is not in the movie?

Anything you can conceptualize or experience or describe or

imagine is in the movie. But is that which is being and beholding the movie in the movie? Don't answer that question, because any answer you can give will be untrue. When every answer dissolves, the truth remains.

P: I took up meditation many years ago, and I do an hour of meditation every day, and that practice helps me to see movies as movies. It helps me to wake up from the story and let things go. It helps me to see that I'm not in the movie. That's my practice – letting go, seeing through the stories. So I feel that there is something to do in order to realize what you're talking about. There is a practice. I consider meditating and letting go my practice.

J: Meditation and what you're calling "letting go" may happen, but it's only another scene in the movie of waking life. The *reality* of what you're describing is not conceptual, but once you formulate it, it becomes a conceptualization: "I took up meditation many years ago and it has had these benefits." It becomes another story. It may be a relatively true story, but it's a story. There's a story that "you" are practicing meditation and that this *causes* letting go and waking up. The *real* letting go is *always* happening. Just simply notice that the last five minutes is completely totally utterly gone – it has vanished. This absolute letting go is so thorough that there really isn't any "thing" formed here in the first place to be let go. But the story is that "you" have to *do* this letting go.

There's nothing wrong with practices. I'm not against them in any way. I'm just inviting you to notice that they happen by themselves, that this happening is dream-like, that there's no "you" who can control the results of such practices, and that the results are also dream-like. There may be tremendous progress within the dream, but in reality, all these practices and seven-step programs are not actually getting you anywhere – you're always right here. You can't ever be anyplace else.

P: Why is there so much suffering, so much cruelty, so much war and crime?

J: This manifestation can only appear in polarities and contrasts. There is no up without down. Unicity includes every possibility. The mind can come up with all sorts of explanations for suffering and there are plenty of them out there. Karl Marx has his explanation. Hinduism has its explanation. Buddhism has its explanation. Christianity has its explanation. But whatever the explanation, the fact is, suffering happens. Cruelty happens. It's part of the show.

Many of the things that we would regard as suffering or misfortune are also blessings. For me, having one arm and being a drunk for awhile have both been tremendous sources of wisdom, understanding, compassion and humor. I wouldn't choose those things or recommend them, but I can look back and see that they're part of the total fabric of this life, and by no means totally bad. In fact, arguably very positive. And similarly, some of the things in my life that you'd say, "Oh, that's really good fortune," have had ill effects as well, if you want to call them that. So whether we judge things good or bad is always a very subjective human judgment.

We look at a newborn baby with awe and wonder. The human baby looks absolutely adorable and beautiful and lovable to our human eye. A tiger might see that same baby the way we see a good hamburger or a nice chicken dinner. And when we humans look at baby mosquitoes hatching, we don't feel the same wonder and awe as when we see human babies or puppies or kittens or butterflies emerging. Seeing mosquitoes hatching, we might even feel aversion or repulsion. These reactions are part of our biology. They are programmed into us for survival reasons – and maybe not even for our own survival.

In his book *Breaking the Spell*, Daniel Dennett begins by talking about why an ant will often climb laboriously up a blade of grass, over and over, like Sisyphus. "Why is the ant doing this? What benefit is it seeking for itself?" Dennett asks. Then he reveals that there is actually no benefit to the ant itself, that the brain of the ant has been commandeered by a tiny parasite, a lancet fluke, that needs to get itself into the stomach of a sheep or a cow in order to complete its reproductive cycle. The ant is serving the lancet fluke. And apparently this is not an isolated phenomenon. Dennett tells us that these parasitic hitchhikers cause their hosts to behave in unlikely and even suicidal ways, all for the benefit of the guest, not the host.

Maybe humans are on the planet to destroy all forms of life and make way for something totally new to emerge. Maybe skyscrapers are as natural as beaver dams. Maybe war is a wonderful natural clearing like forest fires. We don't really know. We're moved to act by forces much bigger (or much smaller) than any single human brain, and every single brain is inseparable from the entire universe. The ant and the lancet fluke are not really two. How is this dream supposed to turn out? Is peace on earth a more desirable conclusion to the present chapter than nuclear holocaust? Is it better for the universe for all of us to "be here now" rather than being entranced in some story? Is it a tragedy when a child dies or when humans drop bombs? From our limited perspective, it seems that it is. But like the ant, our actions may be nothing more than the influence of a parasite. Who knows? In any case, it's the cosmic opera. This whole appearance is a kind of art form or play. Taken seriously and personally, it can seem very tragic. The bottom-line is that we don't *really* know *anything* about *anything,* and we're not in control. And when we relax into that, we discover it's not a problem.

P: It seems to me that we do have one choice, and that's the choice to observe and pay attention to whatever is happening. We can't control *what* that is, but we can choose to be present to it and observe it.

J: Does choosing to be present and observe work for you? Do you find that you can always make that choice?

P: Well, maybe not always.

J: It works when it works, and it doesn't when it doesn't. If the desire to observe is stronger in one moment than the desire to sink into the story, then this "choice to observe" seems to work. But if the desire to sink into the story is stronger in that moment, then that's what happens. We can't control what desire emerges in any given moment, or how our neurochemistry and our genetics and our conditioning will respond to it.

P: So then we can choose to let it be as it is.

J: Can you? Actually, it *is* as it is – always – but you may or may not feel "at peace" with what is going on. And no one is in control of what feelings and reactions pop up.

P: What is there if there's no self?

J: What is there if there's no self? There s *this!* [Joan gestures to indicate everything]

P: What's "this"?

J: *This!* [Joan gestures again to include everything] What *is* this? We don't know. We can come up with many possible answers to that question, like it's a bunch of people at a meeting about nonduality happening on a blue-green planet in the solar system, or it's an illusion, or it's a dream, or it's a brain experience, or it's a subatomic particle dance, or it's all consciousness, or it's unicity, or it's a bunch of sensations, but right now, those are all words and concepts. What this actually *is* cannot be packaged up in any word, can it? What *is* it?

No word-label, no concept, no answer will ever really satisfy that question. Only the answer-less-ness of this moment, just as it is, can truly answer the question.

And *this* [Joan gestures again to include everything] isn't abstract or intellectual or mysterious or ellusive until we start analyzing it and thinking about it. The bare *beingness* of it, the *presence* that is undeniable here now, *this* is vibrantly alive. It needs no explanation, no solution, no meaning beyond simply the fact of being as it is.

P: How did you come to the understanding that there is no choice?

J: Only in a story is there *someone* who comes to an understanding. But if you want me to tell you a story, I'd say that my father told me when I was a very young child that everything was determined by everything else and could not be otherwise, that there was no individual control or free will, and that made total sense to me at the time. He told my mother the same thing, and it *never* made any sense to her, so why this understanding clicks with one person and not another is unknowable. But with me, even as a child, it made sense. It seemed, and it still seems, impossible to deny. Then, later in life, I was drawn to a teacher, Toni Packer, who talked about seeing through the me-illusion and seeing that there is no free choice. With her encouragement, I starting paying attention to how simple decisions and choices actually happen. I'd be sitting in a chair, and I'd pay very close attention to how the decision to stand up actually emerged and unfolded. I saw that I couldn't find anybody who was doing it. I also observed my fingerbiting compulsion, and my efforts to stop, and again, I didn't find anyone in control of it.

But like I say, this is all a story – it requires memory and tremendous abstracting of what actually happened to come up with such a story. When you (choicelessly) asked this question, the thinking mind (choicelessly) scanned back over the movie of "Joan's Life," picked out a few memories, and then assembled those findings into a coherant narrative called "The Story of How Joan Discovered There Is No Free Will." And that, too, is a story! The story of "How the Mind (choicelessly) Scanned Back Over the Movie of Joan's Life and Assembled Those Findings into a Narrative." Stories upon stories. In this instant, *nothing* happens. This instant is so instantaneous that it is gone before anything perceivable or conceivable has had time to form or happen. All forms are gone before they even form. There is only seamless flux.

P: Is there any possibility we could have just a tiny bit of something that looks like choice? Couldn't we have like 1% of control?

J: 1%? Sounds like a really bland, watery kind of lowfat milk or something. [laughter] What is scary about having no control?

P: I don't think it's fear. It just seems that I can direct my mind one way or another.

J: It *seems* that way. But the impulse to put your attention here or there comes up by itself. Watch closely and you will see this. There is no "you" in control of where your attention wants to go or where it goes. You may *think* there is, if a thought arises like "I can put my attention on my big toe," and then your attention goes to your big toe, and then thought says, "See! I *do* have control." But where did the thought-impulse come from to do that?

P: So is there no such thing as progress or impovement?

J: *In* the dream, yes, there is *apparent* progress, relatively speaking. Humanity has gone from ox carts to jet planes, and from spears to our incredibly precise guided weapons systems that only killed tens of thousands of civilians accidentally as collateral damage. So that's progress, eh?

Just look at a tree. It seems as though it grows up from a tiny seed into a huge tree, and thus goes through a process. But what is it that is the same throughout this process? Is there an entity in there that is changing from a seed to a tree? How can something change and still be the same thing? It doesn't really make sense. So there's apparent progress. But in the end you die. Where is the whole journey then? Am I really any closer to unicity now than I was when I was a drunk? Wherever we go, Here we are. It's always Now.

I feel different in some ways every moment, but in some essential way, every moment is always exactly the same. It's always *this* moment, this one eternal present moment that is always Here/Now, ever-changing but ever-present. The same aware presence, the same beingness, is here now as when I was one day old. But the movie is always changing.

P: Where does the soul come in or is that just a word or concept too?

J: What do you mean by the soul?

P: The spark of life within me.

J: The spark of life within you – what is that? And is it "within" or where is it? *What* is it? Does it have an owner? Is it separate from the life everywhere?

P: I don't own it, but it's there.

J: Who is this "I" that doesn't own "it"? What is "it"? Clearly there's life here – there's energy here. *Something* is here. But it's like the ocean and the waves. The waves are not separate from the ocean. They're an activity *of* the ocean, just as we are an activity of this boundless wholeness. But we *think* we are a separate wave, independent from the other waves and separate from the ocean, and then we worry, "How can I find the ocean? How can I experience water? What will happen to me after I wash up onto the beach? Will I be reincarnated? Do 'I' have a soul?" But what are we even talking about? As Nisargadatta used to say, we are discussing the wedding plans of the child of a barren woman.

A Useless Message

The sound of rain is so magical, isn't it? All those delicate, wet sounds – trickling, splashing, gurgling. Rain expresses everything I'm trying to say so much more elegantly and simply. We could sit here and listen to it. Or maybe we can listen to these words that pour out of our mouths in the same way we listen to rain, without expecting them to save us, without trying to understand them, without wondering what use they have or what purpose they serve, without analyzing and dissecting them, but simply with a kind of open enjoyment that appreciates them just as they are – playful sounds like rain.

Of course, unless we're hearing a foreign language we don't understand, it is virtually impossible to hear words as pure sounds in the same way we can hear rain. Words instantly create a whole world in the imagination. That's the beauty and the magic of words, that magical ability to materialize things in the mind, and this mental materializing happens as naturally as the rain.

If we have been meditating for a while, we may have the idea that the rain is something natural and good, and that thoughts are something unnatural and not so good. Rain is spiritual; thoughts are not. But is this true? Or is thought simply appearing here like everything else in the universe, all of it one seamless whole arising? Are thoughts, skyscrapers, moon rockets and cluster bombs any less natural than bird cheeps, ant hills, beaver dams and asteroids?

Can we see that the mental movies that words unfold in the imagination, the pictures they paint, are simply another appearance in consciousness that is *essentially* no different from the sounds of rain and the colors and shapes of this room? There's nothing inherently problematic about words, thoughts or imagination. They *can* generate enormous suffering, but that suffering is as natural as viruses, bacteria, volcanoes, and tornadoes. The vaccines we create and the systems of yoga and meditation we invent are all part of nature as well. Thinking is part of how the universe is functioning, and seeing through the thoughts is also part of how the universe is functioning, and all of it is happening as naturally as rain. *All* of it is one seamless flowing whole.

I saw a cartoon once where there were two cavemen and one said to the other, "I've got a great idea. Let's divide the world up into little squares and sell them." That's thought. And we may *think* that real estate development was a good idea or a terrible disaster, but actually, it's just something humans do, the same way bees make honey and ants build hills and squirrels gather nuts. Humans sell real estate and pave over the planet.

The ants are doing their little job, the squirrels are doing their little job, and human beings are doing our little job. And we really don't know the larger purpose of our little job, if there is one, or how our being here and doing what we do fits into the whole universe any more than the ants know any of that about their little job. We think we're a whole lot smarter than the ants, and relatively speaking, we are, but we're still totally clueless when it comes right down to it. The parasites and viruses are doing their jobs, the cancer cells are doing their jobs, the hurricanes and black holes are doing their jobs. We can evaluate and judge and label some of these activities disease and some of them health. That is part of what this thought process does — it sorts, evaluates, judges, ranks, organizes and categorizes, and that's useful in many situations. It's a survival system. It's part of what is happening, and it is as natural as the earth circling the sun.

We can't grasp this happening or pin it down. The sound of rain, the listening silence, aliveness of being here — it speaks for itself. *Everything* is unicity speaking — the chairs, the clouds, the squirrels, the rain, these words, the words of George Bush, the bombs falling on Iraq, the airplanes hitting the Twin Towers — the whole show is unicity speaking.

P: What about those who say everything is illusion?

J: Something has to be here to say that. There is undeniably *something* appearing here, even if it's an illusion. Even an illusion or a mirage or a dream has some reality. It's not what it appears to be, but nonetheless, *something* appears even if it is an illusion or a mirage. The whole appearance of waking life can be called illusory in the sense that it's not "out there" as a solid, enduring objective reality as we think it is. That's what is meant by saying it is dream-like. But there *is* something real in this moment that cannot be denied, and *that* is the truth. What is that?

You can't deny being here. This might all be a dream, but the *fact* of this dreaming is undeniable. You might say that the bodymind as we conceptualize it is an illusion, but you can't deny that there is consciousness or awareness or presence or beingness – that *something* is here. You could say that any idea you have about *what* this is, is an illusion, but it's undeniable *that* this is. Even if you deny your own existence, you have to be here to deny it – there has to be something here even to call it an illusion. So what is that something that cannot be erased or denied or doubted? What is it that is ever-present in every experience and that remains in deep sleep when everything perceivable and conceivable has disappeared completely?

Anything you get hold of as a possible answer is another dream object that will vanish in deep sleep. The only real answer is beyond words and ideas and pictures. But that doesn't make it mysterious and obscure. It simply can't be objectified or grasped. It's not a relative thing. It's absolute. It has no other, no outside, no inside, no cause, no effect. It cannot be seen, and yet everywhere you look, you see nothing else.

There's always only Now. You're always Here. I don't mean here at the Yoga Center, I mean you're always Here – whatever location appears, it always appears Here. There's no way you can get out of Here/Now. You can go running down the hall and you'll still be Here. It will still be Now. Here/Now is what you *are* – it's what *is*. It's *all* there is.

P: What about death?

J: Death is an idea. There is no one who dies, and there is no one who is born. On the ocean, a wave appears and disappears, but the ocean doesn't go anywhere. The ocean is waving. Likewise, the universe is people-ing.

When we see a dead body, it is like an abandoned husk or a shell that is no longer alive. Something is not there any more, but what *is* it? What *is* that spark, that aliveness? And where has it gone? Is it actually absent, or is it right here in the *seeing* of what appears to be inert and inanimate? The wave has merged back into the ocean, which it never really left. The aliveness doesn't go anywhere, the space doesn't go anywhere, but this particular wave, this particular dream, has dissolved back into what it always has been. And this husk that's left, this dead body, it also goes back into the atmosphere, back into the earth, in one way or another.

The beauty of life is in the lightness of being. It's not all solid and serious and frozen. It's shimmering and dissolving, appearing and disappearing. It's *alive* – the exquisite sounds of rain, the wonder and love that I see in your eyes – the seeing that is seeing itself everywhere. And yet, try to grasp this miracle and it is like trying to grasp a cloud or a handful of water. The fluidity of it is the beauty of it. The suffering is in trying to freeze it. Fixation and grasping – that is suffering.

P: So is that where hatred and aggression come from? I like to think that meditation is a way of learning not to be aggressive. I do it in order to bring peace into my life and into the world.

J: Yes, hatred and aggression arise out of fixation and grasping, or we could also say, they arise out of infinite causes and conditions, like everything else. Meditation also arises out of infinite causes and conditions. And while I might agree with you that meditation can be a helpful tool, once we start *thinking* of it that way, we have begun to grasp and fixate. Thought abstracts one thing (meditation) out from the totality and suggests that this one thing causes some other thing that it has abstracted out from the totality (a decrease in aggression). But in fact, *everything* is the cause and the effect of everything else. There isn't really any separation. It all appears choicelessly and could not be otherwise in this moment than exactly how it is. You are not choosing to meditate. Meditation is happening.

Who directs the trees to drop their leaves? We can imagine some director – God or whatever – but it's only an imagination. And it's all appearing Here/Now. Leaves dropping, bare branches, new buds – meditation, peace, aggression, wars. All of it is one seamless flow, one undivided whole.

P: I'd like to be closer to that flow, whatever that is.

J: You *are* the flow! You're not *in* the flow – you *are* the flow – there is *only* flow. Thinking you'd like to be closer to the flow is like the wave wanting to get closer to the water, or the wave wanting to stabilize as water, or the wave wanting to embody water. The wave *is* water. Yes, in the movie of waking life, different activities can seemingly produce different experiences, some of which might feel very flowing and some of which might not feel that way. Yoga or meditation will produce a different experience than hitting yourself over the head with a hammer. But every experience is equally the flow. There is nothing separate or solid *in* the flow or *outside* the flow. There is *only* flow. Even the experience of stuckness, obstruction and resistance is nothing but flow. You can't find the flow because you never left it and you're not separate from it. You can't lose it because there is nothing apart from it. As long as you are trying to escape or gain control, that is suffering. Brief moments of hope followed by endless disappointment and frustration. But when the controlling mind finally gives up, then you discover freedom in the last place you would have expected it – right here – right in the middle of this unresolved, messy, imperfect, ordinary moment. You are no longer imagining that you are a form trying to survive as a form, or trying to possess and keep other forms. You are the wholeness that has no form and every form.

P: How do you know all this?

J: *Nobody* knows this. This is all simply one possible description of the present moment. This description appears here the same way the sounds of the rain appear here. It is equally useless, equally without meaning or purpose. It's simply a beautiful display.

P: Yes, but how do you know all of this is true? To me, it sounds like a possibility, it might be true, but I don't feel the certainty about it that you seem to feel.

J: Everything we say can be doubted. But the bare actuality of Here/Now cannot be doubted.

P: Yes, but how do you know that?

J: You know this too. This isn't about finally feeling certain that you've got the right answer or the right belief system. Discard everything that can be doubted. What remains?

This is the reality you cannot doubt. When you stop trying to control it, understand it, or escape from it by seeking something else, you discover the jewel. And you realize that the jewel was never not here.

P: I discard everything, and there's this simple presence and the sound of rain, and it's nice for a moment, but so what? Why is this "the truth" or "the jewel"? I don't get it.

J: This is what the mind does. It says, "So what? What's the big deal? What does this do for me? There's got to be more than this. What's next?" Is it possible to *see* those thoughts *as* thoughts and to let them go? Once we try to grab hold of this simple presence and make it into something that I can believe in, or something that will *do* something for me, then immediately we're off into suffering again. And that, too, is only the flow. It's just a passing dream. No big deal.

P: Don't you think that tradition is important in some way? In Zen, for example, you can't just set yourself up and start teaching – you have to be asked by your teacher and approved and given permission. It seems like nowadays, everybody and his cousin is giving satsang, and I'm not sure if most of these people are any more awake or any more enlightened than I am.

J: There is this undeniable aliveness or presence that's here right now, and you don't need anybody to tell you that. This awareness, this beingness is undeniable. It is not something you possess, nor is it something that anyone else can transmit to you, nor does it require anyone else to confirm it or certify it for you. You don't need to read a book or go to a teacher or get dharma transmission to know that you're here – not "you" as somebody with a name – but this nameless presence, this seamless being that includes everything.

Certified teachers in a well-established lineage may be confused and deluded, so there is no guarantee that being certified means you are on the mark. The Buddha was not a Buddhist. Jesus was not a Christian. They both spoke from direct seeing and direct knowing. Buddha said to be a lamp unto yourself. There is no outside authority. And there are no permanently enlightened people. Lineages and certifications are appearances in a dream. What is real is beyond doubt and requires no dream-like certification.

I'm not speaking against teachers. I've had many wonderful teachers – some I've known in person, some I've worked with very closely, some that I've known only through their books. Teachers are wonderful. But every moment is your teacher. Life is your teacher. And a true teacher doesn't make you dependent upon them. Instead, they are trying to show you that you lack nothing, that what you seek is already here.

My main teacher, Toni Packer, once said to me that it was better not to have dharma transmission or certification because without these you had to rely on yourself. You had to rely on presence, awareness, listening, being present, being awake now – and not on some *idea* that you were certified.

P: Can you discuss any techniques you recommend?

J: I recommend exactly what is arising right now, just as it is! What else is there? Unicity needs no techniques to be what is already is.

P: What do you do? For example, when you're upset or there is a powerful story coming up, what do you do?

J: All kinds of different things can happen. Sometimes there's a thought, "I will sit in my chair and be with this," and sitting quietly happens. Sometimes I bite my fingers or check my email or eat chocolate. There is a range of things that can arise, but there's no one here who can make one or the other happen. And what doesn't seem to be here any more is a story or a belief that I've got to be having that peaceful relaxed experience in order to be okay – or in order to be a spiritual success.

P: I have a strong impulse to be compassionate and relieve suffering. That's why I meditate, and I would imagine that a spiritual teacher would be motivated by wanting to relieve suffering. Buddha seemed to be motivated by that – teaching people the way to wake up – being a Bodhisattva. Do you have no desire to relieve suffering?

J: Honestly, no. Maybe that's what's happening here – maybe suffering is being relieved – I don't know. But if it is, then I am not doing it. Thankfully, I have no idea that I am doing this to relieve suffering. I've noticed that often when we *think* we are being helpful, we're actually being very unhelpful and it's really all about building up our own sense of importance. Being a helper can be a real ego trip, and it can involve a lot of paternalistic, condescending feelings about those "others" who need help. The greatest help may be in seeing that no help is needed, that nothing is actually broken however broken it might seem.

When we think something has helped us, in some way, it is always a story. For example, I used to go to this acupuncturist, and one time I had some big problem, but he wasn't there, and so I didn't get a treatment, and then I felt great the next day. The problem I had been having was totally gone, and I realized that if I had gone and had a session, I would have attributed my feeling better to the acupuncture, and I would have thought, "Wow, that really worked. It was well worth the hundred bucks." I am not saying acupuncture is useless – I just mean that we often overlay the idea of cause and effect when we really don't know what causes one thing or another. There's a noticing that certain things *seemingly* produce certain effects. That noticing is part of what happens and it may or may not be true. It's a conceptual overlay. And it all arises on it's own.

Quite honestly, I don't hold meetings or write books with the idea that I'm helping people. Whenever that idea creeps in during a dialog with somebody, as it occasionally does, I immediately notice that something false is happening. I'm buying into the illusion, projecting my own discomfort onto somebody else, and it doesn't work. But of course I'm not speaking *against* things that can be helpful to people. I'm simply pointing to the bigger truth that nothing is really broken and that whatever we are moved to do or not do, it all happens choicelessly out of infinite causes and conditions.

P: But it seems to me that spiritual teaching is about learning to come back to here and now – learning how to wake up from agitation, how to not take it personally, how to see through the idea that I am a separate person and recognize that I am boundless awareness. I would say, teaching that to others, as you do, is compassionate action.

J: Yes, in a way you can say so. But if I start to imagine that what I'm doing here is "compassionate action," and that I am offering you the solution to some real problem that needs solving, then that would only be perpetuating the suffering by confirming the reality of both the imaginary problem and the one who seems to have this problem. Right now, in all honesty, I don't see anyone who needs fixing. I don't see anything broken. And from the vantage point of unicity, there is nothing *other* than compassionate action – even the erupting volcano or the madman shooting people in a shopping center is all a movement of one seamless whole, the heart of which is unconditional love.

P: Teachers say, "Feel what arises, stay with what arises," as a technique. Something happens by not resisting what is arising.

J: Yes, and for a long time that was what I talked about and offered. And sometimes I still talk that way because it has its place. But more often now, I point to the fact that there is no "me" in control of resisting or not resisting, and that whatever appears, there is only unicity. I've seen how well-intended solutions, such as "feel what arises, stay with what arises," can become one more version of our lifelong endeavor to improve and get somewhere and be a success and do it right. Now we have this new task – when suffering arises, we have to "be present," and "feel it in the body" and "be aware of awareness," and so forth, and it gives us a sense of hope and purpose and meaning in one moment, and then in another moment, it becomes a way of beating ourselves up for not doing it right, for failing and falling short again and again. When you see that the whole movie of waking life is a dream-like appearance going nowhere, then something relaxes. Your character has any number of unresolved imperfections. The icecaps are melting. Things are messy. So what? You stop being so fixated on solving the problem of life. Watching *The Sopranos* is as spiritual as going on a meditation retreat. The separation has melted away. There is simply what is, as it is.

P: You must believe that the message you are presenting is in some way important for us to hear.

J: Actually I don't. I can honestly say that I don't believe it's important for you to hear it, although if you're hearing it, then there is no choice – this is what is happening and it could not be otherwise. I can truly, honestly, say that I have no idea why I'm doing this talking and writing and dialoging with people. I enjoy doing this, it's fun, it's entertaining, and it seems to be what is happening in this life. I can make up a story about how I got into it or why I do it, but it would only be a story. It happens. I hold meetings. I write books. I have no idea how it affects anyone else or if I'll still be doing it tomorrow.

This meeting is delightfully useless, like the sounds of the rain. That's the beauty of it. It goes nowhere (now/here). It accomplishes nothing. It simply is. I read somewhere that Alan Watts called himself a spiritual entertainer, and I rather like that job description. Clearly, I wasn't cut out for anything more useful like building houses or producing babies.

P: Do you suffer less than you did twenty years ago? Aren't you better off now?

J: Really, I haven't gotten anywhere. I am right here. I've always been right Here. We so want this to be going somewhere better. We want this to be useful. We want to have hope that there's more to life than this moment. We want it all to have purpose and meaning and a brighter future. But when that all falls away, it is so freeing – to be utterly useless – to be totally helpless – without purpose – simply this absolutely wonderful, terrible, messy, unresolved, irresolvable, amazing, horrible, gorgeous, indescribable aliveness, exactly as it is.

You Can't Get Any Closer to Here than Here

No squirrel is worried about the meaning of existence or getting enlightened or saving its soul or saving the planet. The newborn baby isn't worried about any of this either. Only the developed human brain – the thought process – is trying to figure out the meaning of life. Why are we here? What's it all about? How did it begin? Where is it all going? Why is there something instead of nothing? And thought provides all kinds of answers to these cosmic questions and every answer it provides can be doubted.

Waking up points to the recognition of what is simple and obvious and impossible to doubt. And we could say that the so-called pathless path is a process of wearing out or seeing through all our misunderstandings about what that means. Enlightenment and delusion are like two sides of a single coin. We cannot have one without the other, nor can we find any place where one ends and the other begins. The seeking mind wants to establish "me" on one side of the coin permanently. But that is a total fantasy. Unicity is the whole coin and there is no "me" in the picture at all.

P: So if I understand you, you are suggesting not resisting anything that happens.

J: There is no one who can chose to resist or not resist. So-called resistance may arise. But that, too, is only another shape that unicity is momentarily assuming. It's not like, "Okay, now I get it. I won't resist anything. That's my new goal, not to resist anything. Just let it all be." It's more like seeing that it already *is* allowed to be, including the resistance, including the suffering, including *everything*, because obviously, it's here, so obviously it *is* allowed to be. But there's no "you" in there who has to *do* that allowing.

P: If there is turbulence in the plane on the way home, I want to attend to the space in which it's happening rather than getting all white knuckled. Is that wrong to have a strategy or an intention or a desire to stay calm?

J: It's not wrong. That strategy is something that is arising, like a cloud that's passing through the sky in a dream. The mind is thinking about what happens if there is turbulence on the plane, and it is thinking, "I'll want to have a good strategy for dealing with that, if that happens." If and when that turbulence *actually* occurs, then some response to it will happen, but there's no "you" who has any control over what that response will be in that moment. And who cares about it? There may be the idea that if "I" were really spiritual, then there could be a lot of turbulence, the plane could even be crashing, and "I" would be totally unaffected, spaciously present in complete equanimity.

Katagiri Roshi said, when he was dying of cancer, "Enlightenment is not dying a good death. It is not *needing* to die a good death." The egoic mirage always wants to look and feel good – be calm while the plane crashes, smile benevolently on my deathbed, meet everything with total equanimity, never get angry or anxious or depressed. But the One Reality includes everything.

So what difference does it make? Obviously it's more pleasant one way, but life is not always pleasant by its very nature. The suffering is in the thought that this is "my" reaction, and "I" want it to be spiritually correct. It all seems very important and very serious. So here we are at the Yoga Center and the mind is busy plotting what to do if there is turbulence on the plane flight home tomorrow. It's so human, and it's quite funny, isn't it? As Mark Twain once said, I've been through lots of terrible things in my life, but fortunately most of them never happened.

P: How does one stop caring? We shouldn't care about what happens?

J: I didn't say, "We *shouldn't* care." I asked, "Who cares?" I didn't mean this question flippantly or dismissively, but as a genuine question. In reference to what is there caring about how I'll react to turbulence? It's in reference to the phantom self, isn't it?

If that caring arises, then it is something that arises, like a cloud in the sky. No big deal. Just another appearance like turbulence or white knuckling or the hissing of the radiator. None of it is personal.

P: So is there nothing we can do?

J: You will do whatever you do – but there is no executive at the helm calling the shots. And nothing you do will get you anywhere other than right here, where you always are. And when consciousness goes, either in deep sleep or in death, all your progress is gone. The whole movie of your life vanishes like last night's dream.

Enlightenment is seeing this. Delusion is not seeing this. When enlightenment is here, we see everything as unicity. When delusion is here, we imagine enemies who need to be vanquished, internal enemies or external enemies. Enlightenment sees no boundary between internal and external, and it sees no enemies. It sees only God. Even in the air turbulence or the anxiety or the white-knuckling, enlightenment sees only God. Enlightenment realizes that we all refer to the same presence when we say "I." This timeless, placeless Here/Now is like St. Bonaventure's sphere: the center is everywhere and the circumference is nowhere. Enlightenment has no problem with anything.

P: Can you give us any instructions on what to do after this weekend is over?

J: *This* is never over. The forms are always changing, but Here/Now is ever-present. Instructions will come. Instructions are always coming. The trees know when to drop their leaves, and in the same way, you always know exactly what to do right now, even if what you are doing is ruminating and wavering over an apparent decision.

P: It sounds like you don't believe at all in free will.

J: I don't see anybody separate from the whole to have free will or not have free will. The *appearance* of free will comes in when thought starts to think, "How am I going to deal with the air turbulence?" That thought posits this phantom me who has a choice.

When we say there is a choice, we are thinking about two hypo-thetical possibilities in an imaginary future. I could either relax and breathe deeply when the air turbulence comes, or I could tense up and panic. The notion that "I" have a choice implies that there is someone here who can make one or the other of those two responses happen. But when the air turbulence actually happens, whatever response arises is the only possible one at that moment. There is no self to be in control or out of control. Everything *is* as it is, and it could not be otherwise. And that includes the *appearance* of decision-making and choosing!

P: You talk about seeing that everything is unicity, and how this is our actual experience right now, but I don't see it.

J: You think you don't see it because thought is telling you that "this isn't it" and you are looking for something else. But even this looking for something else is nothing but unicity. You can't get any closer to Here than here. The seeking mind keeps trying to work it all out intellectually – thinking and thinking and thinking about "no self" and "free will" and "unicity" and trying to figure it all out. It compares Eckhart Tolle to Tony Parsons, and Buddhism to Advaita, and it thinks and thinks. Or the seeking mind goes to work on self-improvement – if only I could stop being anxious during the air turbulence, or if only I could stop smoking, or if only I could be better at intimate relationships, or if only I could be more mindful, more compassionate, more generous, *then* I would be enlightened. *Then* I would see unicity.

All of this is unicity. The suffering is in imagining that there is something outside of unicity. The suffering is in the quest for self-improvement and control. Control is only an issue if you think of yourself as a separate part.

P: But you are free of suffering and I am not. I want to be free too. But I keep having these panic attacks.

J: There is no "Joan" who is free of suffering and no "Susan" who is not free. That is all a thought-story, and *that* is suffering. *But it's imaginary.*

For years I regarded my fingerbiting compulsion as a sign of how neurotic I was, a sure indication that I was not enlightened. I saw it as a shameful stain. I hated it. I worked and worked to cure it. I did therapy. I did meditation and inquiry. I did bodywork and somatic awareness work. And over the years, the habit has diminished – it happens less frequently, the wounds are less severe. At age 30, I imagined that someday it would be gone. But now, in middle age, I realize it may continue to happen off and on until the day I die. But that possibility no longer bothers me. Yes, it would be nice if it stopped forever, but maybe it won't. Life isn't always as "nice" as we would like it to be. Life includes thunderstorms, earthquakes, panic attacks, fingerbiting, air turbulence, tsunamis, volcanoes, viruses, predators ripping apart their prey, parasites colonizing their hosts, suns exploding. The only real peace and freedom is the peace and freedom that *includes* all of this, not the peace and freedom that we associate with sunny weather and moments of bliss. That kind of peace and freedom is always temporary, always fragile, always in danger of being upset. That kind of peace and freedom can't tolerate the screaming children, the noisy leaf blowers, the horrific wars, the excruciating pain, the addictions and compulsions, the moments of panic, the incredible injustices of life. That kind of temporary peace is at war with reality.

Messy, unpleasant stuff still happens for the Joan character. What has changed, and not in a dramatic once-and-for-all experience, but gradually, imperceptibly, over what appears to be time, is that the search for improvement has fallen away. I still take my vitamins and go to the gym. That's not what I'm talking about. Going to the gym happens or it doesn't, just the way fingerbiting happens or it doesn't. But with fingerbiting, there's no belief any more that it is a sign of failure and worthlessness. There is no longer a *need* to fix it. When it happens, it happens. The stories *about* it have fallen away. It needs no cure.

P: I still have stories, and I want my stories to fall away, too.

J: Okay, so let's start right here. "I still have stories, and I want my stories to fall away, too." *That in itself is a story!* This is like me thinking that fingerbiting is an obstacle that has to go away before "I" can be truly free. These stories that you think have to go away are like fingerbiting or white knuckling on the plane – they are some kind of weather that the thinking mind is taking personally and holding up as an obstacle to freedom. So let's look right now and see if there is any real obstacle, right here, right now. Is there?

P: But you said that your freedom came when the stories fell away.

J: Yes, and now the mind has managed to turn *that* into a new story about why you are not free. In *this* story, "stories" have now become the imaginary problem, the imaginary obstacle. But where are these stories right now? Is this obstacle real? And is the one who seems to be obstructed by it real? Where is this one right now? Can you find this obstruction or this one who is obstructed? Or is there actually only the boundlessness of Here/Now in which fingerbiting and white knuckling and stories and air turbulence and this meeting and the whole universe appears and disappears?

P: This is very radical.

J: Yes. Radical, to the root. It is the simple recognition that there is no problem. In Reality, nothing is broken.

Not Making Something Out of Nothing

What are we doing here? What is life all about? What matters?

I notice that whenever I ask questions like this, the first thing that happens is that the mind goes blank. There's no answer. Only open space. Listening silence.

And then maybe the thinking mind starts grinding away, looking for the correct answer. Let's see, what is life all about? What am I doing here? But maybe the truest answer is that first instant when there's no answer at all.

Words are so slippery because as soon as I *say* that, then the mind can think, "Okay, 'the first instant,' 'listening silence' – *that's* what I'm looking for, *that's* what I have to get, *that's* what I have to *do* all the time, *that's* the answer to my problems, *that's* what will save the world." And then we think, "Is this it? No, I don't think so. I think I *had* it an hour ago, but now I've lost it. How can I get it back? I wonder if the person next to me has it. What good will this listening silence do for me if I'm in prison being tortured? Will it hold up then? Maybe this nonduality stuff is all just another pipe dream. Maybe I'm totally fucked after all."

Thought can so quickly turn nothing into *something*. Something to believe in or to doubt. Thought can even turn silence or emptiness or boundlessness into an idea of *something* solid and separate. So, can there be a simple noticing of that habitual movement of thought? Not noticing it once and for all and then finally it's gone forever, but noticing it now and now and now, *as it arises* – that mechanism of thought that wants to grasp life, control it, figure it out. "Do we have free will?" or "How does Krishnamurti compare to Nisargadatta?" Thought loves to think about "me" and how I'm doing. Thought says, "If only I could go on retreat for six months, I could really get this."

In *seeing* that grasping for what it is, and in seeing how useless it is, the thinking mind may relax its grip and our whole being may open and fall silent. And then (if only for a moment) there is the utter simplicity of what is – sounds, sensations, breathing – simple presence. Bare being. But if we start to *think* about this utterly simple presence, what happens? We're grasping again. Trying to figure it all out.

We search for meaning and then feel meaningless. We search for success and feel like a failure. We try to believe and we are filled with doubt. We search for enlightenment and feel unenlightened. We imagine a weed-free life without dirty laundry, and we try to invent this, and we create weed-killers that destroy the planet. But of course, enlightenment has nothing to do with the absence of weeds or with perpetual ecstasy. It is simply the falling away of the whole attempt to get somewhere else (as if we could ever be anywhere other than Here/Now). When all of that is seen for the foolish tail-chase that it is, something relaxes and lets go, and there is simply *this* which defies all attempts to box it up in concepts, maps, and descriptions. And *this* is not a problem, even when it hurts, or tenses up, or has a panic attack, or has to do another load of laundry.

We always want to arrive at some final place where there's no more ambiguity, no more confusion, no more doubt, no more weeds, no more laundry, no more depression, no more fear, no more anxiety, no more boredom, no more problems. But is that the goal? To find a perfect life? To be totally dead at last?

We only need to look out the window to see how unrealistic that goal would be – just notice the weather: thunderstorms, clouds, clearings, sun, rain, hot, cold, wet, dry. Always changing. *Whatever* is appearing here, whether it's thunder, rain, clouds, clear skies, boredom, anxiety, happiness – it is impossible for it *not* to be the way it is! It *is* as it is! *All* of it impersonal weather. Am "I" in control of the clearing and clouding? Or is there a clearing and clouding happening here that isn't about any of us as individuals?

There is space here for everything. Have you noticed? Do our apparent problems stick around forever? Or do they turn out to be nothing at all?

How Free Are We?

The universe is not bound by its content, because its potentialities are infinite; besides it is a manifestation, or expression of a principle fundamentally and totally free.

— Nisargadatta Maharaj

How much freedom do we really have? Instead of immediately rushing in with our preferred answer that we are convinced is true, can we leave that question open and unanswered? For me, it is a beautiful koan that continues to unfold and open. Is it possible to wake up, right now, from all the thoughts, ideas, beliefs and habits of mind and body that recreate and reincarnate "the same old world" and "the same old me" moment by moment out of thin air, out of habit?

Nonduality, Buddhism and Advaita are all in some way about cutting through the imaginary limitations and problems created by conceptual thought — *seeing* how we habitually and unconsciously choose bondage over liberation, *seeing* how we are doing our suffering. Waking up is discovering another possibility.

Of course, when I say that "we" do these things, I'm not talking about the phantom self, which doesn't really exist. So it's not about blaming ourselves or others for "choosing" bondage or creating suffering. This "choice" happens out of infinite causes and conditions. It happens out of ignorance. It is a kind of hypnotic entrancement, not some personal failure. But it *is* possible, when it is, to *see* how this "choice" gets made, to become conscious of how we do our suffering, to wake up from this entrancement. Just as delusion is not a personal failure, awakening is not a personal success. It is the dissolution of that very *idea* of separation, limitation and ownership. Waking up is the activity of the True Self—boundless awareness, the intelligence at the heart of everything.

Here/Now is totally open and unpredictable. Awareness has no boundaries and no limits. The survival mind keeps trying to locate and solidify itself, get a grip, figure everything out. *Trying* to end this reincarnation of suffering is more of the same habitual movement of the mind. But the *seeing* of that movement *as it happens* is outside the habitual loop. The *seeing*—the awareness—is free and unbound. Here/Now, before thought, we cannot say what is possible and what isn't. This moment is absolutely new. It has never been here before.

All solidity and limitation is imaginary. The whole movie of waking life is a dream-like appearance, an imagination, a play of consciousness. Perhaps this is what the miracles in the New Testament point to, that with faith in God, anything is possible. We can walk on water and move mountains. Of course, for me, "faith in God" doesn't mean *belief* in some supernatural force outside of ourselves, and true freedom doesn't mean walking on water.

The biggest miracle is Here/Now—every moment of ordinary life. When we really *see*, when we're awake, *everything* is extraordinary. What makes it miraculous is not the *content* but the *awareness* that beholds and illuminates and breathes life into the momentary forms. Awareness is what we love in the beloved. When we dissolve into this openness that is always Here/Now, we act from a place that is unbound. When we wake up, the whole world wakes up, because we are not separate.

No one is the same from one instant to the next. Everything changes. But thought solidifies people and things in the mind, so we *think* we're the same person we were yesterday, and we think we know who that person is—a compulsive fingerbiter maybe, or a loser, or an enlightened sage, or someone with money issues, or a seeker. When we sit down to breakfast with our significant other, or go to work and run into our boss, we imagine that we're talking to the same person who was there yesterday or the day before. But no person has ever really existed as anything other than ever-changing thoughts-images-stories-sensations-shapes appearing in consciousness.

When we talk about how the past is completely gone and no one is the same from moment to moment, that doesn't mean we should deny history or stop planning intelligently for the future. If every time I run into a certain person, he hits me over the head, it's useful to be able to remember that. Remembering history is useful. We don't have to reinvent the wheel every day. The danger with history is in the solidification – making absolute what actually isn't. If I am convinced that this person will *definitely* hit me over the head because that's what he has always done before, and so I assume that he always will, then something goes awry that doesn't have to. Then we have the Israeli/Palestinian conflict. Because even though I might be careful around somebody who (so far) always hits me over the head, in fact, he might *not* do that the next time, because he is not really the same person who was there before and I'm not the same person either. If I can meet the person who is here now openly, without knowing who he is in this moment, that openness actually creates a space for him to change, whereas if I see him as an aggressive, "bad" person, he may very well conform to my image. In so many ways, we influence and create each other because we aren't really separate. If I see that infinite causes and conditions drove this person to hit me, then I will approach him with compassion and unconditional love rather than with blame and hatred. In the Rule of Saint Benedict, the monks and nuns are instructed to treat everyone they meet as Christ. As Jesus said, Whatever you do unto the least of these, you do unto me. Love begets love, and hate begets hate. Waking up is breaking the cycle of hate and opening the door of possibility.

We can't *make* this kind of openness and love happen on command anymore than we can move mountains on command. It doesn't work that way. But it may be possible (when it is) to *see* how we get mixed up, to *see* the false as false, to *see* how we move away, how we postpone, how we create and recreate our apparent bondage. By giving nonjudgmental, loving attention to what we are doing and how we are doing it, everything changes naturally. This giving of attention is like breathing – we can't really say whether we are breathing or being breathed. The attention I'm talking about is open, spacious awareness, not thought, analysis and rumination. It is not a task or a practice. It is our true nature. It has no cause and it seeks no result.

Is it possible in this moment to drop all of our ideas about ourselves and the world? Is it possible to fully enjoy the delightful sounds of rain or the amazing tastes and aromas of a cup of coffee? And maybe to enjoy not only the rain and the coffee, but also the wonderful and terrible messiness of human life with all its perfection and imperfection – this whole astonishing movie of waking life – without needing it to be any different from exactly how it is, and without imagining that anything has to stay the same. That is true freedom.

Cosmic Play

The composer John Cage, who was a very Zen guy, had a symphony where there was no music other than the naturally occurring sounds in the auditorium – people coughing and rustling their programs – and the sounds of silence. *That* was the symphony. I bet many people in the audience were very disappointed that night, or mystified, or maybe even angry. They paid good money for this! But there were probably at least a few people there who heard and enjoyed the symphony. When you really *hear* ordinary sounds, it *is* like a symphony. The car horn, the bird cheep, the cicadas, the wind in the leaves, the vast listening silence.

If you really *look* at any supposedly ordinary thing like this glass of water here, you find an amazing universe. Of course, if you think to yourself, "It's just a glass of water. I've seen it a million times before. It's nothing important," then you don't really *see* it, and chances are, you'll find it very boring and unspectacular. But actually, we've never seen *this* glass at *this* moment ever before. And if we really start to look carefully, there's an astonishing visual symphony here – you could look at this water glass for hours. [Joan holds it up] Look at it! The colors, the reflections, the liquidity, the light. It's infinitely interesting and delightful. And we can have the same experience even with things like pain, depression or addiction. If we're not resisting something and trying to get away from it, then suddenly, amazingly enough, it's actually interesting, even when it hurts.

But if the mind takes what I've just said and decides, "Okay, this is my new project – my new method – to always be interested in everything," it won't work. Because there's an agenda. There's an expectation of results. And so, of course, it's disappointing. And then we think, "Why can't I get interested in my headache?"

[sound of a car starting up]

The sound of that car engine turning over – it really is that simple. *Rrrrhhhhmmmmm* – one, undivided *rrrrrhhhhmmmmm*. Just this!

The sound of children's voices, a ball bouncing on the sidewalk, cars whooshing past. It doesn't get any more enlightening or any more nondual than this.

Everything perceivable or conceivable is here for an instant and then – *whoosh* – it's gone! You zero in on any sensation, really watch it closely, and you can't find anything solid there – only ever-changing, shimmering, vibrating, pulsating movement. The past is completely gone. The future does not exist. Nothing is solid. It's one shimmering, disappearing dream-world.

Words make it seem otherwise. We speak of Chicago, but what exactly *is* "Chicago"? Is it the soil, the air, the ever-changing inhabitants, the ever-changing government, the cultural happenings, the ceaseless rivers of traffic, the buildings that are being built or demolished, remodeled or torn down? The sidewalk that is cracking and crumbling as a tree root pushes up under it? What *is* Chicago? Undeniably, there is *something* that we call "Chicago," but when you try to take hold of exactly *what* it is, you can't actually get hold of anything solid. Two visitors to Chicago on the same day will experience two totally different cities. Which is the real Chicago? The same is true with Lake Michigan and the Pacific Ocean and the United States of America and the chair you are sitting in and you as a particular person. What exactly *is* any of it? Where are the boundaries? Where does the city of Chicago end and Lake Michigan begin? Where does the land become the lake? The tide goes in and out over the wet sand – where is the boundary? On the map, it looks solid and clear, a definitive black line. In actuality, you can't find any exact or enduring boundary. Everything is moving and inseparable.

What exactly *is* "your wife" (or your husband, or your boyfriend, or your domestic partner, or your lover)? How real is he or she? Yes, *something* is in the bed with you, so to speak, but what exactly *is* it and where does "it" begin and end? What exactly *is* "your wife"? Sensations, shapes, colors, smells, subatomic waves and particles dancing, cells dividing, organs pulsating and oozing, lungs contracting and expanding, blood flowing, heart pumping, oxygen and food and ideas and words and sounds and fluids coming in and going out – sensations of touching – where exactly in all this ceaseless movement, change and interaction is "your wife"?

This aliveness does not hold still. A friend of mine who was a surgical nurse described the shock of interns making their first cut in a living body. They've studied the anatomy book, they've dissected the cadavers, but now they're cutting into a living organism and suddenly everything is slippery and pulsating, blood is gushing out, everything is moving. This is real life. Nothing holds still. It's a mess. And yet right in the heart of this impermanence, this messiness, this thoroughgoing flux, there is true stillness, order and intelligence.

P: It's amazing that everything comes from nothing, but is Nothing so damned bored it has to do this? Some experience just seems so miserable. And yet I guess the Nothing is just doing it because it wants to. Pretty weird.

J: This is the problem with words. We talk about no-thing-ness, and next thing we know, the mind has created a Giant Thing called "The Nothing," sort of like God or Zeus, some entity that is sitting up there in heaven deliberately doing all of this out of boredom or for amusement or maybe to teach us a lesson – that's a popular idea, that life is like a giant school system. *There is no one doing any of this.* There is only *this* [Joan gestures to include everything]. And when you dive deeply into *this*, you find no-thing at all. So can we for just one moment drop all these stories and ideas about cosmic school systems and God and Zeus and Consciousness and Unicity – let it *all* go – and see what remains. *That* is the truth!

P: I feel I have to accomplish things and improve myself.

J: That's all part of the mirage. The whole of human history and evolutionary development and progress and "you" as a separate something that is going somewhere and improving – it's all a mirage.

P: This is really starting to confuse me.

J: That's good. We're finally getting somewhere. [laughter] [*tweet tweet tweet* – a bird cheeps] *Tweet tweet tweet* is not confusing. You can try really hard to figure it all out and get something out of it and make something of yourself, or you can enjoy this whole show like the beautiful play it is. It's all play.

P: Lately I find that I really don't know if the war in Iraq and George Bush and hunger in America are "real" or an illusion. I'm starting to suspect I can't know.

J: What is real in this moment right now? That's a wonderful question to live with.

This seamless flow of presently appearing images and sensations gets divided up by thought into what we come to think of as solid, independent, persisting things, like "Chicago" and "my wife" and "George Bush" and "Iraq." On top of these conceptually imagined "things," the thinking mind piles beliefs, ideologies, and stories – most of them based on second or third hand information taken on faith. What facts we believe, what sources we consider reliable, what qualities we see in another person, how we frame or interpret a situation, all have to do with our past experiences, our conditioning, our genetics, our neurochemistry, our hormone balance, our moment in history, our social class, our particular vantage point. To someone else, what we imagine to be "the same event" looks completely different. More accurately, there really is no such *thing* as "the same event." We go to a movie with our best friend sometimes, and when we leave the theater it seems as if we have each seen two entirely different movies, and in fact, we have!

What is real? When we see how fluid it all is, it's hard to take ourselves quite so seriously.

P: You've often said there are no obstacles, only the illusion of obstacles. I'm reading a book by a Tibetan teacher who suggests that a really good question to ask is what prevents me from being free right this moment.

J: That *is* a wonderful question to live with – what is preventing me from being free right this moment? Is this apparent problem or this apparent obstacle real? Is there a "me" who isn't free?

If I am compulsively biting my fingers, for example, what is preventing me from stopping? Not to *think* about that question, but to actually look and listen and see. And if I can't stop, then to wonder, is this biting preventing me from being free? Is it actually a problem? It may be painful and unpleasant. It may be an obstacle to my better ideas of what I "should" be doing with my time. It may be causing some injury to my fingers or my teeth. It may be keeping me from getting things done. It may make me tense. But so what? Even if I were to bite off my whole hand and die from it, is that a problem? To whom is it a problem? *And how does the experience of compulsive fingerbiting change if the belief that it is a problem drops away?*

What about depression? Is that a real problem? As with compulsive fingerbiting, depression is unpleasant and may be causing some harm to the body – the brain, the digestion, the heart may be suffering. It may even lead to losing one's job or ending up homeless. It could even end in suicide. But is any of this a real obstacle? An obstacle to what?

We might think that global warming, child abuse, genocide, and things of that nature are certainly real problems – obstacles to life, to human survival, to happiness and well-being. But then, from the perspective of unicity, would it matter if the whole universe explodes?

This isn't to say that we won't do whatever we are moved to do to heal ourselves or the world, or to correct errors and fix problems. We do what the universe moves us to do. But we will do whatever we do in a very different spirit when we recognize that we are being moved by larger forces, that we don't actually know what the universe needs or how it all works or what "should" or "should not" happen next, and when we really see the interdependence and wholeness of everything – the unicity. Otherwise, we are fighting for "my way" very much like a two-year-old throwing a tantrum, and we are forever fighting against an illusory "other" who is really our own shadow and our own projection. We are always trying to achieve the impossible: a world of up without down, good without bad. The universe couldn't actually show up without these apparent polarities. Consciousness *is* variety and differentiation.

P: This notion that "it's all unicity" brings up great discomfort in me. I'm trying to understand better why it does. Is it because it just seems obvious to me that global warming and child abuse are antithetical to happiness and well being, even given the positive personal transformations that sometimes happen in the midst of such horror? I seem unable to free myself from the thought that, though I *want* to see it all as an illusion and beyond our ability to understand and somehow all fundamentally perfect, I can't. And I think I can't because I have a fear that to do so would be to justify these horrors and give up the last shred of goodness and humanity that I may still have.

J: First of all, statements like "everything is perfect" or "it's all unicity" are verbal pointers. Whether they are true or false depends on how we are hearing them and where we're coming from when we say them. Are we coming in that moment from the awareness, presence and open listening that *is* wholeness and perfection? Or are we coming from a mental spin up in our heads? Are we expressing what is genuinely true for us at that moment or merely regurgitating something we're heard as a comforting slogan to make us feel better?

I know from my own experience the fear that you're speaking about, that if I give up (or see through) this belief that "this should not be," if I let myself see how insubstantial and dream-like the world is, then somehow I will end up being complicit with evil and injustice. But is this true? Is this really what happens?

There is a significant difference between the compassionate

sensitivity that recognizes suffering and wants to respond, on the one hand, and a belief that "this *shouldn't* happen," on the other. To say it "should not" be the way it is, is to fight against the universe. The universe *is*, in fact, often painful and cruel. That "NO!!!" to the universe comes from (and reinforces) the sense of being a separate self. That sense of separation *is* suffering, and it generates more and more suffering.

When we see clearly, we not only see that abuse is hurting the victim, but we see that it is hurting the abuser as well. We also see that the abuser had no choice. We don't hate the abuser and feel the urge to make him suffer through punishment and revenge. We may want to lock the abuser up and keep him out of circulation, but we don't do it in a spirit of anger and hate that comes from believing that "he did this deliberately – he could have made a better choice – he should suffer for his sins." Unfortunately, our criminal justice system and global politics are still very much rooted in these kinds of ignorant assumptions, all based in the idea of the independent, autonomous self with free will.

Of course, on the level of relative reality, we can say that people "should not" abuse children or pollute the environment. But, in fact, those things *do* happen. They happen out of infinite causes and conditions. When you stop believing that "this should not happen," it does not mean that you then pick up the opposite belief that "this *should* happen." Nor does it mean that you cannot take action of some kind in response. But if you do act, it will come from a different place – a place that I would call love rather than hate.

Bernie Glassman, a Zen teacher and social activist, speaks of taking action without the idea of a cure. That is very different from the mind-state I often had as a political activist. I thought I knew what was best for the world. I knew what was "right," I knew how the universe *should* be working, and I was going to fix things. There was a great deal of violence, anger and self-righteousness in that attitude, and it often created more problems than it solved. Light and dark, oppressor and oppressed are not two. They can't really be pulled apart. Everything contains everything else.

What I feel moved to do is part of how the whole universe works, but so is George Bush and what he feels moved to do. We are inseparable aspects of one whole being. And the truth is, even as I telephone the White House opinion line, I actually don't know what "should" happen next.

Much of our dialog seems to turn on the word "should."

We think certain atrocities and injustices "should not" happen.

But do we think that cancer cells "should not" attack an organ? Or that crows "should not" eat the babies of other birds? Or that a volcano or an earthquake "should not" have killed people and plants and animals, perhaps in an extremely slow and painful way? Or that an asteroid or an ice age or whatever it was "should not" have wiped out the dinosaurs? Or that a parasite "should not" live on the host and make them behave in suicidal ways? Or that certain ants "should not" work less than other ants in the colony?

Our ideas of "should not" around Hurricane Katrina all have to do with the things we attribute to humans: the flawed levies, the flawed emergency response, the flawed insurance coverage, and so on. But does anyone think the hurricane itself "should not" have happened? If so, only in the sense of it being a by-product of human-caused global warming.

In our thinking, we seem to remove humans from the rest of nature (ant hills are natural, skyscrapers are not), and we insert that mirage-agent at the helm who freely chooses to abuse children or commit genocide. Then we have that "should" and "should not" idea. We pull the universe apart conceptually and decide that some situation "should not" be the way it is. But does reality actually work that way?

Remember, letting go of "should not" does not mean picking up "should." It does not mean we now believe that child abuse "should" happen, or that we won't act to stop it. We're simply acknowledging and accepting the reality that (like it or not) it *is* happening.

Finally, is anything ever *really* being hurt or destroyed? Relatively speaking, of course the common sense answer would be yes. But that is a question of live with, to wonder about, to look into deeply, to meditate upon, and not to answer with a *belief* one way or the other.

I suspect there may be something worth exploring in that place where the idea of "unicity" makes you uncomfortable. To really look deeply and *see* what is real in this moment and what isn't. This understanding cuts through any sense one is holding onto of moral indignation or self-righteous victimhood. And this can feel very threatening to that false sense of encapsulated selfhood that is fighting to survive. We are so afraid that seeing suffering as a dream will make us heartless and complicit in the cruelty somehow. But is that true? Does this understanding lead us to be cruel and insensitive? Is that your actual experience?

Nonduality: What Is It?

Thinking about nonduality and trying to figure it all out frequently gives us a headache, but we are so convinced that thinking will eventually work, that we keep doing it again and again however much it fails us. It's like any addiction – we keep imagining that maybe one more hit will finally satiate the hungry ghost. So thought keeps on chasing its tail around and around the treadmill, faster and faster.

This treadmill activity is very frustrating and unsatisfying as everyone here has noticed, I'm sure. Truth is what cannot be doubted, what requires no belief. This is so obvious, so simple, so immediate, so ordinary, and so utterly inescapable that we keep *seemingly* overlooking it by seeking something special or trying to figure it out. Even then, we can't ever *really* overlook it because it is all there is. But when that search drops away, when we stop trying to figure everything out, when we let go of everything we can doubt, what remains?

P: I notice that I want certainty, that I am still looking for certainty.

J: Well, let's explore certainty. The mind wants certainty. That's its job. It's a survival instinct. But what is certain? Are you absolutely certain that you are here? Not you as Joe or you as a man, but you as aware-presence, call it what you will. Are you absolutely certain about *being here*? Do you have any doubts about that?

P: Here in Joan's apartment or just being?

J: Just being. Joan's apartment is appearing Here/Now. Here/Now is another word for awareness or presence or being. Do you doubt this awareness, this presence, the bare fact of being here?

P: No, I don't have any doubts that I am.

J: That's the only thing I've discovered about which there can be undeniable certainty. "I am" or "this is." Everything else you can start to question. But *being here* is absolutely undeniable. And of course, by *being here*, I don't mean "all of us" being in "Joan's living room." Joan's living room is appearing Here/Now. "All of us" are appearing Here/Now. By "being" or "here" or "being here," I mean this aware presence that cannot be doubted. Here/Now cannot be doubted or avoided. Interpretations or explanations or descriptions of what this is can all be doubted, but the *fact* of it, the *suchness* of it, cannot be doubted.

P: We keep slipping into identification with thoughts. What causes that?

J: Anything I say in response to that will fall into the category of things that can be doubted. Any notion of cause and effect is always a conceptual overlay. But with that caution in mind, I'd say that thinking appears to be part of what the brain naturally does. It is a survival tool. Thought seems to pose as the voice of "me." So our thoughts *seem* like they come from "me" – the thinker, the author, the executive at the helm. And if thought posits a thinker, then there must be one! We *think* that we are authoring our thoughts, and what our thoughts tell us usually *seems* very believable to us, very credible – an objective report on reality.

Another way we seem to slip into identification with thoughts is when we are suddenly addressed as the character in the play. I'm sure you've all had this experience. One minute there's nothing going on, just listening to the wind in the leaves and the songs of the birds – impersonal boundless presence – and then suddenly someone walks up to you and says, "Joan! What have you done with the last thirty years?" I recently ran into a high school friend I hadn't seen in thirty years who actually asked me this. Then all of a sudden, there's this kind of inner contraction or narrowing down as consciousness seems to remember, "Oh, yes. I'm Joan," and then trying to think, "What *have* I done with these thirty years?" And the mind starts trying to remember and reconstruct and put together a brief narrative to satisfy the question, and as this is happening, consciousness seems to become more and more absorbed in the story and the thought of being this Joan character, and as the story of her life reassembles and solidifies itself, perhaps various judgments and evaluations of the story begin to arise ("I haven't done enough with my life," or whatever it might be), and suddenly that impersonal boundless presence seems to have disappeared and been replaced by this thought-story-sensation of being Joan.

This typically happens many times in any ordinary day – starting with the moment of waking up in the morning and remembering who we are in the play.

But again, that whole explanation that just poured out of my mouth is a story, and it can be doubted. And the whole world it describes is a kind of dream-like appearance. What can't be doubted is the bare *fact* of this appearance, the *suchness* of it, the *beingness* of it, and the ever-present Here/Now in which it all appears.

[Sound of horn honking several times]

Beep Beep Beep [Joan imitates horn] Undeniable! *What* that sound is you can have a million questions and doubts and uncertainties about, but the bare *IS-ness* of it, *that* is undeniable. And no explanation or description is the same as the thing itself.

P: Is there a difference between thoughts and the sounds of birds or traffic?

J: Well, is there? What's your experience? I find that there's a palpable energetic difference between thinking and sensing, or between thought and awareness. One is simple and beyond doubt, the other spins an imaginary world that is complicated and full of doubts and suffering.

They each feel very different in the body – one is spacious and open; the other has a more encapsulated and contracted feel to it. But at the same time, thoughts and bird sounds are both forms of one energy. Both are momentary, dream-like appearances in awareness, as are the sensations of expansion and contraction. All of these different appearances are empty of substance. There is no *essential* difference between compulsive thinking, shooting heroin, and the song of a bird. So, in that absolute sense, they are all One. We can find relative differences or we can find absolute oneness. I would say, don't overlook or deny either side of the coin. The absolute contains the relative but isn't bound by it. And the absolute doesn't deny the relative or mix them up.

[*Two participants get into an increasingly heated argument over whether thought produces anxiety or whether anxiety is a neurochemical change that produces anxious thoughts. Joan says nothing, simply allowing it to unfold. At the same time as this argument is escalating, the sound of a loud siren from the street outside keeps getting louder and louder. After the siren has finally passed and faded away, Joan speaks.*]

J: Rather than getting into the content of what's going on, maybe we can simply notice that there's tremendous energy here, and that it's not personal to the two of you who happen to be having this argument right now. The whole argument was like that siren – a human version of that sound, that wailing energy. We don't take the siren personally, whereas we do tend to personalize an argument or a conflict. But both are simply energetic appearances like weather. Because we don't take it personally, the siren has already disappeared completely. But this argument may be lingering in many of our minds, especially for the two of you who were caught up in it. Because we take something like that personally, we could be chewing on it for hours or even years in some cases.

What is happening right now? Not just for the two of you, but for all of us? *Is* the mind still chewing on this? Do we consider this heated argument an unfortunate distraction from where the meeting should have gone? Does it make us uncomfortable? Do we feel an urge to fix it?

Do we wish the feelings that may be lingering would go away? Do we have ideas about someone being at fault? Do we think one viewpoint was right and the other wrong? Can we perhaps simply notice this whole disturbance, including all these possible reverberations, without needing *any* of it to be different in any way from exactly how it is? Can we notice that this space of Here/Now allows everything and has room for everything?

Nothing has really been damaged by that little flare up of energy, has it?

P: The thought arises here that it would have been good if that had not happened.

Another participant (*returning to the room*): I was in the bathroom. What did I miss?

J: Finally something happens here and you miss it! [laughter].

You'll Never Get It

P: I know that the snake is really just a rope, but how can you see that when you think you don't see it?

J: By recognizing that it doesn't matter whether you see it or not.

P: It doesn't?

J: It matters relatively, *in* the dream. But when the dream ends, what happens to the dream characters and their imaginary problems? Without the sense that you have to find a solution, there really isn't a problem.

P: So the search for a solution is the problem.

J: Even that is not really a problem. That, too, is simply what is appearing. Searching for a solution is part of the survival mechanism, but it's *all* only a movie, and the movie has no *fundamental* seriousness or reality. It plays for awhile and then it ends. The me who thinks it is terribly important to wake up from the movie is part of the movie. It's real as a movie, just as a dream is a real dream, and a mirage is a real mirage, but it is unreal in the sense that the content or story that it unfolds has no actual, independent, inherent, objective reality, no substance, no permanence.

P: I want to do something to remember this.

J: It's hopeless. Forgetting and remembering are both in the dream. In seeing that, there may be a relaxing, and in that relaxing, the discovery that there is no problem to solve.

P: But relaxing doesn't happen here.

J: Then there's non-relaxing or tensing up. So what?

You can't control this appearance called life. And you don't *need* to control it. You are totally helpless. When you finally see that absolute helplessness, it's surprisingly liberating.

You know those inflatable punching bags we used to have when we were kids – they were shaped like a person or something, and you'd push them over, and they'd pop back up? The thinking mind is like that – it keeps popping up. Looking for a solution, looking for the answer that will finally satisfy the cosmic itch.

P: So then the technique is to recognize –

J: There it is, popping up again! But it's okay. That, too, is only unicity. It's a game, a play of hide and seek.

P: It was really strongly ingrained into me as a child that it matters what I do. This is serious business here!

J: Yes, in the movie of waking life, it all seems very serious. Global warming, plagues, wars, famines, one hideous injustice after another, and under it all, the need to survive and procreate and keep this pattern going. My one and only chance to make something of myself and do it right! That's the dream. And it seems so serious, so important, so real. But in spite of all the horrors and atrocities, in the end, it all disappears.

P: Like in deep sleep.

J: Yes. And in deep sleep it isn't just the whole show that disappears, but more importantly, the one who is observing the show and trying so hard to figure it all out and do it right, the one who thinks it really matters what "I" do. That phantom is completely gone in deep sleep, and it's a huge relief!

P: For a moment there, I thought I got it.

J: You'll never get it. It's hopeless. You will never get it. You *are* it. There's *only* it.

P: If I wanted to be in a movie, it sure wouldn't be this one.

J: You're not in a movie. The movie is in you.

We have only a few minutes left, so maybe we can sit silently and notice what doesn't require any effort at all.

[long silence]

It's snowing.

There's No Way Out of Totality

When we look into a mirror, we see a reflection – an image, shapes and colors, a visual sensation – and we say, "That's me." But what we don't see is the seeing. We don't see awareness. We mistake an image or a sensation for what we are, and we overlook the boundless awareness or the presence in which it all appears.

When you look across the room and see somebody else, you say, "I see Lucy." But again, you're seeing an image – shapes and colors. You aren't seeing the seeing that is seeing you. What you see and identify as "Lucy" is nothing but an image, a shape, a sensation, along with an overlay of memories and ideas and stories that you have about "Lucy."

In a sense, we could say that looking at the world is like looking in a mirror. Everything you see – the whole world – is a reflection of you. But you can't ever see the seeing. You can only see the reflections, like the stars in the night sky, and by the time they register, they are images from the past. The seeing – the present moment – is invisible. It is too close, too immediate, too all-inclusive to be seen.

Much of what we call spirituality or religion is engaged in trying to perfect the character *in* the movie by changing the story and trying to improve the outcome. Then there are more "advanced" kinds of spirituality where we are trying to wake up from the movie and identify as the screen. And of course, this is a whole new movie about "me" becoming the screen. It's another version of trying to perfect the character and change the story. There's still the mirage of an imaginary *someone* who hopes to be pure awareness and not Joe Blow.

There are many shifts that occur in the movie of waking life. If you drink a cup of coffee or a glass of wine, there is a shift. If a car almost hits your car and adrenalin floods your system, there is a shift. If you are a teenager with raging hormones, or a woman who is premenstrual or menopausal, there are many shifts. If your blood sugar drops, there is a shift. If the sun comes out on a cloudy day, there is a shift. The primary, root illusion is that there is *someone* who "has" these shifts, that there is *something* that is shifting.

The appearance can only appear in contrasts and polarities. Our suffering is wanting up without down, searching for perpetual sunshine. But if there were perpetual expansion or perpetual pleasure, it would no longer be pleasure. If there were an orgasm that went on forever it would quickly turn to suffering, like those six hour erections they warn you about in the television commercials for those erectile dysfunction drugs. If you had to eat chocolate cake for 24 hours straight, what was pleasurable for five minutes would turn to tremendous suffering in the space of an hour. There's no such thing as continuous pleasure and it wouldn't be pleasurable if there were.

The flower opens and then it closes. We enjoy curling up and hiding under the covers. Sometimes we want to close and sometimes we want to open. We enjoy movies. They're fun, they're entertaining, they can even be enlightening. Sometimes we want to lose ourselves in a story. There is no such thing as perpetual expansion or constant mindfulness. And any *experience* of expansion is always part of the dream-like movie of waking life, the world of reflections and appearances. When we really *see* that nothing is solid or fixed, that it's all empty, that unicity is all there is, then we're not at war with life anymore. We're not trying to be awake "all the time." But anywhere you *look* for this discovery is too far away. Anything you *do* to achieve it is too much and too late. It's much closer than that.

P: I believe that there is a shift, or a letting go, or an acceptance that matters. In fact, it makes all the difference in the world. You've said so yourself. When we resist what's here, then we have moved out of alignment with all that is, and we suffer. It seems to me that spirituality and religion are about moving back into alignment.

J: Yes, in a sense that's all very true. But now I'm pointing to that same truth in a different way. Only *in* the movie, *relatively* speaking, can you *apparently* go in and out of alignment with something else. To be in or out of alignment there needs to be two. For unicity, the question of alignment makes no sense, for there is nothing outside of unicity.

P: So are you saying that we never really are out of alignment?

J: The one who could be in or out of alignment is a mirage. *Relatively* speaking, *in* the movie of waking life, your vertebrae can be out of alignment, or the brakes in your car can be out of alignment, or "you" can be lost in stories – second-guessing yourself, hesitating, resisting, being angry or defensive or whatever – and you can *think* of that as "you" being out of alignment with unicity. But nothing exists outside unicity, and nothing can ever *really* be out of alignment with *what is.* Any relative "out of alignment" that exists *in* the movie is in perfect alignment in Reality. Even the apparent mistakes are part of a larger perfection, and *all* of it is only an appearance. In deep sleep, the whole universe disappears.

P: If everything's truth, then what do you need meetings like this for?

J: These meetings are truly useless. Use implies two. Relatively speaking, I can use a hammer to drive a nail into a board. But the driver, the hammer, the nail, the board, and the driving are all one whole undivided being, one inseparable flow – call it whatever you want. The boundary lines are notional. Boundlessness is all there is, *in spite* of whatever hammering and manipulating occurs, never *because* of it. You cannot become what you always already are.

P: But if that's not seen, then there is fear, anger, suffering.

J: Yes, and on a global scale, *in* the dream, that could snowball into a war or genocide or any number of horrific nightmares. But that too is simply boundlessness appearing as war and genocide.

P: Why is it okay to be in suffering? Why is that okay?

J: I'm not saying anything is okay or not okay, only that there *is* suffering, and only *in* the dream-like appearance.

P: And there's no way out of that?

J: The way out and the one who needs a way out exist only *in* the dream. The whole problem of being stuck is imaginary. It's like at night, you dream that you and five other people are being chased by a tiger. You are terrified. In the morning, you wake up. Are you still worried about the fate of the other five people and whether they are safe?

You're hoping for a way out, but there isn't a way out. In the dream, the tiger seems real, and in the dream, you run like hell, and you are terrified. It's unavoidable. It's the cosmic fun. But it's not really happening except as a dream event, and there is no one who can actually die or be eaten. Not ever. You wake up and see that you were never in any real danger. The tiger, the others, it was all a dream. But still, you can't avoid dreaming.

In the movie of waking life, there are genocides, cancers, ice ages, shipwrecks, hurricanes, wars, plagues, all manner of death and destruction, but unicity is never harmed. The forms break down, but emptiness is unharmed. What we truly are is never born and never dies. Seeing this is liberation. But unicity includes the nightmare of bondage as well as the dream of liberation. You cannot escape or control the dream world. But when you see that there is no need to escape or control, that nothing real is happening, then you relax. And if you don't relax, then you tense up. It doesn't matter either way. Unicity includes every possibility. And in the end, it's all a dream.

P: I think there are dream characters that are animated by an awakeness, and I think there are other characters that are more caught up in the dream.

J: *In* the dream, there are relative differences among characters, and these differences matter relatively, *in* the movie. But every night in deep sleep, the whole dream world vanishes into thin air. We can discuss the differences in dream characters, but it makes no difference. It's all like a dream. It vanishes into thin air. I'm pointing to what is prior to the dream, what is Here/Now.

P: Don't you suffer less when you're less identified with the character?

J: What is this "you" who imagines being more or less identified or suffering more or less? That imaginary you *is* the mirage.

P: Why are we trying to wake up?

J: Because we're dreaming that we are asleep. It's entertainment in the dream. The "Trying to Wake Up" dream.

P: Well, it's kind of a pain in the neck actually –

J: Yes, it can be.

P: But I've gotten to this point where I can't seem to go back to whatever I was before.

J: That's all *in* the dream. You have always been Here/Now.

P: It's not a comfortable place that I'm in.

J: You're not in any place. All places appear in you. All places appear Here/Now. And they are all appearances in a dream.

Another P: I was praying for my son once when he had a medical problem and all of a sudden I knew he was fine – and he was. So what is that, just part of the dream?

J: Yes.

P: So it wouldn't have mattered what I did?

J: We can say everything you did mattered absolutely because you couldn't have done anything else. In the dream world, everything is the cause and the effect of everything else. Everything matters absolutely or nothing matters at all – you can say it either way. What does it mean, "mattering"? It seems to mean something about whether something was important or necessary or essential in some way. The whole universe was essential for your son's recovery. If one tiny dust mote had been different, *everything* would have been different. The whole idea of cause and effect is a conceptual overlay, a way of thinking about things. We try to isolate out one thing and say that it "caused" some other thing, but everything is one seamless whole without division. Only in thought can we seemingly tease it apart and then think that one imaginary thing caused another imaginary thing. Only in thought can we think that maybe the prayer *caused* the recovery. Actually, they are one whole happening – the illness, the prayer, the recovery, and everything else in the whole universe.

P: Our whole family prays to God. And then one day, I thought, I am God. There is no God out there. Adyashanti said that you could pray to the coke can and the same thing would happen.

J: As far as I'm concerned, God is another word for the groundlessness of being. God is the true "I" to which we all refer when we say "I am." "I am God" is megalomania and delusion if the "I" refers to me, Jane Doe. But "I am God" is the deepest truth when "I" refers to the boundless awareness being and beholding everything. Here/Now, there is no "me," only God, this undivided aliveness [Joan gestures to include everything] that no word can ever represent or contain. *Everything* is God and God *is* everything. God is the unconditional love that allows everything to be as it is, including all the changes and the desire for change.

P: It was much easier to have a God I could pray to and have him fix things for me.

J: Well, you can still pray to God – you're just praying to yourself.

P: Praying to myself is nuts.

J: Maybe not. In a sense, every conversation you have is a conversation with yourself. This meeting is a meeting with yourself. You are meeting yourself as everyone in this room and as the bird songs and the cicadas and the traffic noise. You are always meeting yourself everywhere. So maybe prayer is simply a way of listening to yourself and hearing yourself, much like writing a book or giving a talk. I am always talking to myself and listening to myself.

P: I feel this fear whenever I get close to dissolving into boundlessness.

J: There is no one to dissolve. There is *only* boundlessness. Even this fear is nothing but boundlessness appearing as fear. When we imagine that we are the bodymind, then we are terrified of nothingness, terrified to be nobody, terrified of the void, terrified of death – but only when we *think* about these things and *imagine* them do we feel terrified. Every night we fall willingly and happily into this nothingness, and there is no one left to be afraid.

Email Correspondence with George

Q: While I can intellectually affirm everything you've written about – it resonates for me – and while I can see some of it, there is still the story that says: "George, you don't really see this for yourself." Take for instance, that there isn't actually an "I" – it's just a construction. While I accept this – almost as a matter of faith – and while I've read over and over about it and inquired over and over, when it comes down to it, I don't see this fact in the same way that I see that a mirage is actually an illusion. I still somehow believe that George is doing the thinking, even though I'm quite aware that I've never been in control of a single thought arising. Body-mind identification is so fundamental.

J: I would challenge the validity of the *thought* that you don't really see this, that it isn't your direct experience. I would suggest that you are like a wave looking for water and claiming you've never experienced wetness directly, you've only read about it. What I am pointing to is what cannot possibly be doubted. It's not intellectual. It's not an idea. It's the unavoidable bare actuality of Here/Now. The thought of being George comes and goes, like the sound of traffic or the light on the carpet. It's simply a passing appearance. There are many moments in any ordinary day when any thought of being George is entirely absent. Of course there is a functional identification with the bodymind that is essential for survival. That isn't a problem; it appears when needed. But the *idea* of being a separate, independent *somebody* is the illusion that dissolves when it is exposed to the light of awareness. You don't need to take this on faith as a belief, but rather, investigate the appearance of this "self" and see if it is real.

In my experience, belief is never satisfying. Doubt is always lurking, especially when the shit hits the fan. That's why I recommend looking and listening and exploring and seeing for yourself. Some people seem to derive complete satisfaction from beliefs. But for some reason, I have simply never been able to believe in something unless I could really see and verify it for myself. I don't know if that's a curse or a blessing, but I've never been able to swallow "the teachings" of Christianity or Buddhism or Advaita or nonduality or Marxism or anything else unless I could confirm them directly.

You say, *"I don't see this fact [that the 'I' is a construction and not a reality] in the same way that I see that a mirage is actually an illusion."* But how do you know that a mirage is an illusion? You see what appears to be a lake in the distance, you run toward it, and it isn't there. In the same way, if you turn to find the "I" who is supposedly reading these words right now, what do you find?

If you do find something, ask yourself what is seeing that? See if you can see the seer. And if you think you're seeing a seer, then ask yourself what is seeing that seer? Eventually, you'll discover that what you truly are can't be found as an object, that you are prior to any object you can find. *Being here* is undeniable, but what *is* this that is here? Isn't it obvious that you as presence-awareness are here prior to any thought-image-story of George?

"No self" doesn't mean you don't still see a form in the mirror that you have learned to call "George," but what is seeing this? No-self doesn't mean that you forget your name or no longer know whose mail to open. It doesn't mean that you can't distinguish between yourself and your wife or that you don't know which mouth to put the food in when you are eating dinner. This functional sense of identity as a particular bodymind shows up as needed. But you notice that there is something bigger – an awareness in which all of this is appearing. And whenever you look closely, you notice that much of time, there is no sense (no thought) of being anybody at all. There is just boundless awareness in which chairs and tables and clouds and dinner parties and all kinds of shapes and forms and activities, including George, are appearing. This has always been the case whether it has been noticed or not.

So what can drop away more and more is the illusory sense of identity that takes everything personally as "my" doing and "my" experience. That false sense of identification as a separate "me" encapsulated inside a particular bodymind (and the accompanying sense of separation from the whole) is the root of all our suffering, personal and global. This sense of encapsulated identity as a separate "me" doesn't drop away *for me*, because that me who wants to be free of me is part of the illusion that drops away. And *nothing* really drops away. False notions are simply seen to be false. The truth has never been absent.

You can't deny being here. You can't deny present awareness. "George" is something that has been learned and practiced – a conceptual construction. You were told that you were George, you learned this. But *being here* and *knowing you are here* is not something you had to learn. It is obvious and irrefutable, impossible to doubt. It requires no belief and no practice.

In truth, you need nothing. But if you find that you don't really believe that, or that believing that is not enough, then the exploration will go on until you are satisfied that the problem is imaginary.

with Love,

joan

Beyond Belief

True spirituality is possible only when you let go of everything.

— Nisargadatta Maharaj

Religion is often about beliefs. But what is being pointed to here is not about belief at all. The breathing right now is not a belief. The sound of the car tires on the wet street — that's not a belief. *Being here* is not a belief. The idea that "I am human being on a blue planet in the solar system" is a belief, a way that thought has organized and conceptualized this present experiencing. But the bare *fact* of being present and aware is irrefutable.

We're not talking about *getting rid* of all beliefs because certain beliefs are useful and functional and necessary. But waking up is about *seeing* that beliefs *are* beliefs and being open to seeing something new. So we may still believe that the earth is round and that if I keep traveling westward, I'm not going to eventually fall off the planet. That's a useful belief. And if I can hold this belief lightly and tentatively, as a scientist might, then I am open to the *possibility* of seeing something new. Waking up is also about seeing how we identify our beliefs as "me" and then defend them to the death, as if our very life were being threatened when our beliefs are questioned.

It's amazing to consider how many things we believe based on secondhand information and how easily we adopt beliefs from other people. The ideas sound good, we trust the source, so we adopt them. And we adopt them not just tentatively, but often quite tenaciously. For example, I believe that human-caused global climate change is happening, and that if it continues unabated, it will result in catastrophic problems. I believe this because my conditioning leads me to trust certain sources of information and not others. And this viewpoint fits with my observations of the world based on what I read about and see reported about hurricanes, floods, droughts, melting ice caps, and so on. But I don't really *see* "climate change" in the same direct and immediate way that I see that chair. I *believe* there is climate change and that it is being caused primarily by human behavior. And I can become quite upset when George Bush and other right-wing ideologues deny climate change and keep right on doing the things that I believe will make it worse. This belief in climate change may prove true, and it may be an essential belief for human survival – if enough people come to believe it, it may end up saving the human race and many other species from extinction. But it's still a belief, however scientifically verified and relatively true it may be. I'm not suggesting that anyone should drop this belief. But is it possible to be aware that it *is* a belief and to be open to new information? Is it possible to see and wonder about how angry and defensive and upset I can get over this? Even if the icecaps melt and human life is wiped off the face of the earth, can I really know this is a bad thing?

It's fine to have opinions and make a case for what we think is right. It's fine to use concepts and maps and beliefs. All of this has a vital function. But can we also recognize how insubstantial everything is, how questionable, how we really don't know *anything* for certain other than being here? Can we be awake to the bare actuality, the inconceivable reality that is totally beyond belief?

P: I had cancer a year ago, and I went through chemotherapy. I found it very interesting to see that I did not experience fear when I was in the moment during the actual chemotherapy, whereas the *idea* of chemotherapy beforehand was quite scary. It made me realize that people who are going through difficult experiences may not be suffering as much as we think they are.

J: Yes. That is a wonderful discovery, how much of our suffering is imaginary.

P: I recently found myself in a very difficult situation at work. I wasn't really present, the mind was full of thoughts, and that effective kind of action "without a doer" did not arise because of my lack of presence. So there is a desire to learn how to act without the doer.

J: All action arises without a doer. There can be the *appearance* of a doer, but all action arises without a doer. The doer is simply a thought that is added on afterwards. *"I* did it," or *"She* did it." Action is simply occurring, and then thought is reflecting on it afterwards and either claiming it or attributing it to somebody else. Thought also passes judgment on this phantom doer: *"I* could have done better." There is no thinker *doing* this thinking; it simply happens. And yes, there *is* a difference between the kind of action that comes out of compulsive conditioned thinking and the kind of action that comes out of open spacious awareness with no thoughts of self clouding the picture. But there is no doer of either one and no one who can control which one happens.

P: But it makes such a huge difference!

J: Yes, in the movie of waking life, it makes a huge difference, the difference between heaven and hell. But unicity includes both heaven and hell.

I used to live and work at a retreat center. Often, before a retreat, various people on staff would be in conflict with each other. There would be anger and animosity, people would be scowling at each other, arguing. Then we would spend seven days in silence, bathed in presence, and at the end of the retreat, there would be this wonderful love. Everyone's face would be so open, so unprotected, so innocent and full of love. It was beautiful. Of course, it didn't last. And it didn't come about from *trying* to drop all the conflicts and *trying* to be open. It was the opposite of that. It was a letting go and a seeing through of the illusion that there was something and someone to defend. And that seeing and that letting go cannot be engineered.

P: But the retreat obviously helped!

J: Yes, maybe so, but if we say that the retreat *caused* the openness then we begin to get mixed up. Next thing you know, we've become a *believer* in retreats! But the retreat itself was actually about *seeing through* beliefs and not doing anything to fix the problems or get to someplace better. It was the absence of all that. What is discovered in the retreat is not the effect of a cause. Awareness, presence, unicity, unconditional love – whatever we call it – this is uncaused.

P: But I can't stay here.

J: Can you leave here?

P: I just did when I remembered my story.

J: Remembering the story happened Here/Now. This is all there ever is.

P: But I don't have any sense of the wide open space when I am in my bubble of delusion.

J: You are not in any bubble of delusion. This imaginary bubble, and this story of you being trapped inside it, both appear Here/Now in awareness. It's all a story, an appearance, a kind of visualization. It has no substance, no reality. Can you see that this notion of you being inside a bubble of delusion is only a mental image?

P: I am reaching for it to be solid and it wants to go away. It requires attention to be sustained.

J: You mean the story, the visualization, requires attention to be sustained?

P: Yes. Otherwise I might look at the sun and feel happy.

J: Ah, so you have to keep attention on the *story* of the bubble for it to stay there.

P: Right. But how can you break out of the story when you are caught in it? I often *feel* trapped.

J: Can you see that right now, that's another story, another mind-generated problem for us to work on solving? *Where is this problem in reality?* We're talking about how to solve an imaginary problem in the imaginary future. You can only solve this problem *now*.

P: I think I've managed to depress everybody.

J: A new story!

P: I feel like I should be able to get this. During the meditation this morning I was okay. I was "just nowing" then. But now –

J: Can you hear the joke here? Back then, I was successfully now-ing, but now, I'm not in the now. [laughter] You are always "just nowing"! There's *only* now.

What Dies? What Wakes Up?

The most essential thing that's being expressed here is that all our problems are entirely imaginary. Of course, I am not denying the *apparent* reality of the pain in your tooth, or the lack of funds in your bank account, or the war being waged in Iraq. I'm talking about the root problem – the idea that we exist as something separate from everything else, the idea that we can screw up our life, the idea that the love, the freedom, the joy, the aliveness that we seek is something apart from us that has to be acquired.

The thinking mind is always on the lookout for the next guru, the next book, the next drug, the next promising thing to try. Perhaps it is an evolutionary impulse, a survival function. And to some degree, within a certain context, it works. We enjoy and benefit from meetings and teachers and books and meditation practices and Feldenkrais lessons and whatnot, but to the degree that we keep seeking salvation "out there" in the future, we are overlooking the only place where salvation really *is* – Here/Now.

And when I speak of salvation, I don't mean perpetual happiness or the disappearance of all our problems. *What disappears is the need for anything to be other than how it is.* When we see that everything is empty of substance, that there is only unicity, then there is no more death, no more personal failure or success. There is no more *need* for things to be different.

P: I'm wondering about this whole notion of unicity or One Self.

What I see is different from what someone else sees or experiences. How can that be without separate selves? I still feel that the seat of my consciousness is different from the seat of your consciousness.

J: Where is this seat? You have to really look and see – is there a seat? Does awareness have a location? It takes thinking to conjure up a seat or a location, doesn't it? We can say that you and I have two different brains, but where did those brains come from in the first place? How did they evolve? How did they grow? What is beholding them both? There is obviously some sort of intelligence that antedates the brain and these particular bodies. Does this intelligence belong to you or me, or is it more accurate to say that we belong to it?

All these different bodies depend on a common supply of oxygen and food and water to survive. We all breathe in and out, sharing the same air. All of us in this room are like waves on the ocean. The whole universe is all very fluid and permeable and borderless. I am made up of you, and you are made up of me, like the jewels in Indra's Net that all reflect the others.

P: But I can feel my body and not your body. For instance, if someone hit me, I would feel it and you wouldn't. That makes me think that we are two separate individuals.

J: If someone hits you right now, there is sensation. For you, pain sensations. For me, visual sensations of watching this happen. *All* these sensations happen in awareness. Awareness is borderless, boundless and seamless. Relatively speaking, within the dream world, we can say that we are two separate individuals and that you were punched and I wasn't. But actually, if you are punched, I am also punched, even if I am on the other side of the world at the time. A leaf falling in Kansas has an effect in Africa because everything is one whole. The dividing lines are imaginary. What happens in Africa, Gaza, Afghanistan and Iraq effects us here in Chicago even if we don't know it. We're not really separate. The different waves are never anything but water, all of them the indivisible activity of one ocean.

P: But my sense is that the experience of awareness is different in me than in you.

J: The *content* is different, like left eye and right eye, two similar but entirely unique movies. But is the *awareness* divided up or encapsulated? Can you actually find the place where inside turns into outside?

This room is full of television waves right now, but the programs can only appear if we have a television that can translate these waves into visual images. If we turned on the television, we'd be able to see these waves unfolded into different programs, all happening Here/Now simultaneously. It would look as if we were seeing actual people in actual locations moving around in real time doing things, although in fact, this would all be an illusion. If we opened up the television, we wouldn't find the characters in the drama, just as, if we cut open your brain, we wouldn't find this living room and this meeting and all these people who seem to be sitting here now. All of this is happening in consciousness, and we can't really find consciousness. It has no location.

If we had six different televisions in this room, we could tune into six different programs simultaneously. We could tune into six different News programs and get six very different versions of today's (supposedly real and substantial) events. In a similar way, each brain and nervous system in this room is playing a different movie.

Are we the television (the bodymind or the brain), or the program (our particular unique movie of waking life), or the character *in* the program (the "me" in the story of "my" life), or the phantom viewer of the program ("me" the observer of my story, the witness), or are we the boundless and seamless unicity that is being and beholding it all? Your movie and my movie are different, but they go together as one seamless whole, like a hologram where every part contains the whole.

P: Is the body a necessary vehicle for awareness?

J: We can get into endless abstract speculation about how the universe works, but where is your question coming from?

P: When the body dies, what happens to that awareness? I once had an out of body experience – there was awareness and I was looking down at my body on the operating table.

J: I've heard many reports of "out of body" experiences and "near death" experiences. I had a brief out of body experience myself once during a car crash – I wrote about it in my last book. But I don't know if we really know what they are or how they work. It seems entirely possible that an "out of body" experience could be a dream or a hallucination or a vision combined with sensory input of some kind, or it could be some kind of neurological event. In fact, I've heard that during brain surgeries, they can now induce these experiences with a probe. They touch a certain area of the brain and the person experiences looking down from the ceiling just as you describe. Those who have out of body experiences always have bodies at the time they are having the experience, just as those who have near death experiences are not actually dead. So while these experiences are certainly real experiences, we should probably be careful about drawing conclusions about what they mean.

What I *can* say is that the way we divide "awareness" from "the body," and "the mind" from "the brain," and "the chicken" from "the egg," and "you" from "me" is all conceptual. Only after we've mentally divided everything up in this way do we worry about what depends upon what, or what comes first, or what causes what, or what survives death. But when we *see* that nothing is really divided up that way, then all these questions dissolve. They don't really matter.

P: What about past lives?

J: Past lives for whom? It's all a story – this notion of "something" that goes from one life to another life. Perhaps all these ideas about the afterlife come from the deep intuition we all share that what we truly are, the wholeness of being, is never born and never dies. Perhaps reincarnation and heaven and hell are primitive ways of conceptualizing and expressing that intuition. But I don't find anything that could reincarnate, unless by reincarnation we simply mean the thoroughgoing flux that is constantly forming and re-forming, reincarnating from moment to moment. After death, the body disintegrates back into the soil, or becomes food for insects, birds and other animals, or is in some way reabsorbed and recycled. In that sense, it lives on forever, but it doesn't live on as "this body." In fact, "this body" is only an idea. The reality of this body is nothing but thoroughgoing flux inseparable from the whole universe. Does awareness continue? Awareness is timeless. It has no continuity. It is Here/Now.

It's easy to slip into philosophical rumination and somehow that never feels very satisfying. Everything we think can be doubted, but the juice – the aliveness – is in what cannot be doubted. When we wake up to Here/Now, the question of past and future lives simply doesn't come up. Every moment is an out of body experience in a way, because you (as awareness) are beholding both the body and the universe.

Without words, there is no division.

Is India More Nondual than Chicago?

Since so-called Eastern spirituality has come to the West, many westerners have rushed to Japan or India or someplace in the Far East to get the real goods. There is nothing wrong with traveling, but what these teachings point to is right here in front of you. You don't need to go somewhere else. In fact, you never *do* go anywhere else. Places appear *in* you, in awareness. They come and go, dream-like.

It has been said that the truth is inside, not outside you. That doesn't mean it's in your intestines or in your emotions, but not in the chair across the room. It means it's in the undivided awareness that beholds intestines, emotions, chairs, birds, and everything else. It points to the realization that there is no boundary, that inside and outside are one whole. In the same way, past and future are inseparable from Here/Now. When I talk about the jewel of Here/Now, I'm not in any way intending to disparage the study of history or the creative envisioning of the future. I'm simply pointing to the fact that it all shows up Here/Now as one indivisible whole that is boundless, seamless, timeless and spaceless.

How to realize that? Well, first of all, notice that the question itself is rooted in the assumption that it is not realized right now. Is that true? What are you imagining that such realization would look like? Perhaps the acquisition or the sighting of an enormous object like a giant dinner plate? Or maybe an experience like being permanently high on drugs? Or maybe some mental understanding like an algebraic equation or a verbal formulation that would be the final answer to every question?

Does it make sense that totality would be an object, an experience or a formulation? Does it make sense that "you" would need to find it?

The truth itself is so simple that the mind habitually keeps overlooking it by looking elsewhere. Endlessly fascinated by glittering distractions (India, Japan, robes, bells, gurus, teachers, retreats, satsangs), we overlook the jewel of here and now. Of course, India, Japan, robes, bells, gurus, teachers, retreats, satsangs – it's all the jewel. There's no escape. But when we think the jewel is in India but not in Chicago, or that we need to go to a retreat or a satsang to find it, then we are like a wave looking for the ocean. The imaginary problem can only be resolved Here/Now.

After wandering all over the world seeking the truth "out there" somewhere, after having amazing spiritual experiences and breakthroughs, we inevitably end up back in our ordinary everyday life. Like Dorothy in *The Wizard of Oz*, we wake up back in Kansas. The whole journey is inside us, and what we are seeking is inside us, too. And when I say inside us, again, I don't mean inside the bodymind – I mean Here/Now.

And that's really what all spiritual teachings are pointing to – that the heart of the matter, the jewel that is being sought is not "out there" somewhere apart from you or in the future. No one can give it to you. You must discover it yourself. And the only thing that makes this discovery seem difficult is how easy it is. It is already perfectly realized.

This moment *is* the Buddha. The thought of "somewhere better" keeps us from seeing that what we are seeking, we already *are*. The postponements, the ways we move away, get subtler and subtler. Wanting to never run off on another journey to Oz ever again is itself running off on such a journey! But luckily, the journey and the one taking it are both imaginary. You never *really* leave Here/Now.

Sometimes people say, "Everything is great when I'm at these meetings," or, "It's all totally clear when I'm off on a meditation retreat, but then I get home and I lose it all." I come back to Kansas and it seems like I'm this screwed up character again. But of course being on a meditation retreat is going to be different from being in the office. Sitting in silence listening to the rain is different from listening to other human beings. And yet both the office and the meditation retreat appear Here/Now in this ever-present awareness. What *is*, is so simple, so unavoidable. Everything *is* as it is, even if what is appearing is confusion or upset.

P: I feel very torn between this teaching in which there is no doer and nothing to do, and other teachings that talk about making something happen, improving yourself and the world, getting enlightened, being more present and aware and all of that. I see it one way on one day, then I see it the other way the next day, and I feel very confused.

J: Where is this problem right now if we don't think about it?

P: I think non-doing is the ultimate truth, but I keep getting sucked back into doing things and thinking I have a choice.

J: Okay, more thinking. That's all a story: "I know that non-doing is the ultimate truth, I keep getting sucked into doing things, I feel confused." This story materializes the phantom "I" like a mirage. Then we worry about whether this phantom will make the right choice and pick the winning answer. Waking up is nothing more or less than *seeing* that whole story for what it is – thought and imagination.

The bodymind can't *not* do things. It is the nature of the bodymind to act. Thinking, feeling, acting, choosing – these things all happen. There is no choice about it. There is the *appearance* of choice. But every apparent choice happens as it does because everything else in the whole universe is the way it is. But seeing that doesn't mean you stop apparently making choices. You have no choice! But you see that the choice "you" appear to make is actually coming from the whole universe and could not have been otherwise. It is the action of totality, not the action of some phantom executive.

P: How can we be here now and get things done? It seems to me that we need to plan and think about the future. We can't just sit around "being here now" all the time, can we?

J: Realizing that Here/Now is ever-present and seeing through the thoughts and stories that generate suffering doesn't mean that you're never supposed to think about the future or remember the past or plan a trip to someplace else. All of those things happen Here/Now. And they are essential to functioning in daily life. If you are Martin Luther King leading the civil rights movement, you obviously need both an understanding of history and the vision of a future without segregation. As he said, "I have a dream." His life was about realizing that dream. That in no way contradicts what I'm pointing to when I talk about Here/Now. To take another example, if you want to punch through a board in karate, you may find it helpful to visualize your hand going through the board. In so doing, you are focused on the future. But as with Martin Luther King's dream, that visualization is happening Now. And whether you *can* visualize your hand going through the board at that moment depends on everything in the whole universe. It may be that a fear of hurting your hand inadvertently pops up instead. Martin Luther King was an activity of the whole universe, as was the civil rights movement. No one can be anyone other than exactly who they are, doing exactly what they do. And that doesn't negate the *apparent* making of choices or the potential usefulness of remembering the past or visualizing future possibilities.

P: When I've felt completely at one and at peace, usually there was very little productivity going on in my work at that time. There were long periods when I felt wonderful – I was traveling around going to satsangs and retreats – but I was going bankrupt [laughter]. So then I thought it was time to do something, to get back into the world and get down to business. But then that tended to feed some sense of being separate. And then I suffer more from not having that experience of beingness. It continues to be a dilemma for me.

J: It's a dilemma only when there's thinking about it, right? In this instant, right now, before you think about it, where is this dilemma? It takes thought to dredge it up. What you describe is the natural rhythm of life. It's like walking – we lose our balance and regain it with every step. We fall this way, then that way. We withdraw from the world, then we plunge back into the world. We inhale, we exhale. That's the nature of the manifestation. And then the thinking mind comes in and creates confusion. We apparently have to decide if inhaling or exhaling is the true way, we have to choose between them. In that example, we can easily see how absurd it is. But choosing between a retreat and business is equally absurd. They happen in a natural rhythm, each in their own time and place. And stress and upset is not a bad thing. It can be every bit as enlightening and enlivening as blissful experiences of expansion and unity. It's all part of the show.

P: But you must have had periods of sustained awakening and all your suffering must have stopped permanently, or else what's the point of all this?

J: I feel pain and upset just like you do. But I notice that Here/Now is ever-present and that it is not divided up into me and you.

It has been said that enlightenment is not final victory, it is final defeat. When we imagine enlightenment, we imagine *me* finally triumphing over all of my imperfections, *me* fearless and imperturbable at last, *me* always happy, completely successful, totally in balance. That's our picture of enlightenment. But for the phantom *me*, enlightenment is not final victory, but rather, final defeat. For the phantom self, enlightenment is complete disappointment. Total failure.

Wholeness doesn't need to be improved – it is already perfect and complete. It's only the little cartoon character who seemingly needs to be improved. And even that is questionable, because what kind of movie would it be if all the characters were without blemish or imperfection? Life itself is always in balance, and that perfect balance includes the imbalance of inhaling and exhaling, loss and gain, falling to the left and then falling to the right. It's all part of the larger picture. Oh, I can hear, "Yes, buts," floating in the air. [laughter]

I was walking in the park early this morning before the meeting. It was a beautiful morning. There were no clouds. It was absolutely clear and still. Little green leaves were just beginning to unfurl. The park was totally empty of people and absolutely quiet except for the beautiful songs of the birds. The water in the pond was as still as glass, and there were beautiful reflections in the water. Everything was sparkling with light. There was no "me," only the immensity of silence and stillness.

All of a sudden, along comes this man walking his dog and talking on his headset telephone in a very loud voice. Immediately there was a tensing up in this body and a feeling of aversion and various judgmental thoughts about this man: "What an egotistical jerk – he's totally missing the beauty of this morning – he's ruining this exquisite silence by talking on his stupid cell phone at the top of his lungs." And then more thoughts: "This is what's happening to western civilization, the world is going to hell."

I'm unpacking all these thoughts and spelling them out in complete sentences so that we can hear them and look at them, but in that moment, in real life, these thoughts happened in a split second like a series of very quick energetic telegrams accompanied by a tensing in the body. We don't think in complete sentences. It's all much more instantaneous, which is why it isn't always that easy to notice what we are thinking. It goes by very fast. That's why meditation is often very helpful in revealing the workings of the thinking mind.

Anyway, after a short barrage of these judgmental thoughts, there was suddenly a different thought: "This, too, is what is. This loud man on his cell phone is also what is." (And we might wonder, what came first, the thought or the realization?) And then a question arose in the mind, "Is it possible to listen to him just as I listen to the birds?" And immediately there was a relaxing that happened, allowing this human voice be there along with the bird voices and the stillness of the morning.

All of it was there – the stillness, the birds, the man on his cell phone, the dog, the aversion – and it was all okay, even the upset and the resistance and the judgment. Suddenly it all seemed beautiful. The man on his cell phone was no longer a problem – he was wonderful. And my own little upset was no problem either. None of it was personal. It was just weather.

It's not like the goal of nonduality or Zen or Advaita is to get to someplace where we never tense up or feel irritated ever again. All of these things that happen are probably rooted in some survival function that gets misplaced in some way. Like this morning, the negative thoughts about this man were not needed for my survival, and all they did was make me unhappy. When they dropped away, I could see the beauty in everything – not just the birds and the stillness, but the man and myself as well. It was quite delightful.

But "I" didn't *make* those thoughts drop away. It all happened spontaneously – the clouding and the clearing – no one is doing any of it.

P: How can you appreciate the moments of non-appreciation? I would have hated the man on the telephone and then started beating myself up for not accepting what is.

J: That's just another layer of thought – taking the first layer (the resistance and the upset) personally and then judging myself for having such thoughts, telling a story about what it means about me – that I'm unenlightened or neurotic or mean-spirited or whatever the story is. But actually, getting bothered by this noisy man is not something "I" did. The whole universe was showing up in that moment as Joan being bothered. Ten other people could have been standing there in the park this morning and not felt bothered by that guy at all, but my particular conditioning is such that what came up here at that moment was dislike and negative judgments. It's an impersonal happening, like the weather. And it's the same with those thoughts you describe about, "I shouldn't have felt that way." That is also an impersonal happening. These thoughts are all so momentary, so insubstantial. They seem so heavy and real and serious, but they can dissolve in an instant! This morning at the park is totally gone! Of course, I can keep the story alive in memory until the day I die, feeling angry at people who talk loudly on their cell phones in public places and telling the story of how they "shouldn't" do this, or else going over and over my shortcomings and how judgmental I am, and feeling bad about myself. That is our human tendency, our human dis-ease, our suffering. So to *see* that as it happens, to wake up from these stories and ideas. Not once and for all forever, because that's just another fantasy, but now. *This* is the only reality.

P: I don't like it when I get caught up.

J: There are a lot of things that we don't like, and there's nothing wrong with not liking things. We have preferences. That's natural.

P: How can you say that there is nothing wrong with not liking things?

J: By nature, we like things that feel good to us and dislike things that feel bad. It's a survival function – so we don't eat the poison berries or the rotten meat, and so we *do* eat the good stuff and do what it takes to reproduce. Obviously what starts as a survival function can go somewhat amuck with brains as complex as ours. So in my experience this morning in the park, for example, my natural preference for quiet had no functional usefulness in that situation – it was only a form of suffering. There's nothing problematic in the preference itself. The preference is fine. The suffering is when we are *attached* to our preferences or *identified* with them – feeling *personally invaded* if someone shows up talking loudly on a cell phone, or feeling *personally insulted* if someone doesn't like the same movie I like, or feeling that I *must* have silence to be happy – then I suffer. But there's nothing wrong with liking one movie more than another movie or having a favorite flavor. There's nothing wrong with having a preference for silence and birdsong in the park. But if I feel I *need* that, as happened in my movie this morning, or if I think that silence and birdsong is spiritually superior, as also happened in my movie this morning, then the man on his cell phone seems to be an assault on my well-being from the evil empire that it threatening life on earth. *That* is a story, and that is unnecessary suffering. When it fell away, I found only beauty everywhere.

But it's not like "my suffering" has now been vanquished

"forever," and from now on, Joan will see only beauty everywhere. That's just another story – the enlightenment myth. I'm not saying there's no enlightenment. But it's not what we think it is. It's not some final, permanent victory for Joan.

P: Sometimes when I'm afraid or agitated, if I can remember to breathe, it helps.

J: And that remembering happens by itself, right? Afterwards we say, "I remembered to breathe," and verbalizing it that way paints the mirage-image of "me" the doer. But in reality, that thought or that impulse popped up by itself. Of course, you were already breathing, but you started paying attention to the breathing. Did the thought actually initiate that shift in attention, or did it describe the shift after the fact? Either way, it all happened by itself – the thought, the impulse, the shift in attention. And as attention shifts to breathing, to pure perception and sensation, thought stops. Instantly, you feel better.

But if you now try to *do* that as a strategy, it doesn't work. Because that's thought again looking for a result. And if you try to cling to the calm experience, that very clinging is agitation. No *experience* is going to be permanent.

P: I don't get it.

J: There is nothing to get. There is simply what is.

P: Here seems difficult to access sometimes.

J: "Here seems difficult to access," is a thought, and it *seems* that way because there's an *idea* of what "here" is. There's an idea that this isn't "here." Can you see the absurdity of that?

P: But don't you have difficulty accessing that space sometimes?

J: What space are we talking about? Here/Now is all there is. You don't have to access it, it's ever-present and unavoidable.

There's some idea that "here" was the experience I had for a moment in meditation when there were no thoughts and I was just feeling the breathing – *that* was "here." But this busy mind full of thoughts, *this* "isn't here." But *all* of this is appearing Here/Now.

P: Paying attention is needed, it seems. Maybe like tuning a radio dial to a frequency – that level of work, rather than a complex strategy.

J: Wherever you tune on the dial, it is always Here/Now. What we're talking about is truly unavoidable and unattainable. It requires no tuning.

P: So it's not work really.

Another P: There is a Feldenkrais lesson in which the instruction is: "Do it like you are wasting your time." I love that because we are so used to goals and agendas.

J: That's beautiful. Yes, we're very programmed to not waste time. That's a cardinal sin in the post-industrial world. Everyone is rushing around multitasking like crazy, working three jobs, barely getting any sleep. And so many of these jobs are all about creating false needs and filling them with toxic junk. I resonate with those old Zen hermits who did nothing all day but watch the clouds. Totally without ambition, totally useless.

P: I have so much fear.

J: The root fear is the story that I won't exist any more, that I'm going to get wiped out.

P: Which is true.

J: Everything we *think* of as "me" is going to get wiped out. This form, the bodymind, will be wiped out, although in fact it has never existed as anything but an ever-changing process. The movie of waking life, consciousness – in the sense of thinking, remembering, sensing, perceiving – all of that will be wiped out, as it is every night in deep sleep. All my memories and stories and accomplishments will eventually be wiped out. My children, if I have them, will eventually be wiped out. Even any *idea* of the Absolute Self or Ultimate Reality will be wiped out. Actually, *all* of that is wiped out every night in deep sleep and we find it enormously refreshing and rejuvenating.

P: So *nothing* survives death?

J: Nothing dies. Nothing is born. The body is only an idea. The actuality of what we call "the body" has no boundaries, no beginning, no ending. And the "me" who is supposedly located inside the bodymind is a bunch of ever-changing thoughts, stories, mental images, memories and sensations. *None* of this survives in deep sleep.

P: But something remains in deep sleep, doesn't it? Pure awareness? Beingness? The Self?

J: None of those words remain in deep sleep. No idea remains in deep sleep. No concept remains. Nothing perceivable or conceivable or experiencable or describable remains in deep sleep. There is no experience and no experiencer in deep sleep. The concern with whether or not something remains, or what it might be, is totally absent. All *sense* of being present is absent. And any *sense* of being absent is also absent. No *thing* is there to be present or absent. And if we say nothing remains, this "nothing" is much too much. Can you feel how freeing this is? What a relief it is?

Because of this liberating quality in deep sleep, some Eastern teachings say that deep sleep is the closest state to Ultimate Reality, and yet, no temporary state is really any closer than any other state to Ultimate Reality. Ultimate Reality does not depend on the presence or absence of any particular state or experience. Ultimate Reality is not one frequency on the radio dial as opposed to some other frequency.

Ultimate Reality has been given many names. But whatever we call it, no word or description applies. We only name or conceive of it in the waking state – or in the dream state. And they're very much the same, waking and dreaming. This naming happens only in waking or dreaming consciousness. But in deep sleep, there is nothing to name, and no one to name it, and no concern about what it is. In deep sleep, nothing stands apart from anything else. Nothing exists. To exist means to stand outside. In deep sleep, nothing is separate to stand outside of anything else. All separation between inside and outside is dissolved. When everything is erased, no such *thing* as "emptiness" or "space" remains.

Zen Master Dogen has this beautiful line in Genjo Koan: "When you see forms or hear sounds fully engaging body-and-mind, you grasp things directly. Unlike things and their reflections in the mirror, and unlike the moon and its reflection in the water, when one side is illuminated the other side is dark."

There is no seer and no seen, only undivided seeing. Nothing is "out there" apart from us, and we are not "in here" looking out, but rather, everything is right here – no distance, no separation – only unicity and immediacy.

In waking consciousness, the lights are turned on, and the ten million things appear – movies roll, plot lines unfold, stories spin, whole universes come into being. And when that side is dark, as in deep sleep, everything disappears. What remains is not perceivable or conceivable. There is no way for waking consciousness to ever see or know what is present on the dark side, for when that dark side is "illuminated," the very waking consciousness that seeks to know the darkness is absent.

There is no duality between the two sides or between subject and object. They do not co-exist, like the moon in the sky and its reflection in the water. They are each absolute. They each fill the whole field. They are not opposites. Each side contains the other completely. The noumenon is not *other* than the phenomenal manifestation. Form is emptiness and emptiness is form.

The whole universe appears as this chair, this water glass, this carpet. When you see one thing, you see the whole universe. When you take care of one thing, you take care of the whole universe. The noumenon or the absolute is not somewhere else. This is it, this very moment.

Consciousness cannot help waking up in the morning. It cannot help the emergence of Joan and her story and the world that appears around her with all its complexity – the beauty and the horror. It cannot help caring about what it cares about, and doing what it does. It cannot control where the attention goes.

Everything that appears is a kind of display, a painting in emptiness, with no substance and no continuity. It disappears completely instant by instant into the nothingness of death and deep sleep. Its beauty, its preciousness lies in its impermanence, its no-thing-ness. This understanding is not some cold nihilism that discards the world, but rather, total intimacy with the world.

This disappearance, this death is every moment. Everything is appearing and disappearing. Consciousness imagines itself encapsulated inside a particular bodymind, and then it worries about death, about "me" coming to an end. And to assuage that fear, it imagines life after death for "me" – heaven, hell, reincarnation, all that nonsense. But the whole problem is imaginary. What is it that would end? It is an idea based on false assumptions. All the problems we have, or seem to have, are problems of the bodymind. They only exist in consciousness, in waking life. In deep sleep, they are completely absent. This is a big clue. At the end of a long life, where did it all go? How real was it? Every night in deep sleep, there is no problem. Where did it go?

And this freedom of deep sleep or death is here right now in the utter simplicity of this moment –*whoosh, whoosh, whoosh* [Joan imitates traffic sounds]. When the stories drop and thought is silent, what problem remains?

Consciousness is painting pictures in emptiness. Like the paintings I did on the sidewalk with water when I was a child, it all evaporates moment by moment. That was very Zen, those paintings I did back then. I loved doing it. My paintings would quickly evaporate, but I didn't mind. I wasn't looking for permanence or achievement. I was simply enjoying the gesture of darkening cement, the activity of painting.

Like those sand paintings the Tibetan monks do. They spend hours and days and weeks meticulously creating an elaborate mandala in the sand. When it's done, they enjoy it for a moment, and then they wreck it! Like children at the beach building sand castles and then smashing them.

Or like the painting of a whole lifetime at the moment of death—*poof!*

The Truman Show

There is nothing to do other than exactly what you are doing, whatever it is. This whole movie of waking life is like a dream. Whatever we appear to gain or lose, wherever we seem to go, it's all a dream. Whether we win or lose, whether we seem to be a king or a homeless person, an enlightened sage or a deluded madman, it's only a dream-like appearance. Nothing really matters in the way we think it does. I don't mean that life is some meaningless, nihilistic waste. Not at all. Life is an amazing miracle. I only mean that all our apparent problems and defeats, as well as all our apparent victories, are moments in a dream. They have no substance, no reality.

But there is something that is real. What is it? Whatever word or idea or image we come up with in answer to that question is only another dream. Even this aware presence that I call Here/Now, this vibrant aliveness, this knowingness that "I am," even this disappears every night in deep sleep. This drop of consciousness that contains the movie of waking life vanishes into thin air along with the one who knows, the one who cares. Nothing remains. And this nothing that remains is not something. It is not our *ideas* of "nothingness" or "blankness" or "voidness." It is the absence of all ideas. It is absolute freedom. And this freedom is Here/Now at the heart of everything.

P: I don't get it.

J: When you say, "I don't get it," you're speaking as the phantom self, and there's a belief that you're supposed to *get* something from this talk. It's supposed to *do* something for you. *Something* is supposed to happen other than what *is* happening. And you've got big ideas about exactly what that should be – final enlightenment or something grandiose like that.

P: Freedom is experienced sometimes.

J: There's no other possible experience really.

P: There isn't?

J: *Everything* is this freedom. You can only *think* that something isn't it, that something is outside the One Reality.

P: So thinking is really the problem.

J: Nothing is a problem. All problems are imaginary. In this dream-like movie of waking life, thinking is vital to our survival. And movies are wonderful. I love the movie of waking life! I love stories and theater and TV shows and novels. We're not trying to banish all of that. We suffer when a story such as "I've ruined my whole life" or "I've lost the Now" is believed and not seen as the story that it is. When this kind of thought is believed, and we start trying to solve this imaginary problem and fix this imaginary self, we suffer. But even that suffering is only a dream-like appearance, as is waking up from that suffering. It's *all* a dream. As one Tibetan teacher said, in the end, you realize you are visualizing (or imagining) *everything*.

But there is something that cannot be visualized, something that remains when everything disappears, something that *is* everything, something that is not something.

P: Life seems to be nothing but fear and desire.

J: Fear and desire are the two primary movements of life in a sense, and both are vital to how life sustains itself. You are afraid of the tiger that's running towards you and desirous of the sex that will continue the species. Psychological fears and addictive desires are something else, a kind of malfunction of our capacity for complex, self-reflexive thought. But *all* of it is a dream, the real tiger and the imaginary tiger, and above all, the one who worries about being eaten.

P: In addiction, you may not want to desire what you desire.

J: Part of addiction is that you have conflicting desires. You want to smoke and you want to stop. When the desire to stop prevails, you make a vow never to smoke again. The next day, when the desire to smoke wins out, you light up. Then the desire to stop comes back and you feel terrible about having slipped. And you feel so terrible about having slipped that you want a cigarette. No dog has problems like these!

The ultimate addiction is the addiction to surviving as this drop of consciousness, this "I am," this form. The deepest addiction is to this sense of being separate and needing to continue. All the other addictions are forms of that root addiction.

P: The world seems to like the extremes of success and failure.

J: Yes, like the woman who stabbed her children the other day. We are fascinated with it. We wouldn't want to turn on the News and hear, "It was another ordinary day here in Chicago. Mrs. Brown cooked dinner for her family. Mr. Brown went to the office and had a routine day. The two Brown children went to school. And that's the news for today."

P: There was a reality program of a family in which the camera was on them day and night and people would tune in to see them sleeping.

J: Like that movie—*The Truman Show*—about a guy whose whole life was a reality TV show. He doesn't know it, but as a baby he was given to a reality TV program. His whole life is lived on a movie set.

Unbeknownst to him, everybody out in the real world is watching his life on television. His wife is actually an actress, and all his neighbors and co-workers are actors, and the town where he lives is a movie set, but he doesn't know that until the very end. It was a great movie.

[Turning to one of the participants] And now, Bob, it's time to break the news to you. This whole group – we're all actors.

Wearing Out the "Yes, buts"

The heart of the matter is so very simple. But we become entangled in our complexity, our sophisticated confusion. We compare this teaching to that teaching, this enlightenment story to that enlightenment story, this blog to that blog, and we get more and more confused. Notice the difference right now between all that mental complexity and this aliveness that is right here – listening, hearing, breathing.

This aliveness is always here. We don't have to work to get it. It is ever-present. Seeking enlightenment is a form of postponement, postponing what can only be realized now. It all boils down to the simplicity of what is, *this* that is always already realizing itself.

P: How do I wake up to that?

J: By noticing how you deny that this awakeness is already present, how you postpone, how you look elsewhere. Asking that question, for example, is a form of postponement and denial. That very question creates the mirage-like problem that it pretends to be trying to solve. See what the mind is doing – how you are looking for a strategy, something to do, to get somewhere else. Because when thought asks, "How do I wake up now?" – the question paints the picture of a "you" who is not awake yet, and "the now" to which it refers is actually in the future, right? So, see how the mind does this. Waking up is simply seeing that this problem is imaginary. There is no one who needs to wake up. Nothing needs to be any different from exactly how it is.

P: Sometimes there's such a yearning for peace.

J: Looking for peace in the future is a form of restlessness and agitation. Here/Now is the only true peace. But Here/Now is the peace that includes everything, even war and conflict and upset. Unconditional love has no enemies. It sees no others. It finds only itself everywhere. If we reference peace to particular circumstances and experiences, like a calm day or the absence of conflict, then we will be endlessly disappointed. We will be at war with reality.

Another P: Can you have both self and no self at once? No self in the background but me involved in acting?

J: "No self" is not some *thing* in the background. In reference to what are we concerned with background and foreground? It's the phantom self again, isn't it? The phantom self *is* the imaginary dividing line. It's not that we *aren't* this bodymind – it's that we are not *limited* to this bodymind. We're not encapsulated *inside* this bodymind. We *are* the bodymind and we are also the whole universe, and we are what remains when the whole universe disappears. Relative and absolute co-exist. When we confuse relative and absolute, we get in trouble. We jump out the window because "it's all one" and there's "no me" to hit the pavement. And that can be a rude awakening!

We wander around seeking some big experience or some final answer, trying to get this all sorted out. And in all of this seeking, we miss the boat in some way. We overlook the obvious. We do this until we don't. At first, we don't even realize we're doing this. But eventually, we know. We become sensitive to it, awake to it. But even then, it's very hard to let this go. It's like any other addiction or compulsion. It's habitual, it's familiar, it's comforting, it's entertaining, and we're afraid of what will be here if we stop. And as with any other addiction or compulsion, any *effort* to stop is part of the addiction, part of the compulsion. That, too, is a movement away from what is, rooted in taking the imaginary problem seriously.

We hear over and over that the truth is right here, that it is not outside of us, that there is nowhere to go and nothing to get, that we already *are* what we seek, that ordinary mind is the way. And the thinking mind says, "Yes, but –" So, in a way, we have to wear out those "Yes, but's." The so-called search, or the so-called pathless path is simply wearing them out.

Of course, some of us try adopting non-seeking as an ideology or a belief system, and we run around saying that we have stopped seeking and there is nothing to get, but that doesn't work if it is only a belief. We become closet seekers, like secret drinkers. So, if seeking shows up, rather than denying it or trying to repress it, simply watch it. See it for what it is. Question the beliefs and stories that underlie it. Look for the "I" that needs to find something or get somewhere. See if this search is really bringing happiness.

There *is* an awakening in a way, something to see through and undo, but the paradox is that when you see it, you realize it has never been absent and you have always been seeing it. You discover that you *are* it, and you always have been. Even the seeking was it. There is no separation between you and the One Reality. There never has been.

P: What was your enlightenment experience like?

J: There have been many experiences, but experiences come and go. I find no one here to be enlightened or unenlightened. Sometimes there is enlightenment Here/Now, and sometimes there is delusion Here/Now. Any "enlightenment experience" or any "enlightened one" is *in* the dream. In the dream, we look outside ourselves for some big event that will make "me" into a nondual gold medalist. We gather enlightenment stories. We avoid by seeking. We postpone. A true teaching stops us in our tracks. It wakes us up to Here/Now. Telling personal enlightenment stories or claiming to be a permanently enlightened person does exactly the opposite. It's like dangling a carrot in front of everyone and telling them there is something they lack. It confirms the reality of the dream rather than undermining it.

P: Being drawn to something like this is what most of us experience.

J: Yes, so really question what you are seeking. The key to enlightenment is to stop postponing this awakening. The problem can only be resolved now. And by "now," I don't mean this week or this year. I mean this *instant*, now. Enlightenment is now or never. Here you are! This is it!

P: How can I know that unicity is all there is? How can I be certain of it beyond doubt? How can I realize or experience it? How can I know if it's true? It sounds possible to me, but I don't feel the certainty that you seem to feel about it.

J: The only thing of which I am completely certain is being here now. This present moment is beyond doubt. When I look for the "I" in "I am," nothing is found. When I look deeply into "this" (presently arising sensations), there is nothing solid, only ceaseless movement, inseparable from the awareness in which it appears. Either way, I find only the immediacy of boundless presence, seamless being. Every night in deep sleep, even the barest *sense* of that disappears. So when these "how can I be sure?" questions come up, I would recommend dropping *everything* you can possibly doubt – every belief, every conceptual model, every description, every map, every ideology, every philosophy – and then discover what remains. *That* is the truth. The utter simplicity of what is, as it is.

If you're looking for *something,* you'll only feel frustrated. The mind wants to see unicity as a particular object, grab hold of it, experience it, possess it, pin it down. It wants to "get it." But the present moment (the absolute, unicity) can't be grasped or gotten. And it doesn't *need* to be grasped or gotten. It is all there is! Liberation is simply the absence of this grasping and fixating and seeking. Or maybe even more accurately, it is the absence of any *concern* about grasping, fixating or seeking.

What remains is a wide open space where nothing is a problem. There is no place for anything to land or to stick. Everything is as it is. This is freedom. It is what Here/Now *is,* our True Nature. It is what remains when the whole universe dissolves.

Doubt and uncertainty is actually a very fertile place. It is the falling away of illusions – false certainties and false beliefs. Of course, it is a tremendously uncomfortable place until we stop running away from it. It is very tempting to fill it up with new beliefs – or with comforting or exciting experiences, substances or adventures. A new project, a new love affair, a new drug, a new religion, a new teacher. Those things can all be delightful, but they never quite deliver the certainty and the freedom that we are seeking. The hangover, the broken heart, the doubt, the disillusionment is always waiting in the wings like death itself.

When we finally let go into the void that we so fear, we find it to be amazingly peaceful, relaxing and joyous. The actuality of this moment is not scary at all.

But the survival mind tends to pop back up. "Where am I?" it asks, trying to reorient itself. "Have I really got it?" It's an old habit. Suddenly the fear and the doubt and the confusion come pouring back in. And we search again for something to fill the hole of uncertainty. It can *seemingly* take time to wear out the mind. But it only takes time when we think about it before or after the fact. The reality is always Here/Now.

P: I really get this when I'm here or on a retreat, but in daily life, I totally lose it.

J: Anything you can get will eventually be lost. Waking up is the discovery of what can't be lost, what remains when all your ideas disappear. It's not *something*. It's the no-*thing*-ness of everything, the groundlessness of Here/Now.

You may have some very beautiful experience on a retreat, but it doesn't last. The bills still have to be paid. The floor still needs to be vacuumed. We still prefer flowers to weeds, and when a rock drops on our foot, it still hurts. Multiplicity and particularity keep showing up. Messiness shows up. This bodymind character shows up and has to go to work and do the laundry and take out the garbage and relate to its rebellious children. Limitation keeps showing up. Headaches, acid indigestion, murky weather, broken plumbing, disturbing news. And we keep telling ourselves, "I'm not Joan. I'm the emptiness. I'm nothing. It's all One." And we *try* very hard to keep seeing that it's all One, that we're nobody, that nothing is happening. And we keep feeling doubtful and longing for certainty.

And then we stop trying to escape and the bubble breaks. That imaginary separation dissolves. There's simply what is, as it is.

It has always been so.

Acknowledgements

I am deeply grateful to Lynne VandeBunte for recording and transcribing the talks that were the groundwork for this book, for encouraging this book and my work in so many ways seen and unseen, and for your friendship and support.

Thank you to D Allen for looking and listening together and asking invaluable questions, for feedback and encouragement on this manuscript, and for your friendship.

Thank you to Judith Cope for your keen editorial eye and friendship.

Thank you to Julian Noyce for publishing my books and doing it so beautifully.

Thank you to Toni Packer for illuminating what matters most with such clarity and being who you are in every way.

I am deeply grateful to Sri Nisargadatta Maharaj. I know him only through books, photographs and video, but he has been (and is) one of my greatest teachers.

Thank you to all the other teachers and colleagues who have contributed to my understanding in some way.

Thank you to everyone I have met with, individually and in groups, without whom this book would not exist, and to all the people who have hosted, organized, or help to facilitate my meetings, and to all those who have corresponded with me or expressed appreciation for the books or the web site.

Thank you from the bottom of my heart to all of my friends. I feel incredibly blessed to know each and every one of you and to have all of you in my life.

Last but not least, thank you to my truly wonderful parents: Dorothy, who taught me to play and have fun and laugh and follow my bliss and love myself and the whole world, and Wallace, who told me that there was no god and no free will, that everything is as it is and could not be otherwise, that there is no essential difference between a person and a table, and that the sun will eventually explode. I bow to you both, my first and greatest teachers.

NON-DUALITY PRESS

If you enjoyed this book, you might be interested in these related titles published by Non-Duality Press:

Awake in the Heartland, Joan Tollifson
The Wonder of Being, Jeff Foster
An Extraordinary Absence, Jeff Foster
Awakening to the Dream, Leo Hartong
From Self to Self, Leo Hartong
Dismantling the Fantasy, Darryl Bailey
Standing as Awareness, Greg Goode
The Transparency of Things, Rupert Spira
Perfect Brilliant Stillness, David Carse
I Hope You Die Soon, Richard Sylvester
The Book of No One, Richard Sylvester
Be Who You Are, Jean Klein
Who Am I?, Jean Klein
I Am, Jean Klein
The Book of Listening, Jean Klein
Spiritual Discourses of Shri Atmananda (3 vols.)
Nobody Home, Jan Kersschot
This is Always Enough, John Astin
Oneness, John Greven
Awakening to the Natural State, John Wheeler
You were Never Born, John Wheeler
The Light Behind Consciousness, John Wheeler
What's Wrong with Right Now?, Sailor Bob Adamson
Presence-Awareness, Sailor Bob Adamson
You Are No Thing, Randall Friend
Already Awake, Nathan Gill
Being: the bottom line, Nathan Gill

For a complete list of books, CDs and DVDs, please visit:
www.newharbinger.com